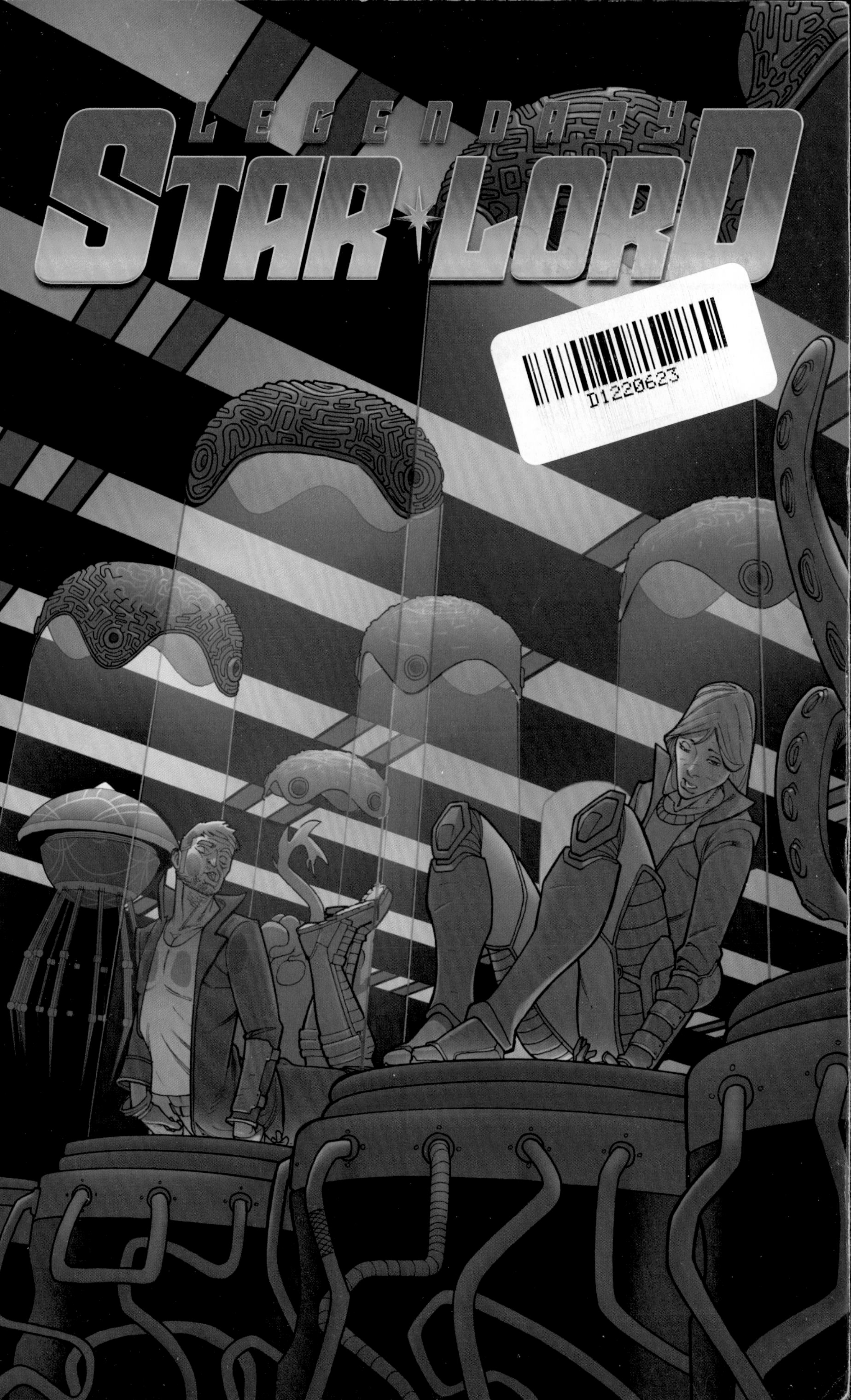
LEGENDARY
STAR-LORD

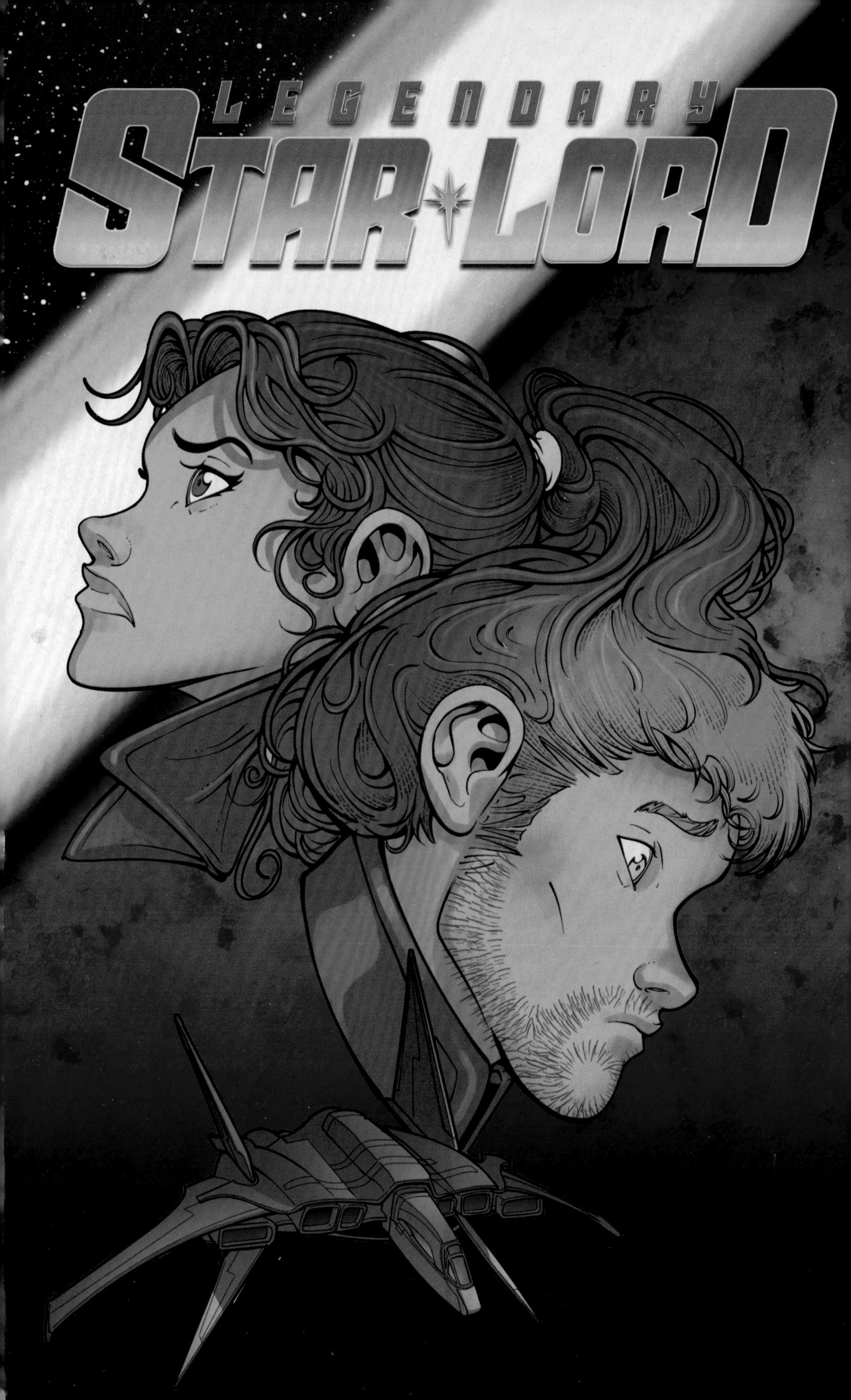
LEGENDARY
STAR-LORD

OUT OF ORBIT

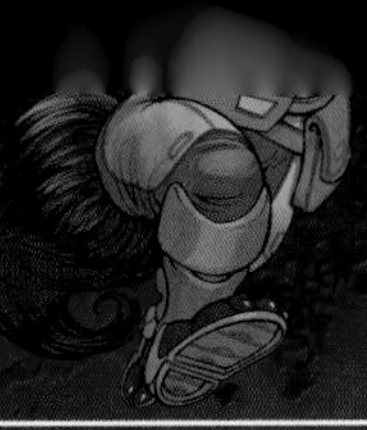

WRITER: **SAM HUMPHRIES**

ARTISTS: **JAVIER GARRÓN** WITH **WILL ROBSON** (#8)

COLORIST: **ANTONIO FABELA**

LETTERER: **VC's JOE CARAMAGNA**

COVER ART: **DAVE JOHNSON** (#6) AND **MIKE HAWTHORNE & JORDIE BELLAIRE** (#7-8)

ASSISTANT EDITOR: **KATHLEEN WISNESKI**

EDITOR: **JAKE THOMAS**

COLLECTION EDITOR: **JENNIFER GRÜNWALD**
ASSOCIATE MANAGING EDITOR: **KATERI WOODY**
ASSOCIATE EDITOR: **SARAH BRUNSTAD**
EDITOR, SPECIAL PROJECTS: **MARK D. BEAZLEY**
VP PRODUCTION & SPECIAL PROJECTS: **JEFF YOUNGQUIST**
SVP PRINT, SALES & MARKETING: **DAVID GABRIEL**

EDITOR IN CHIEF: **AXEL ALONSO**
CHIEF CREATIVE OFFICER: **JOE QUESADA**
PUBLISHER: **DAN BUCKLEY**
EXECUTIVE PRODUCER: **ALAN FINE**

EGENDARY STAR-LORD VOL. 4: OUT OF ORBIT. Contains material originally published in magazine form as STAR-LORD #6-8; and AVENGERS #28, #51 and #174. First printing 2016. ISBN# 978-0-7851-9625-9. ublished by MARVEL WORLDWIDE, INC., a subsidiary of MARVEL ENTERTAINMENT, LLC. OFFICE OF PUBLICATION: 135 West 50th Street, New York, NY 10020. Copyright © 2016 MARVEL No similarity between any of the ames, characters, persons, and/or institutions in this magazine with those of any living or dead person or institution is intended, and any such similarity which may exist is purely coincidental. **Printed in Canada.** ALAN NE, President, Marvel Entertainment; DAN BUCKLEY, President, TV, Publishing & Brand Management; JOE QUESADA, Chief Creative Officer; TOM BREVOORT, SVP of Publishing; DAVID BOGART, SVP of Business Affairs Operations, Publishing & Partnership; C.B. CEBULSKI, VP of Brand Management & Development, Asia; DAVID GABRIEL, SVP of Sales & Marketing, Publishing; JEFF YOUNGQUIST, VP of Production & Special Projects; AN CARR, Executive Director of Publishing Technology; ALEX MORALES, Director of Publishing Operations; SUSAN CRESPI, Production Manager; STAN LEE, Chairman Emeritus. For information regarding advertising in

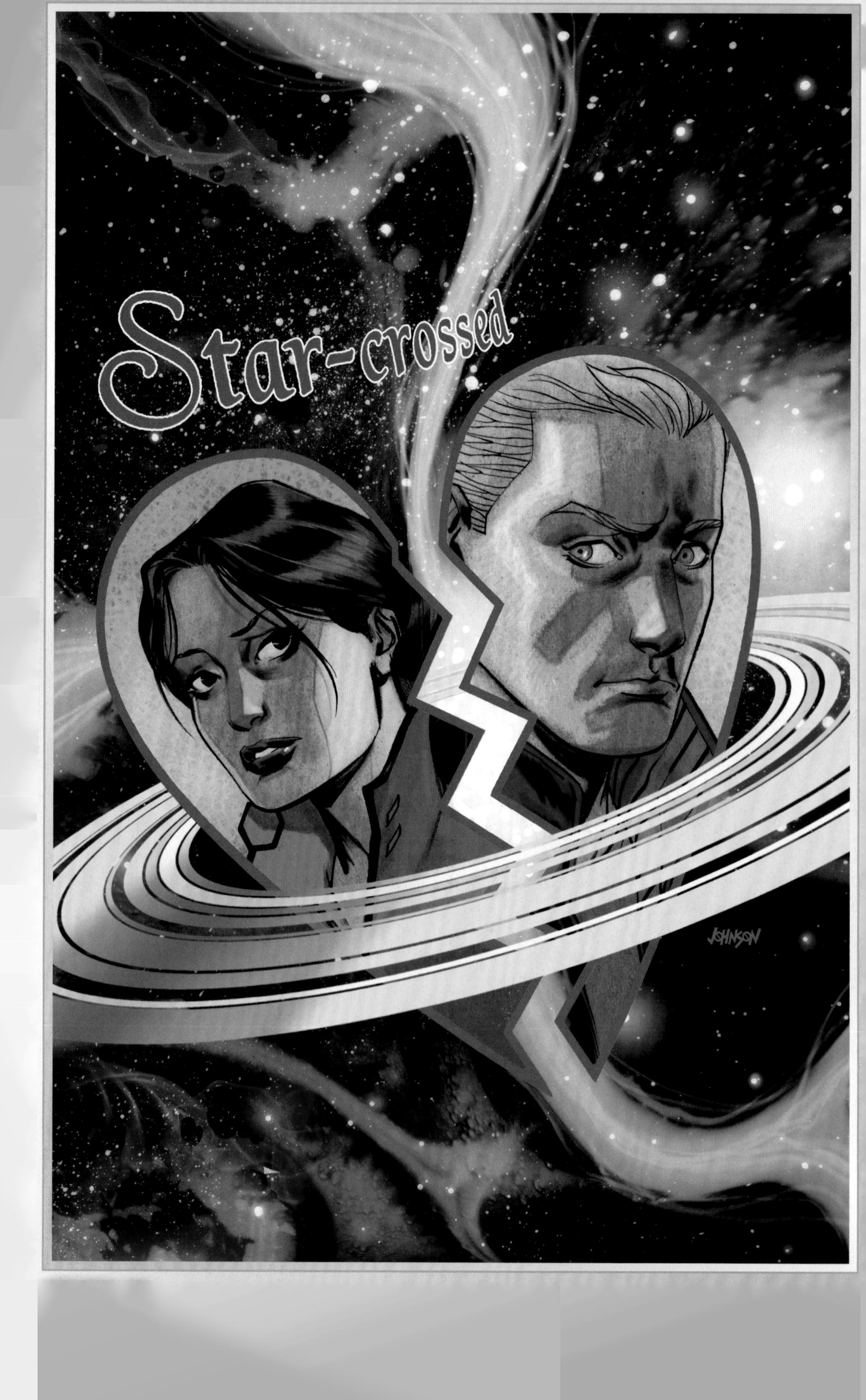
Star-crossed
JOHNSON

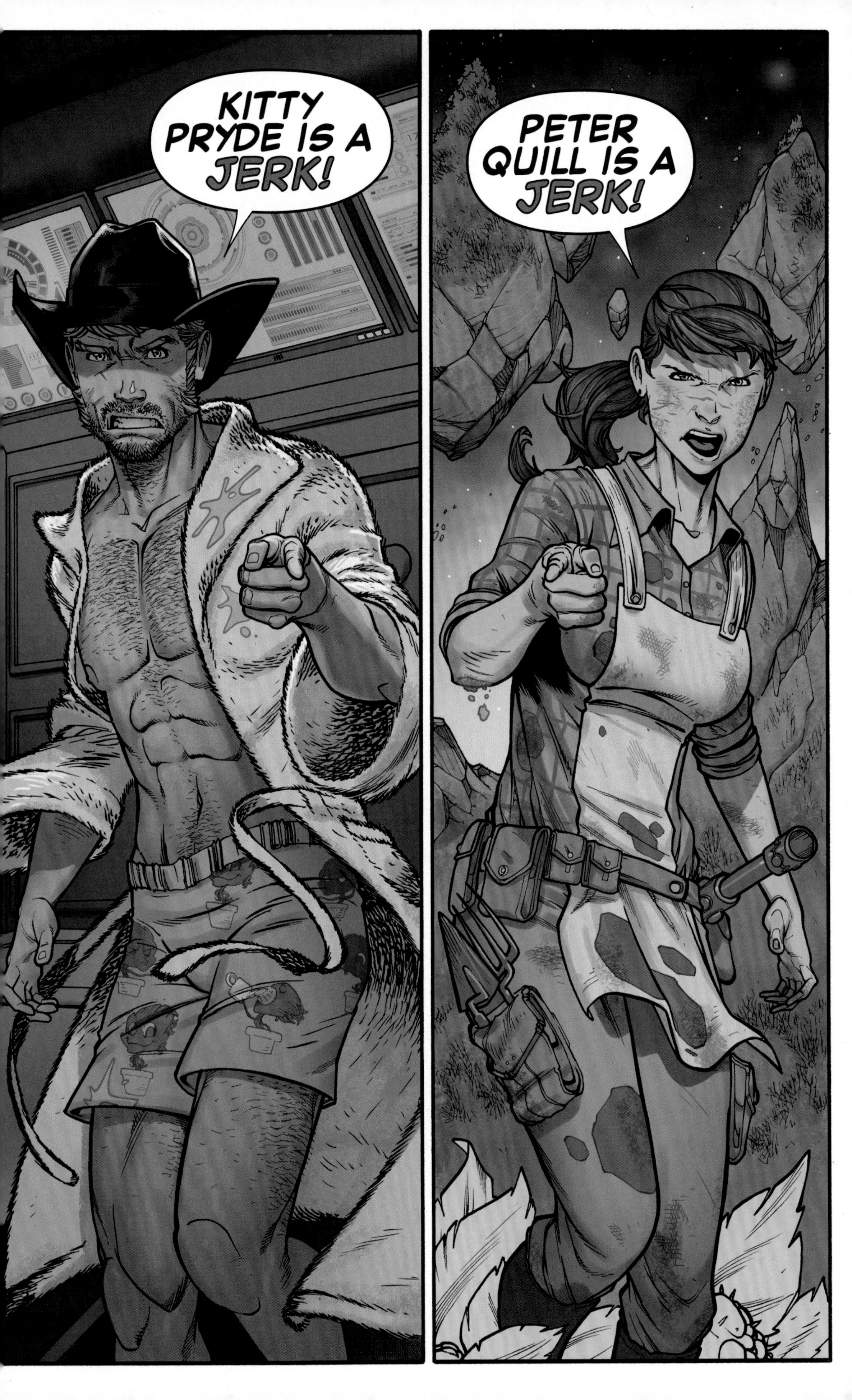
KITTY PRYDE IS A JERK!
PETER QUILL IS A JERK!

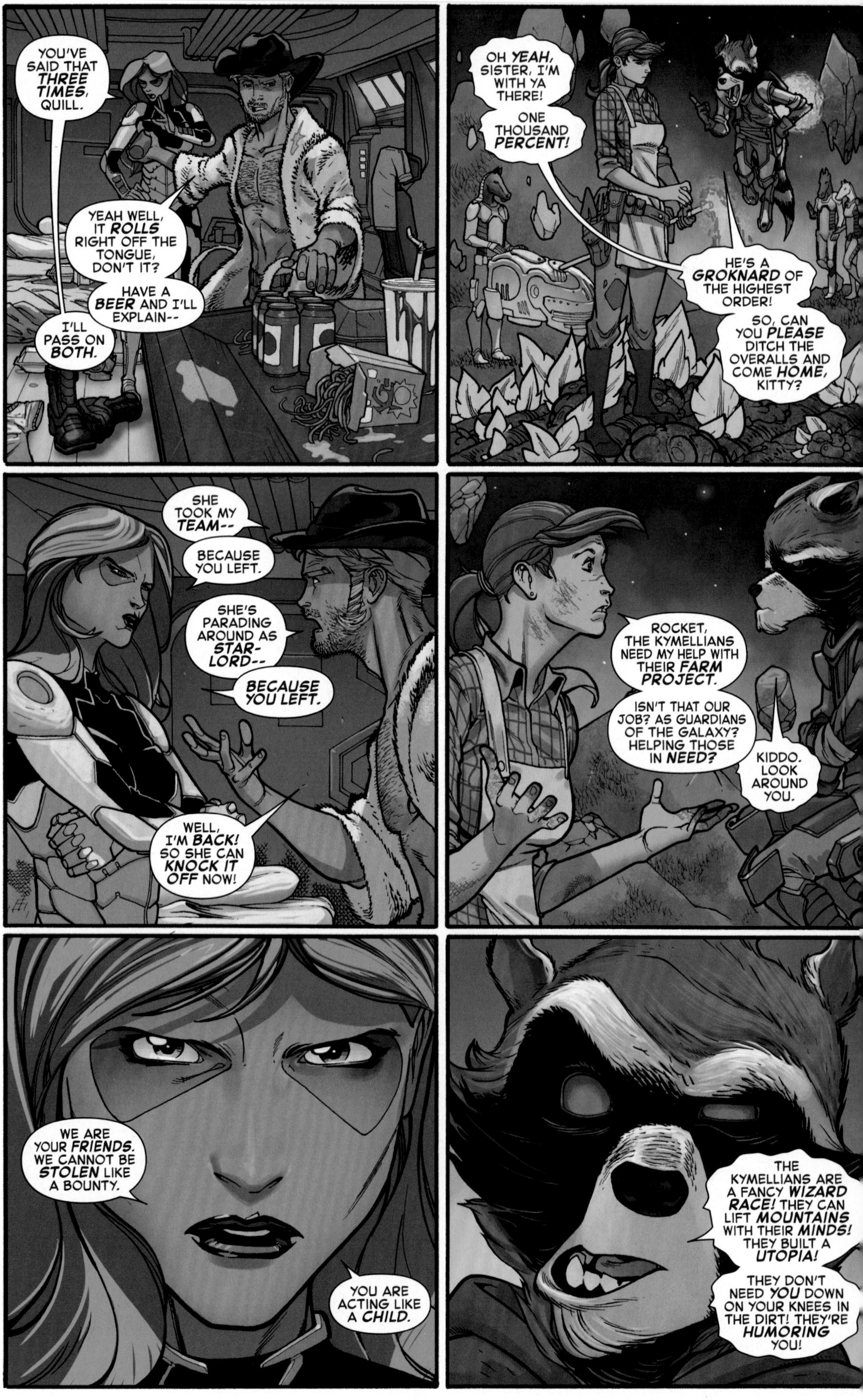
YOU'VE SAID THAT THREE TIMES, QUILL.
YEAH WELL, IT ROLLS RIGHT OFF THE TONGUE, DON'T IT?
HAVE A BEER AND I'LL EXPLAIN--
I'LL PASS ON BOTH.
OH YEAH, SISTER, I'M WITH YA THERE!
ONE THOUSAND PERCENT!
HE'S A GROKNARD OF THE HIGHEST ORDER!
SO, CAN YOU PLEASE DITCH THE OVERALLS AND COME HOME, KITTY?
SHE TOOK MY TEAM--
BECAUSE YOU LEFT.
SHE'S PARADING AROUND AS STAR-LORD--
BECAUSE YOU LEFT.
WELL, I'M BACK! SO SHE CAN KNOCK IT OFF NOW!
ROCKET, THE KYMELLIANS NEED MY HELP WITH THEIR FARM PROJECT.
ISN'T THAT OUR JOB? AS GUARDIANS OF THE GALAXY? HELPING THOSE IN NEED?
KIDDO. LOOK AROUND YOU.
WE ARE YOUR FRIENDS. WE CANNOT BE STOLEN LIKE A BOUNTY.
YOU ARE ACTING LIKE A CHILD.
THE KYMELLIANS ARE A FANCY WIZARD RACE! THEY CAN LIFT MOUNTAINS WITH THEIR MINDS! THEY BUILT A UTOPIA!
THEY DON'T NEED YOU DOWN ON YOUR KNEES IN THE DIRT! THEY'RE HUMORING YOU!

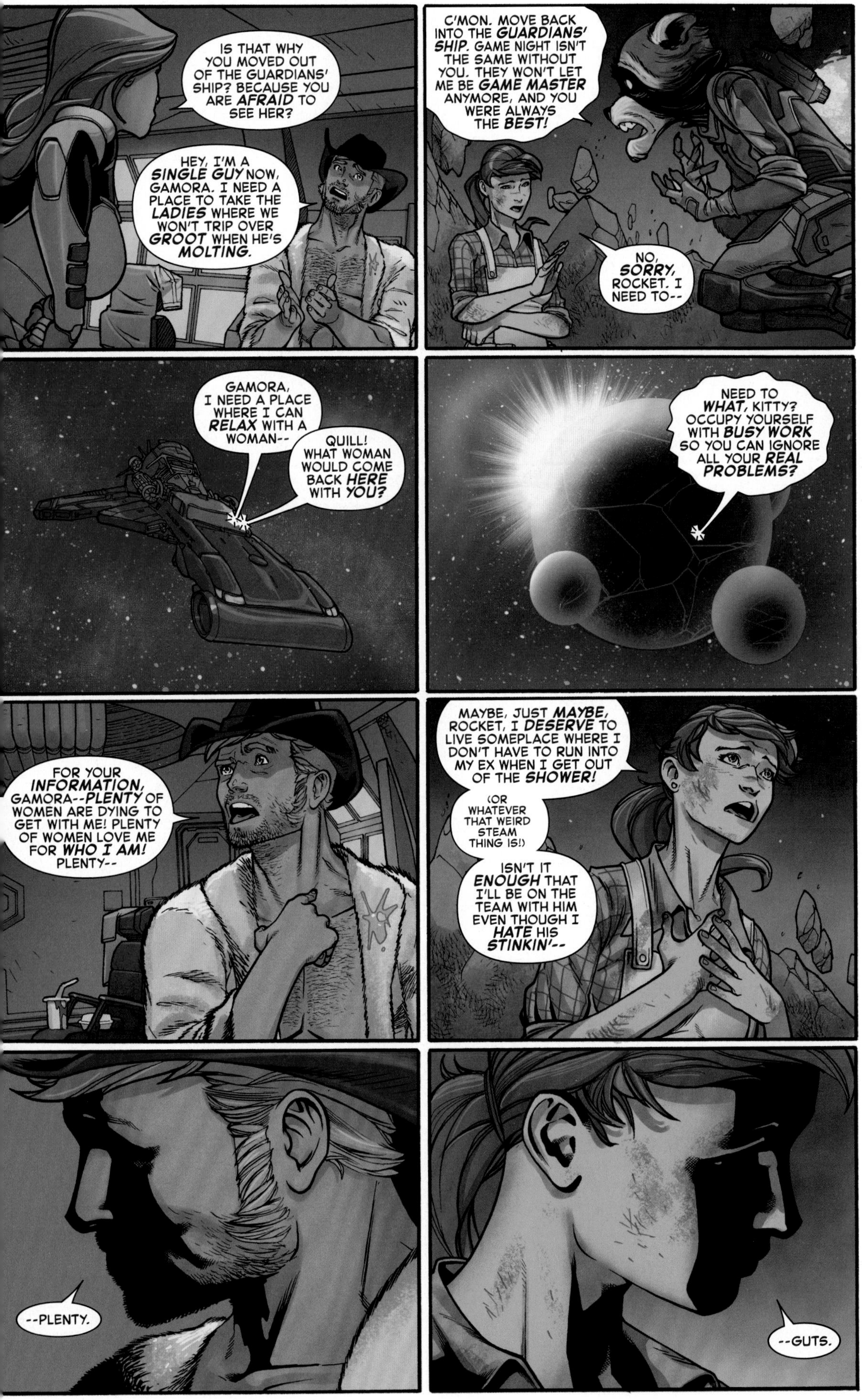
IS THAT WHY YOU MOVED OUT OF THE GUARDIANS' SHIP? BECAUSE YOU ARE AFRAID TO SEE HER?
HEY, I'M A SINGLE GUY NOW, GAMORA. I NEED A PLACE TO TAKE THE LADIES WHERE WE WON'T TRIP OVER GROOT WHEN HE'S MOLTING.
C'MON. MOVE BACK INTO THE GUARDIANS' SHIP. GAME NIGHT ISN'T THE SAME WITHOUT YOU. THEY WON'T LET ME BE GAME MASTER ANYMORE, AND YOU WERE ALWAYS THE BEST!
NO, SORRY, ROCKET. I NEED TO--
GAMORA, I NEED A PLACE WHERE I CAN RELAX WITH A WOMAN--
QUILL! WHAT WOMAN WOULD COME BACK HERE WITH YOU?
NEED TO WHAT, KITTY? OCCUPY YOURSELF WITH BUSY WORK SO YOU CAN IGNORE ALL YOUR REAL PROBLEMS?
FOR YOUR INFORMATION, GAMORA--PLENTY OF WOMEN ARE DYING TO GET WITH ME! PLENTY OF WOMEN LOVE ME FOR WHO I AM! PLENTY--
MAYBE, JUST MAYBE, ROCKET, I DESERVE TO LIVE SOMEPLACE WHERE I DON'T HAVE TO RUN INTO MY EX WHEN I GET OUT OF THE SHOWER!
(OR WHATEVER THAT WEIRD STEAM THING IS!)
ISN'T IT ENOUGH THAT I'LL BE ON THE TEAM WITH HIM EVEN THOUGH I HATE HIS STINKIN'--
--PLENTY.
--GUTS.

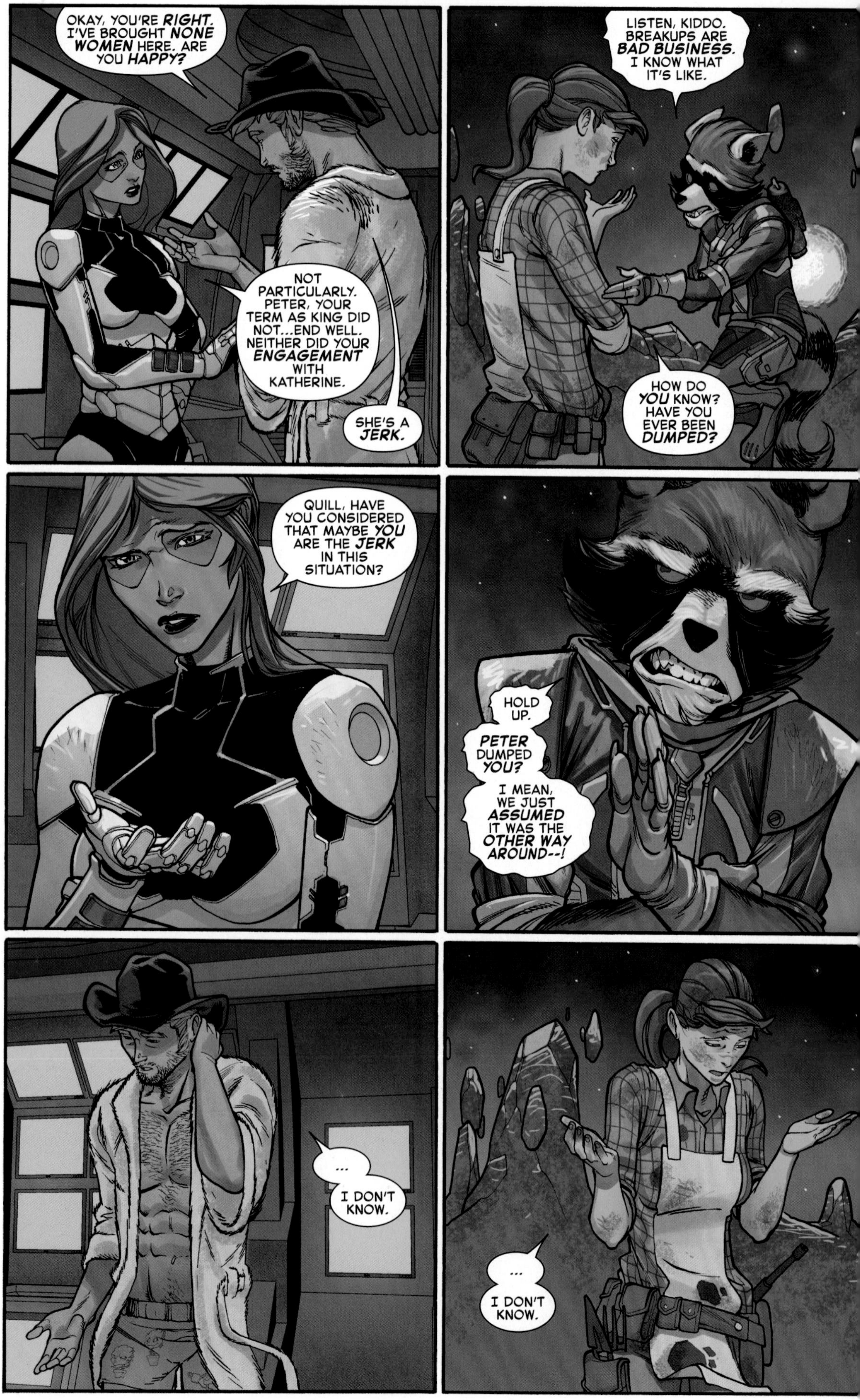
OKAY, YOU'RE RIGHT. I'VE BROUGHT NONE WOMEN HERE. ARE YOU HAPPY?
NOT PARTICULARLY. PETER, YOUR TERM AS KING DID NOT...END WELL. NEITHER DID YOUR ENGAGEMENT WITH KATHERINE.
SHE'S A JERK.
LISTEN, KIDDO. BREAKUPS ARE BAD BUSINESS. I KNOW WHAT IT'S LIKE.
HOW DO YOU KNOW? HAVE YOU EVER BEEN DUMPED?
QUILL, HAVE YOU CONSIDERED THAT MAYBE YOU ARE THE JERK IN THIS SITUATION?
HOLD UP.
PETER DUMPED YOU?
I MEAN, WE JUST ASSUMED IT WAS THE OTHER WAY AROUND--!
...
I DON'T KNOW.
...
I DON'T KNOW.

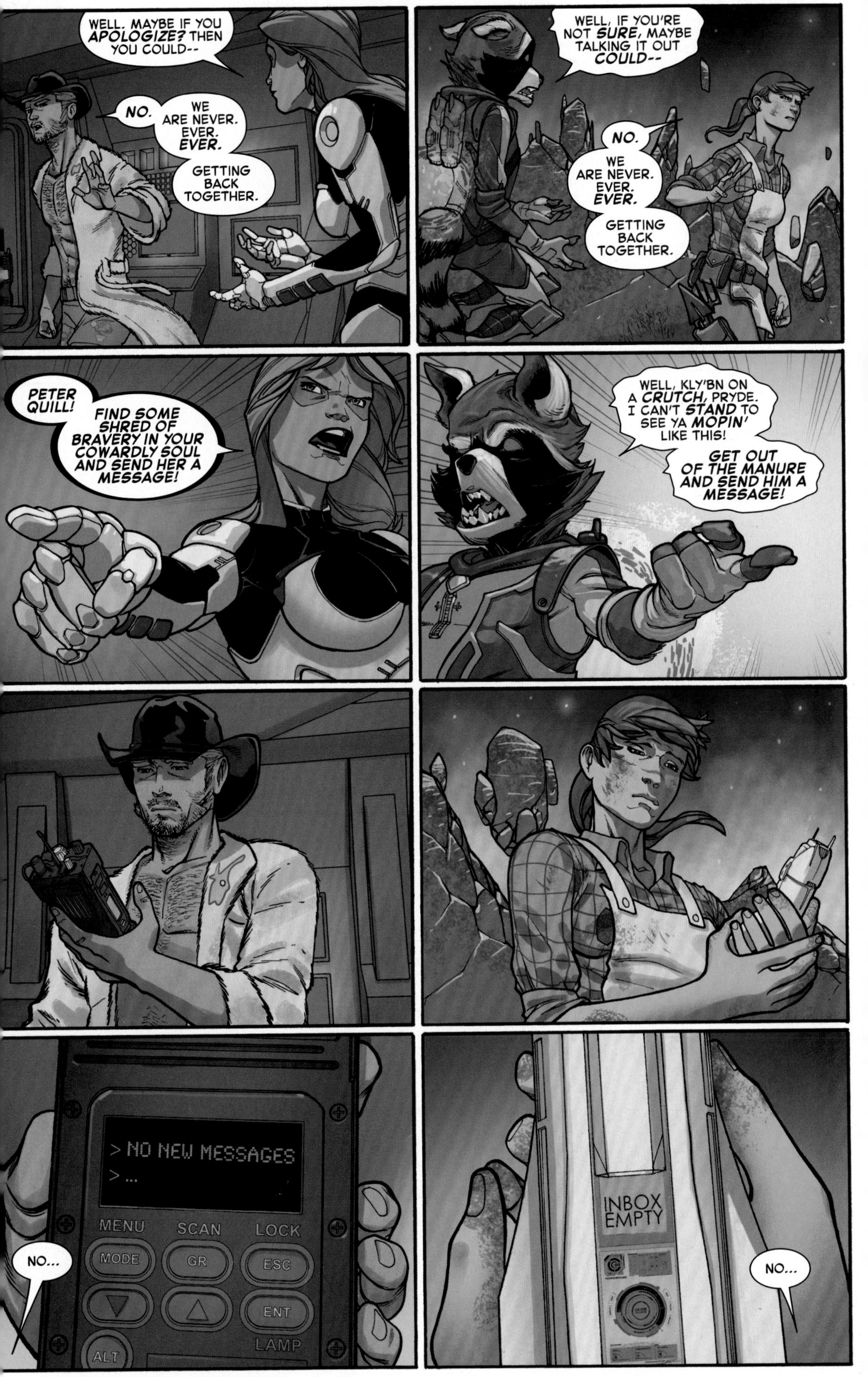
WELL. MAYBE IF YOU APOLOGIZE? THEN YOU COULD--
NO.
WE ARE NEVER. EVER. EVER.
GETTING BACK TOGETHER.
WELL, IF YOU'RE NOT SURE, MAYBE TALKING IT OUT COULD--
NO.
WE ARE NEVER. EVER. EVER.
GETTING BACK TOGETHER.
PETER QUILL!
FIND SOME SHRED OF BRAVERY IN YOUR COWARDLY SOUL AND SEND HER A MESSAGE!
WELL, KLY'BN ON A CRUTCH, PRYDE. I CAN'T STAND TO SEE YA MOPIN' LIKE THIS!
GET OUT OF THE MANURE AND SEND HIM A MESSAGE!
> NO NEW MESSAGES
> ...
MENU
SCAN
LOCK
MODE
GR
ESC
ENT
LAMP
ALT
NO...
INBOX EMPTY
NO...

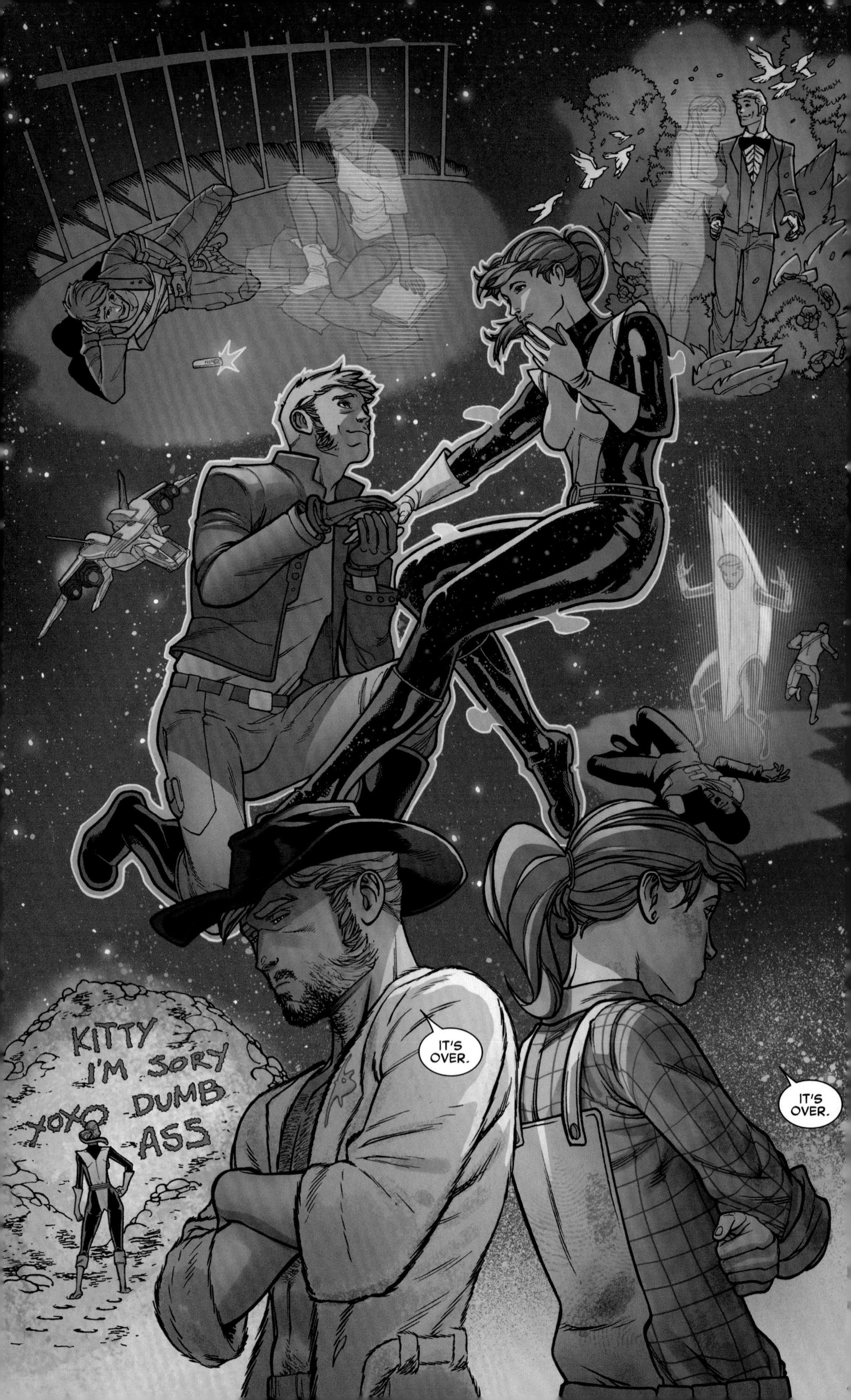
KITTY
I'M SORY
DUMB
ASS
XOXO
IT'S OVER.
IT'S OVER.

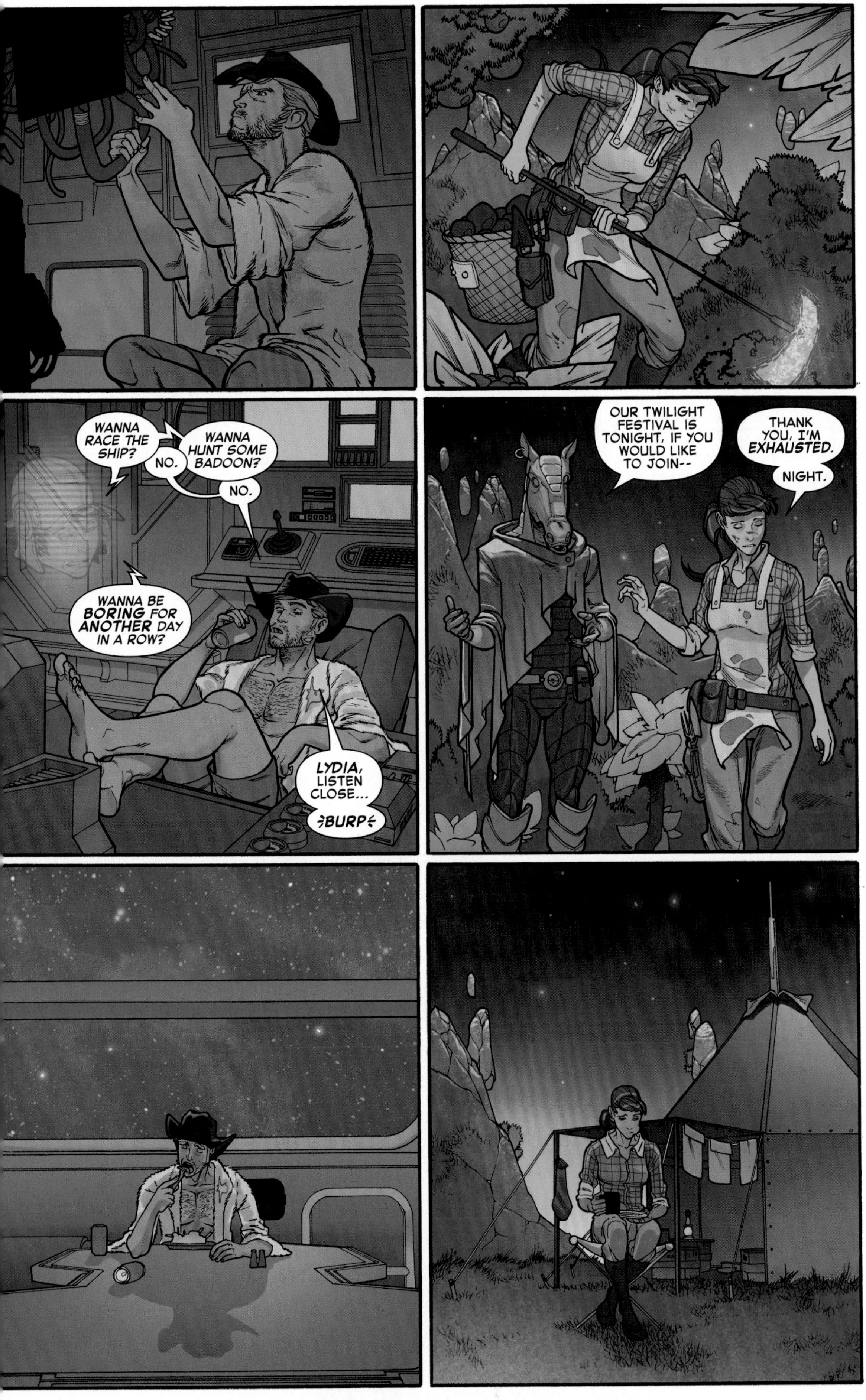
WANNA RACE THE SHIP?
NO.
WANNA HUNT SOME BADOON?
NO.
WANNA BE BORING FOR ANOTHER DAY IN A ROW?
LYDIA, LISTEN CLOSE...
BURP
OUR TWILIGHT FESTIVAL IS TONIGHT, IF YOU WOULD LIKE TO JOIN--
THANK YOU, I'M EXHAUSTED.
NIGHT.

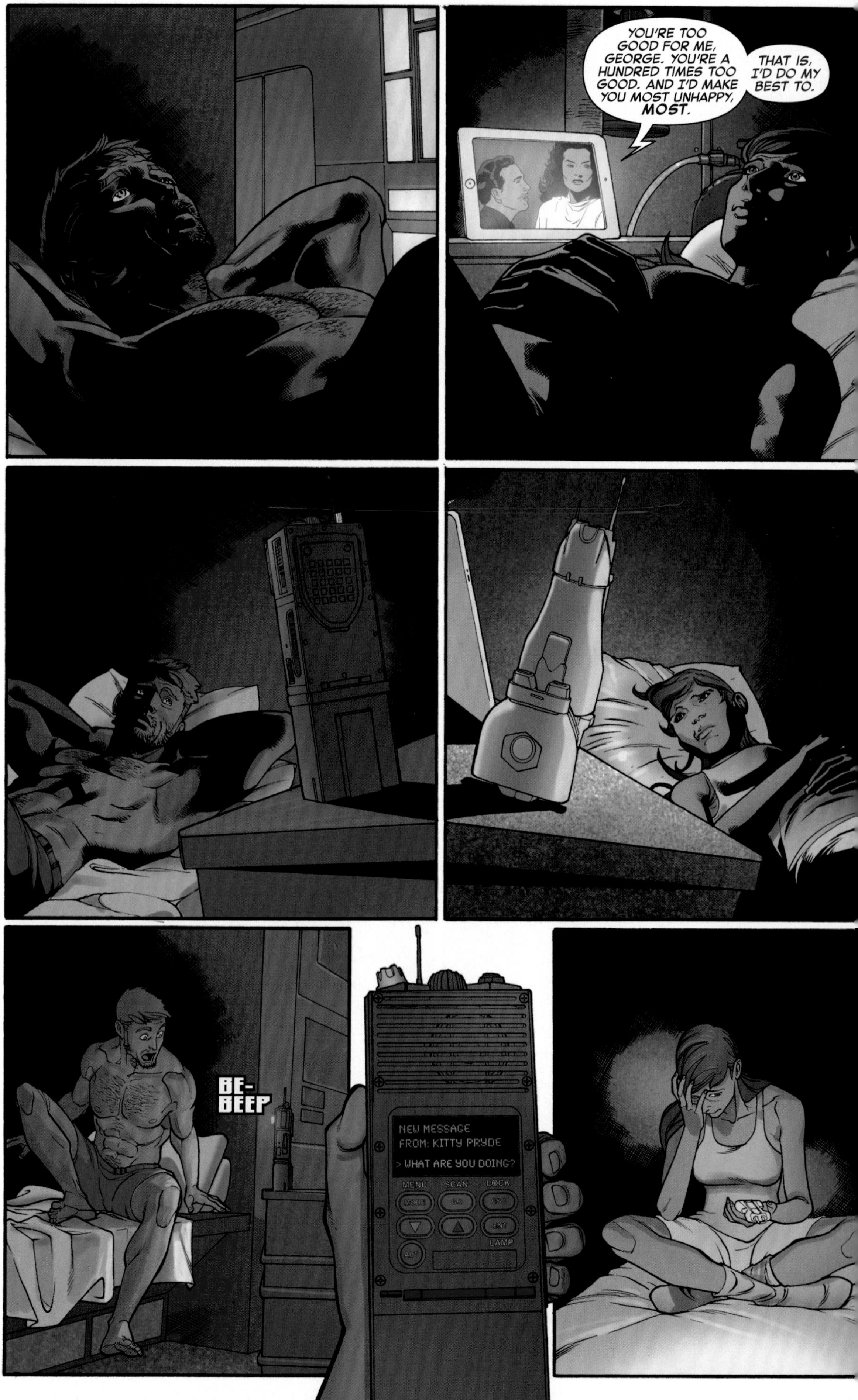
YOU'RE TOO GOOD FOR ME, GEORGE. YOU'RE A HUNDRED TIMES TOO GOOD. AND I'D MAKE YOU MOST UNHAPPY, MOST.
THAT IS, I'D DO MY BEST TO.
BE-BEEP
NEW MESSAGE
FROM: KITTY PRYDE
> WHAT ARE YOU DOING?
MENU SCAN LOCK
LAMP

TAK TAK
TAK
KITTY
> WHAT ARE YOU DOING?
>> HEY THERE LOL ;) NOT MUCH
JUST CHILLIN WHAT ARE YOU |
MENU
SCAN
LOCK
GR
TAK TAK
TAK
PETER
What are you doing?
...
TEMPERATURE
TAK TAK TAK TAK

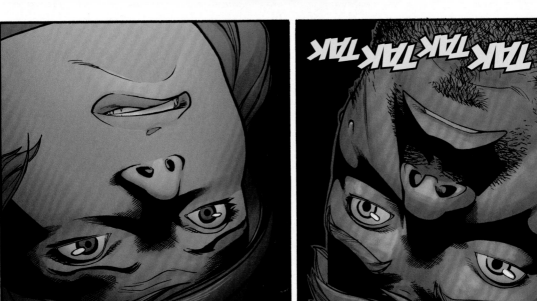

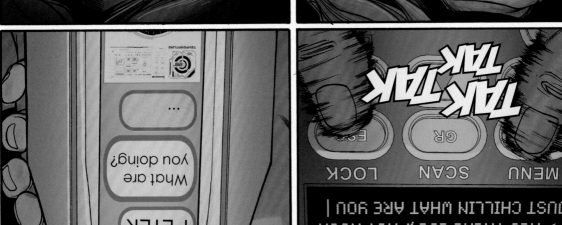

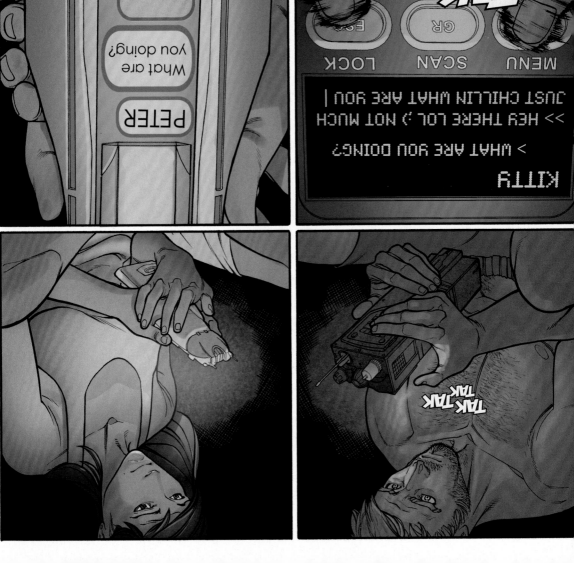

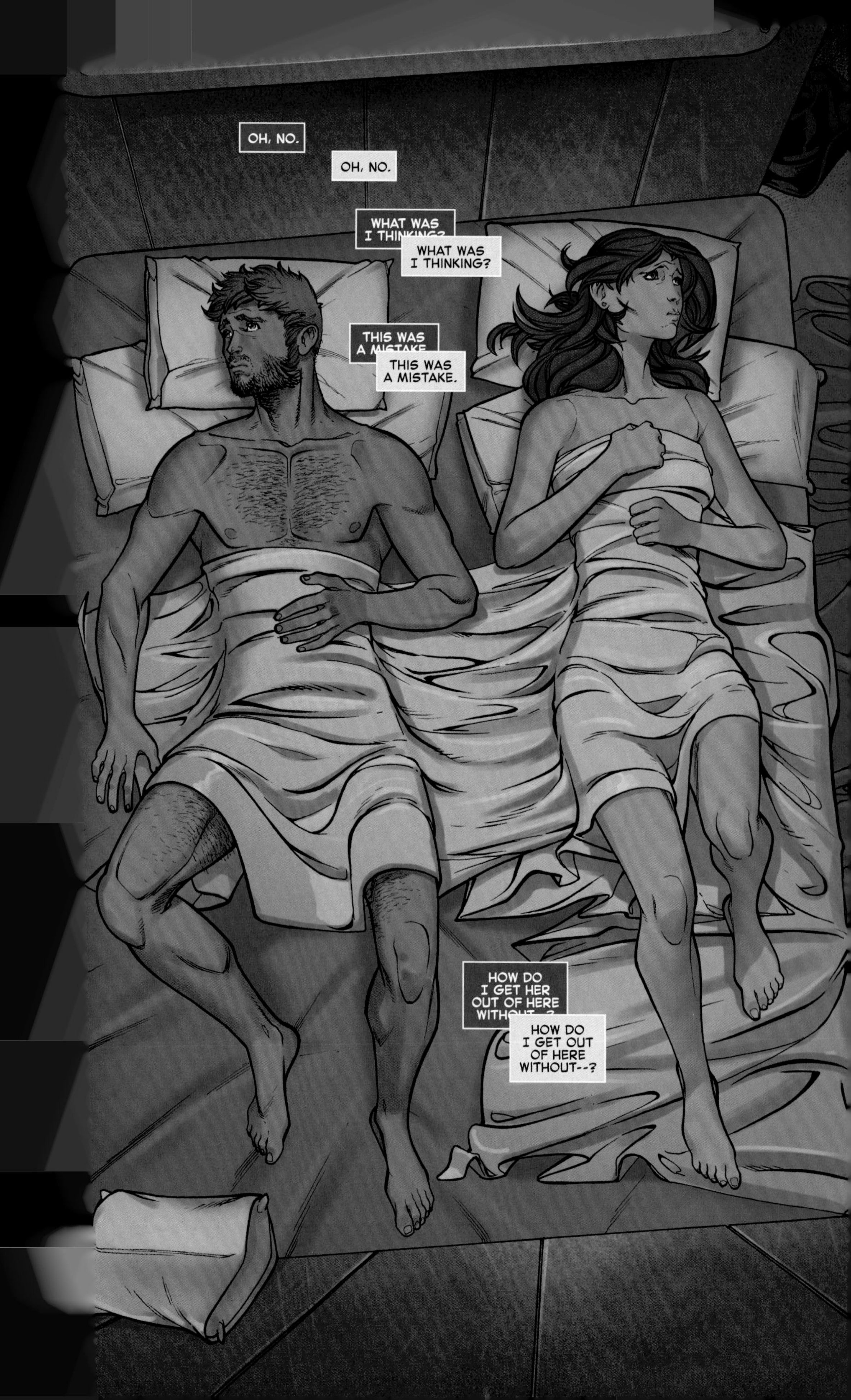
OH, NO.
OH, NO.
WHAT WAS
WHAT WAS I THINKING?
THIS WAS
THIS WAS A MISTAKE.
HOW DO I GET HER OUT OF HERE
HOW DO I GET OUT OF HERE WITHOUT--?

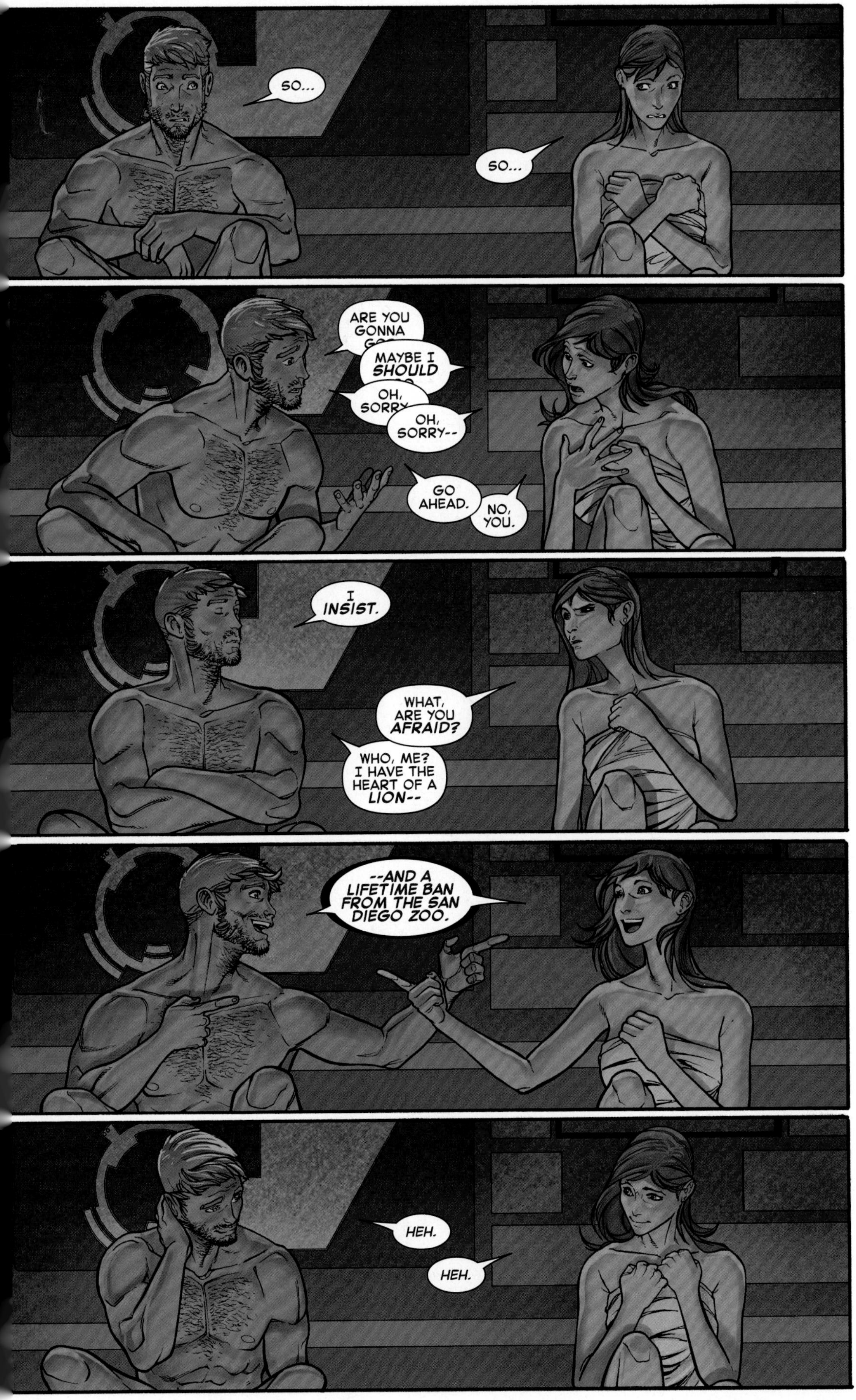
SO...
SO...
ARE YOU GONNA
MAYBE I SHOULD
OH, SORRY
OH, SORRY--
GO AHEAD.
NO, YOU.
I INSIST.
WHAT, ARE YOU AFRAID?
WHO, ME? I HAVE THE HEART OF A LION--
--AND A LIFETIME BAN FROM THE SAN DIEGO ZOO.
HEH.
HEH.

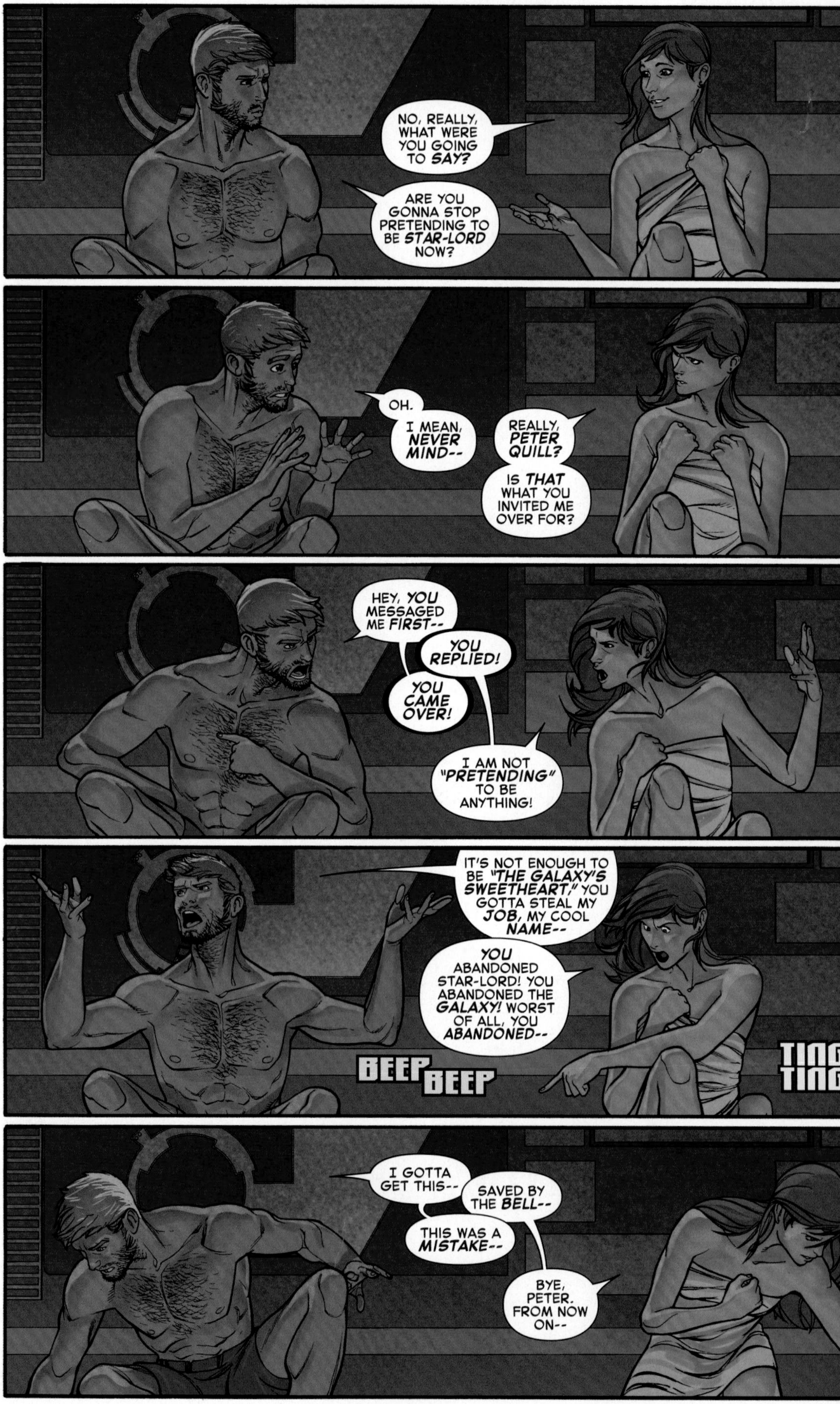
NO, REALLY, WHAT WERE YOU GOING TO *SAY?*
ARE YOU GONNA STOP PRETENDING TO BE *STAR-LORD* NOW?
OH.
I MEAN, *NEVER MIND--*
REALLY, *PETER QUILL?*
IS *THAT* WHAT YOU INVITED ME OVER FOR?
HEY, *YOU* MESSAGED ME *FIRST--*
YOU REPLIED!
YOU CAME OVER!
I AM NOT *"PRETENDING"* TO BE ANYTHING!
IT'S NOT ENOUGH TO BE *"THE GALAXY'S SWEETHEART,"* YOU GOTTA STEAL MY *JOB*, MY COOL *NAME--*
YOU ABANDONED STAR-LORD! YOU ABANDONED THE *GALAXY!* WORST OF ALL, YOU *ABANDONED--*
BEEP BEEP
TING TING
I GOTTA GET THIS--
SAVED BY THE *BELL--*
THIS WAS A *MISTAKE--*
BYE, PETER. FROM NOW ON--

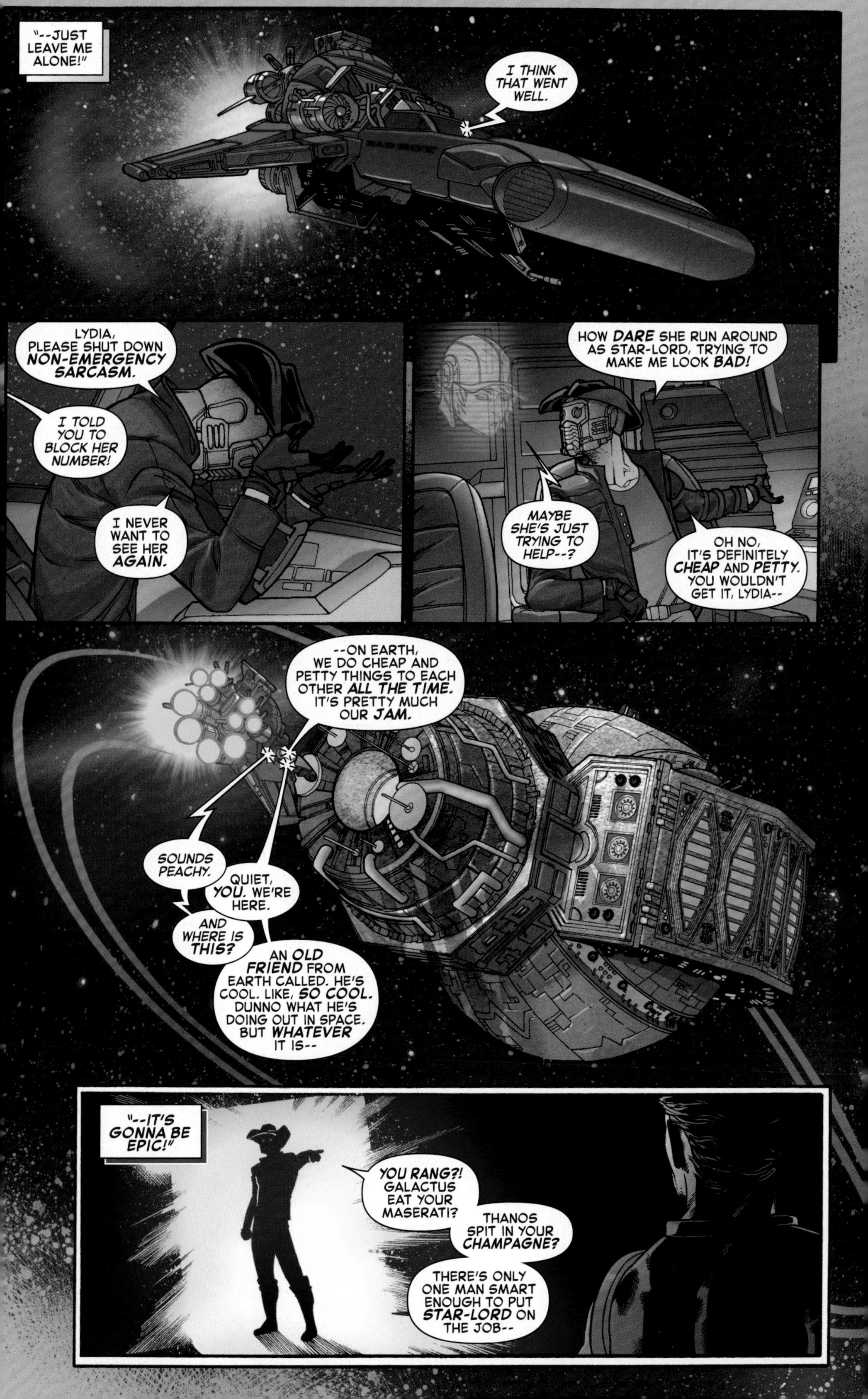
"--JUST LEAVE ME ALONE!"
I THINK THAT WENT WELL.
LYDIA, PLEASE SHUT DOWN NON-EMERGENCY SARCASM.
I TOLD YOU TO BLOCK HER NUMBER!
I NEVER WANT TO SEE HER AGAIN.
HOW DARE SHE RUN AROUND AS STAR-LORD, TRYING TO MAKE ME LOOK BAD!
MAYBE SHE'S JUST TRYING TO HELP--?
OH NO, IT'S DEFINITELY CHEAP AND PETTY. YOU WOULDN'T GET IT, LYDIA--
--ON EARTH, WE DO CHEAP AND PETTY THINGS TO EACH OTHER ALL THE TIME. IT'S PRETTY MUCH OUR JAM.
SOUNDS PEACHY.
QUIET, YOU. WE'RE HERE.
AND WHERE IS THIS?
AN OLD FRIEND FROM EARTH CALLED. HE'S COOL. LIKE, SO COOL. DUNNO WHAT HE'S DOING OUT IN SPACE. BUT WHATEVER IT IS--
"--IT'S GONNA BE EPIC!"
YOU RANG?! GALACTUS EAT YOUR MASERATI?
THANOS SPIT IN YOUR CHAMPAGNE?
THERE'S ONLY ONE MAN SMART ENOUGH TO PUT STAR-LORD ON THE JOB--

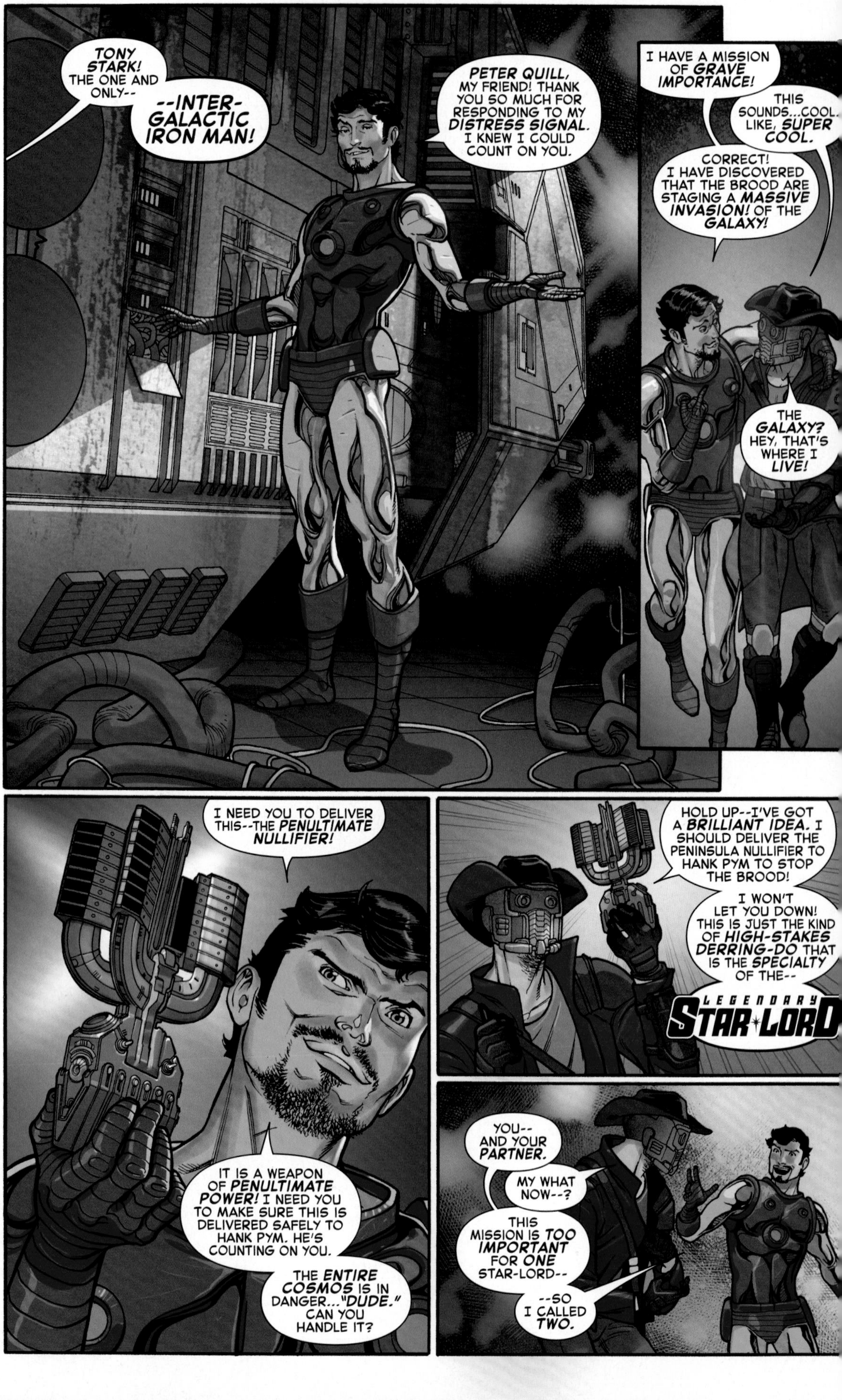
TONY STARK! THE ONE AND ONLY--
--INTER-GALACTIC IRON MAN!
PETER QUILL, MY FRIEND! THANK YOU SO MUCH FOR RESPONDING TO MY DISTRESS SIGNAL. I KNEW I COULD COUNT ON YOU.
I HAVE A MISSION OF GRAVE IMPORTANCE!
THIS SOUNDS...COOL. LIKE, SUPER COOL.
CORRECT! I HAVE DISCOVERED THAT THE BROOD ARE STAGING A MASSIVE INVASION! OF THE GALAXY!
THE GALAXY? HEY, THAT'S WHERE I LIVE!
I NEED YOU TO DELIVER THIS--THE PENULTIMATE NULLIFIER!
IT IS A WEAPON OF PENULTIMATE POWER! I NEED YOU TO MAKE SURE THIS IS DELIVERED SAFELY TO HANK PYM. HE'S COUNTING ON YOU.
THE ENTIRE COSMOS IS IN DANGER..."DUDE." CAN YOU HANDLE IT?
HOLD UP--I'VE GOT A BRILLIANT IDEA. I SHOULD DELIVER THE PENINSULA NULLIFIER TO HANK PYM TO STOP THE BROOD!
I WON'T LET YOU DOWN! THIS IS JUST THE KIND OF HIGH-STAKES DERRING-DO THAT IS THE SPECIALTY OF THE--
LEGENDARY STAR-LORD
YOU--AND YOUR PARTNER.
MY WHAT NOW--?
THIS MISSION IS TOO IMPORTANT FOR ONE STAR-LORD--
--SO I CALLED TWO.

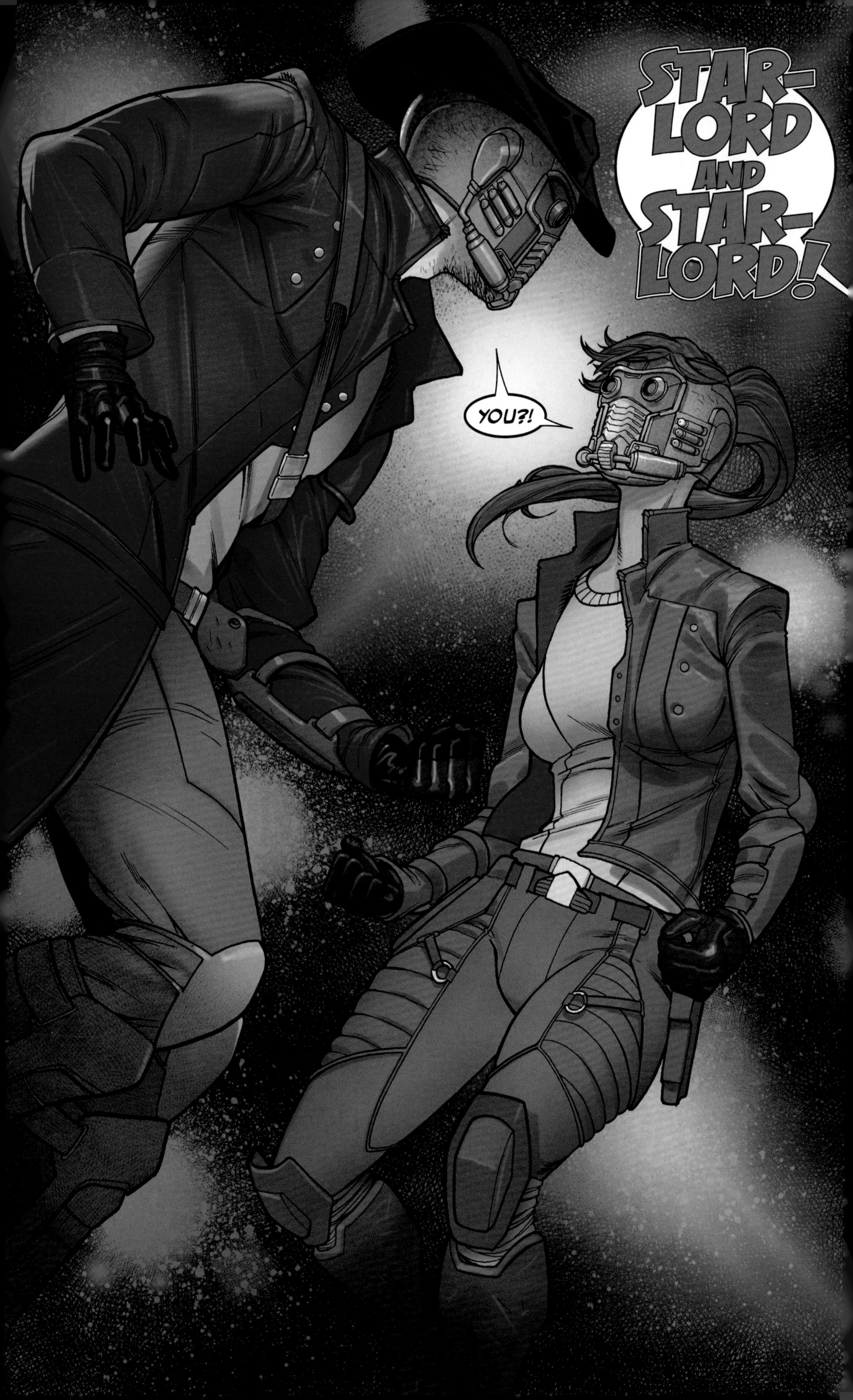
YOU?!
STAR-LORD AND STAR-LORD!

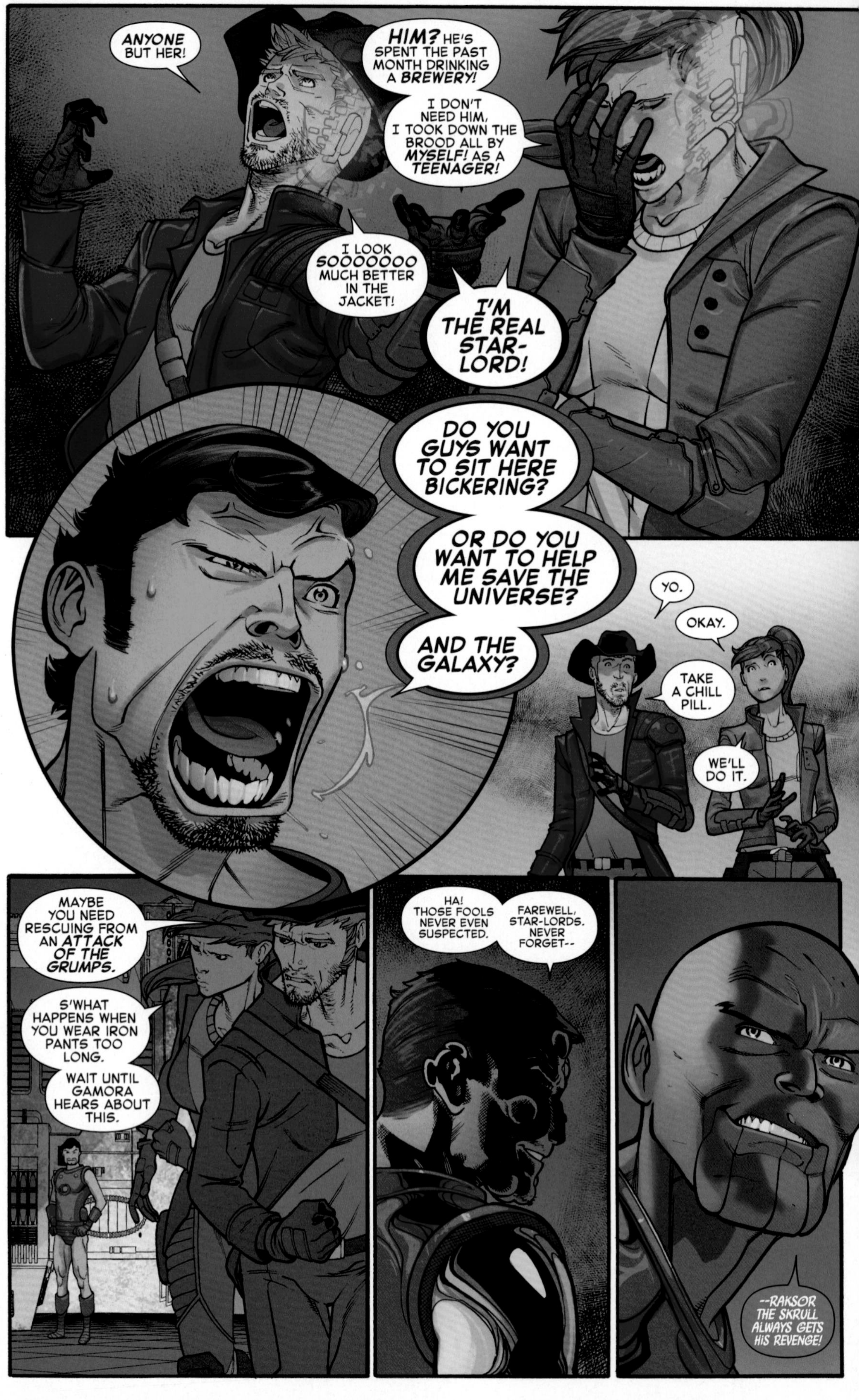
ANYONE BUT HER!
HIM? HE'S SPENT THE PAST MONTH DRINKING A BREWERY!
I DON'T NEED HIM, I TOOK DOWN THE BROOD ALL BY MYSELF! AS A TEENAGER!
I LOOK SOOOOOOO MUCH BETTER IN THE JACKET!
I'M THE REAL STAR-LORD!
DO YOU GUYS WANT TO SIT HERE BICKERING?
OR DO YOU WANT TO HELP ME SAVE THE UNIVERSE?
AND THE GALAXY?
YO.
OKAY.
TAKE A CHILL PILL.
WE'LL DO IT.
MAYBE YOU NEED RESCUING FROM AN ATTACK OF THE GRUMPS.
S'WHAT HAPPENS WHEN YOU WEAR IRON PANTS TOO LONG.
WAIT UNTIL GAMORA HEARS ABOUT THIS.
HA! THOSE FOOLS NEVER EVEN SUSPECTED.
FAREWELL, STAR-LORDS. NEVER FORGET--
--RAKSOR THE SKRULL ALWAYS GETS HIS REVENGE!

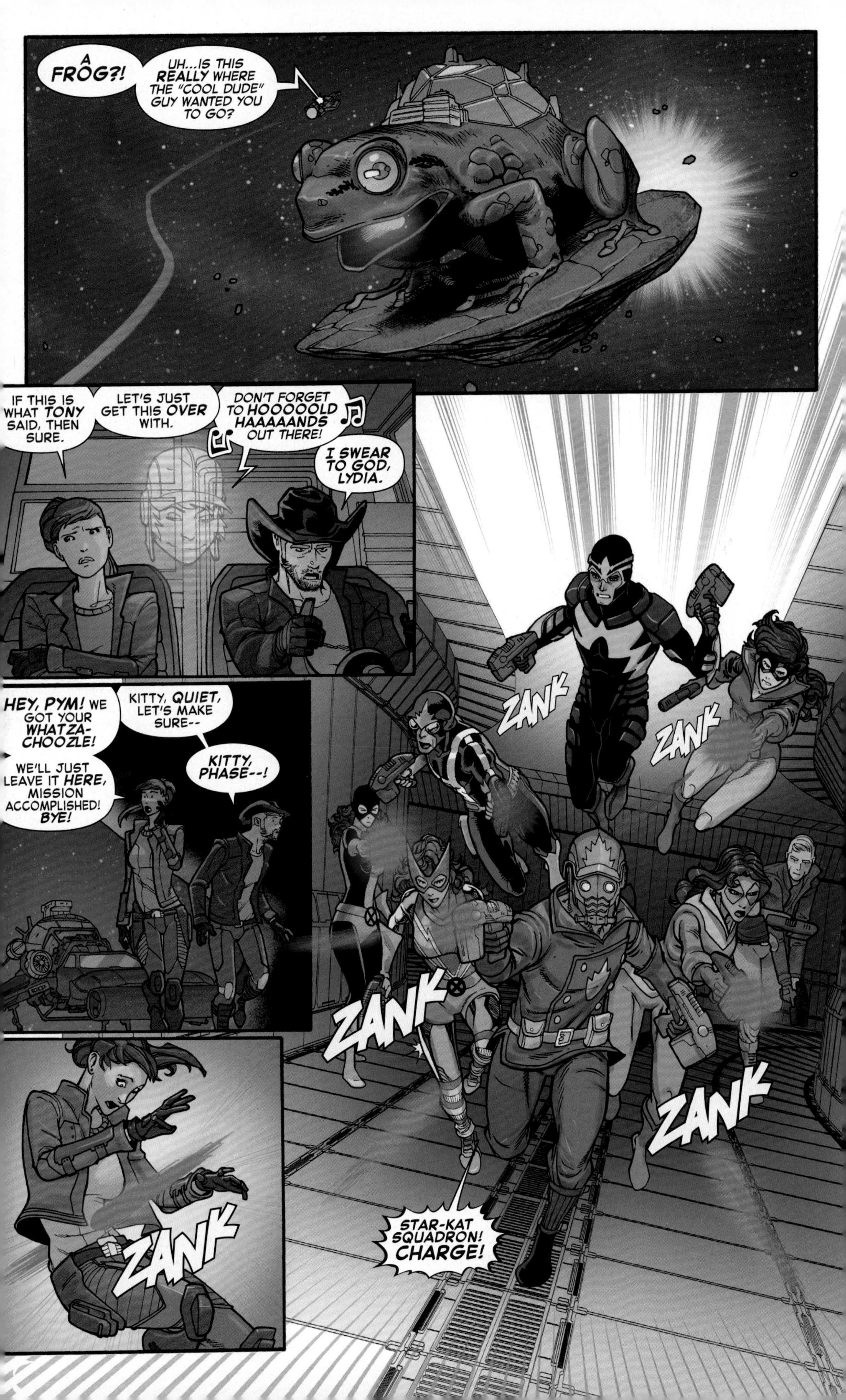
A FROG?!
UH...IS THIS REALLY WHERE THE "COOL DUDE" GUY WANTED YOU TO GO?
IF THIS IS WHAT TONY SAID, THEN SURE.
LET'S JUST GET THIS OVER WITH.
DON'T FORGET TO HOOOOOLD HAAAAANDS OUT THERE!
I SWEAR TO GOD, LYDIA.
HEY, PYM! WE GOT YOUR WHATZA-CHOOZLE!
WE'LL JUST LEAVE IT HERE, MISSION ACCOMPLISHED! BYE!
KITTY, QUIET, LET'S MAKE SURE--
KITTY, PHASE--!
ZANK
ZANK
ZANK
ZANK
ZANK
STAR-KAT SQUADRON! CHARGE!

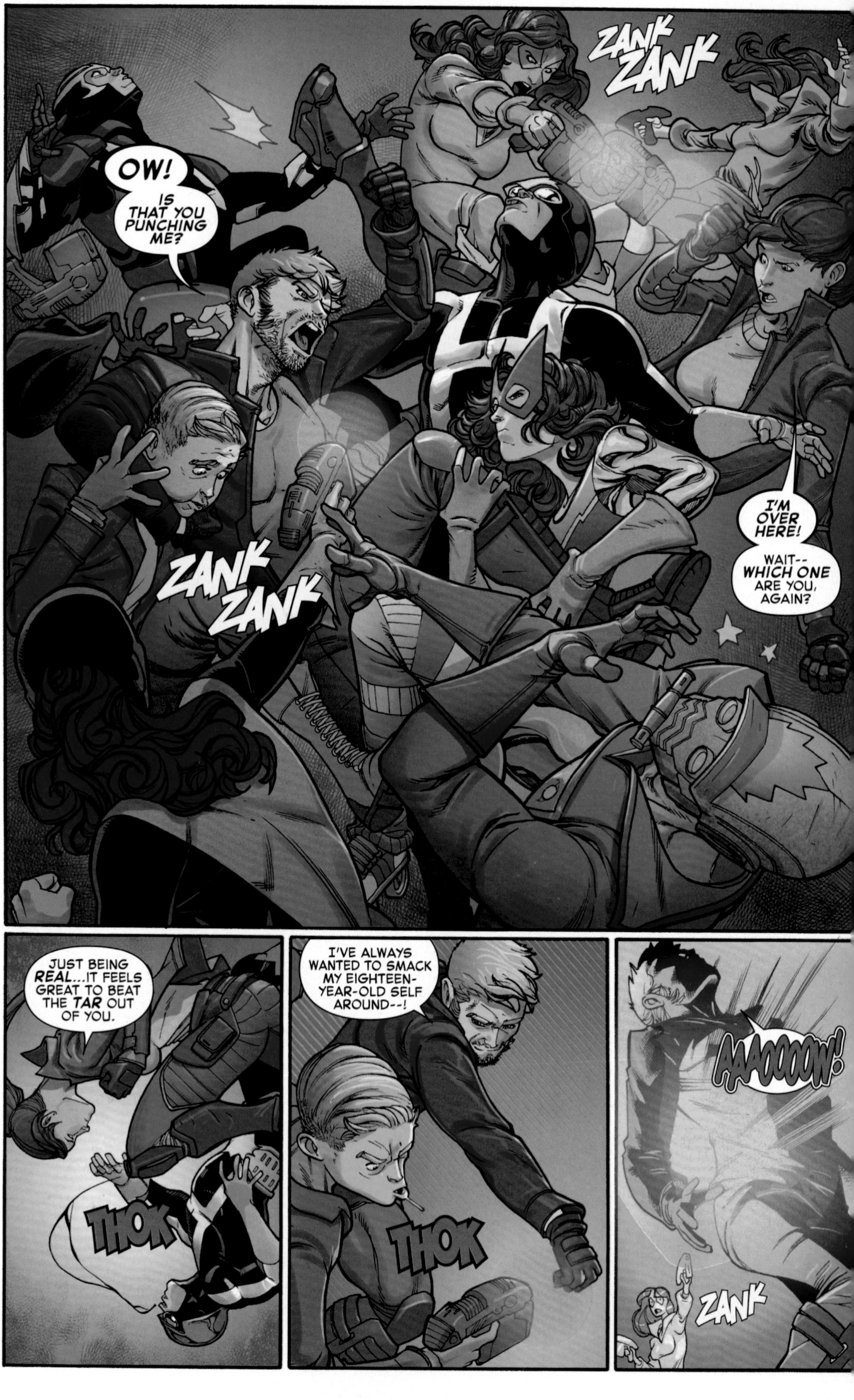
ZANK ZANK
OW!
IS THAT YOU PUNCHING ME?
ZANK ZANK
I'M OVER HERE!
WAIT-- WHICH ONE ARE YOU, AGAIN?
JUST BEING REAL...IT FEELS GREAT TO BEAT THE TAR OUT OF YOU.
THOK
I'VE ALWAYS WANTED TO SMACK MY EIGHTEEN-YEAR-OLD SELF AROUND--!
THOK
AAAOOOOW!
ZANK

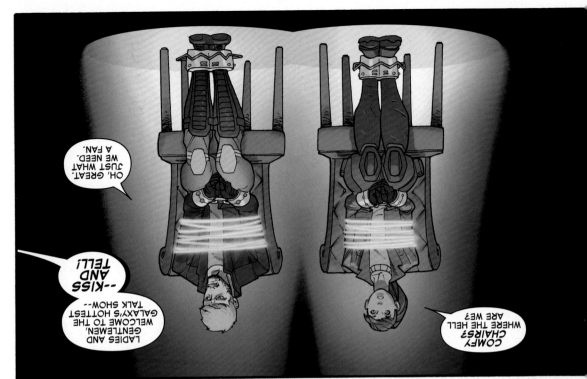

OH, GREAT. JUST WHAT WE NEED. A FAN.

COMFY CHAIRS? WHERE THE HELL ARE WE?

LADIES AND GENTLEMEN, WELCOME TO THE GALAXY'S HOTTEST TALK SHOW-- --KISS AND TELL!

WHOA, WHO INTERRUPTED MY DREAM?

WHY YESSSS, ROCKET, I WOULD LOVE TO LAMBADA WITH YOUUU--

...UGGGH MY HEAD.

--PETERRRR, THIS IS YOURRRRR FAUUUULT...

UH-OH--

PETER!

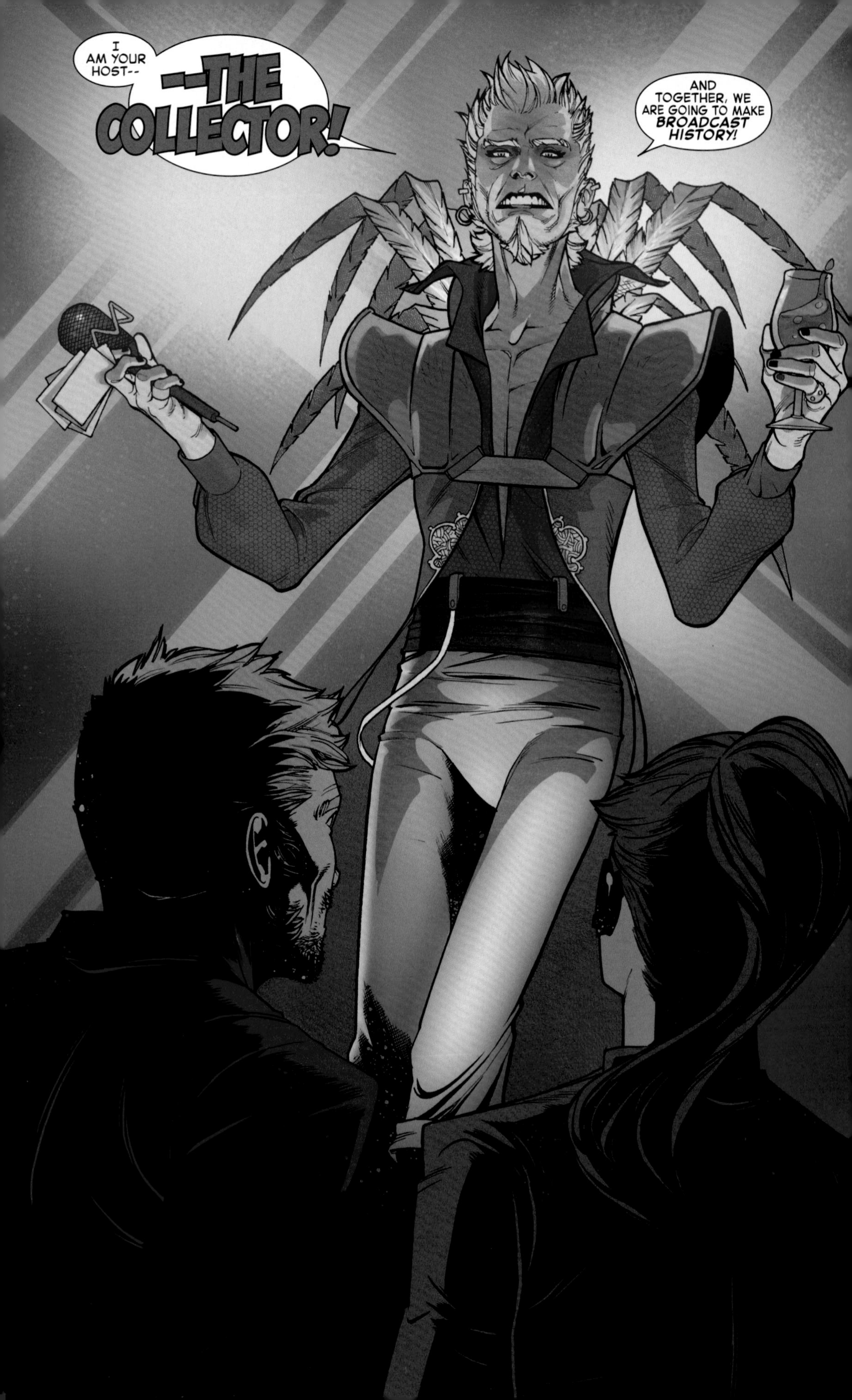
I AM YOUR HOST--
--THE COLLECTOR!
AND TOGETHER, WE ARE GOING TO MAKE *BROADCAST HISTORY!*

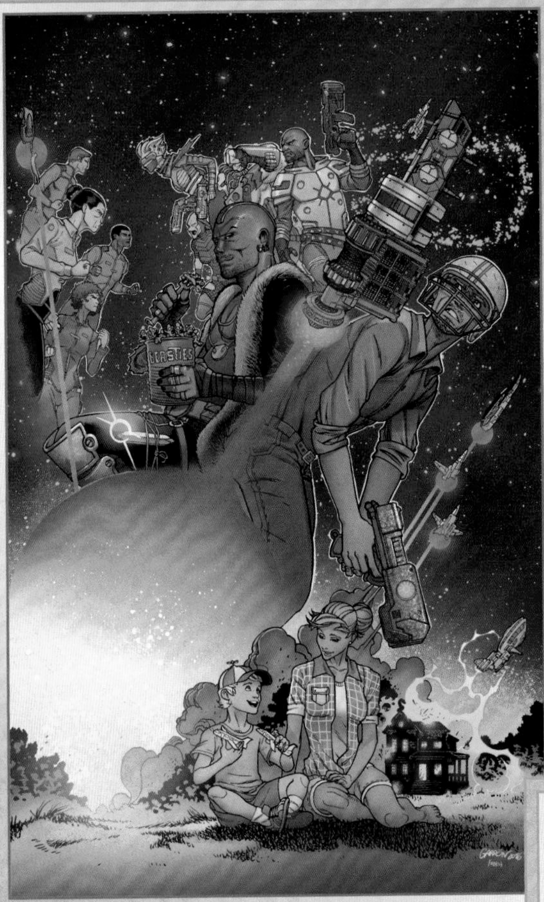

CLASSIES

#6 STORY THUS FAR VARIANT BY
AVIER GARRÓN & ANTONIO FABELA

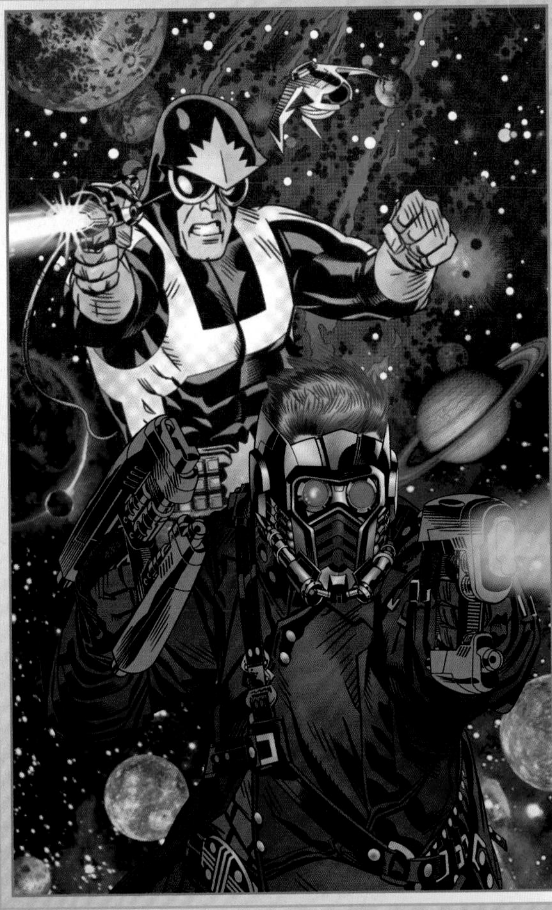

#6 CLASSIC VARIANT BY MICHAEL GOLDEN

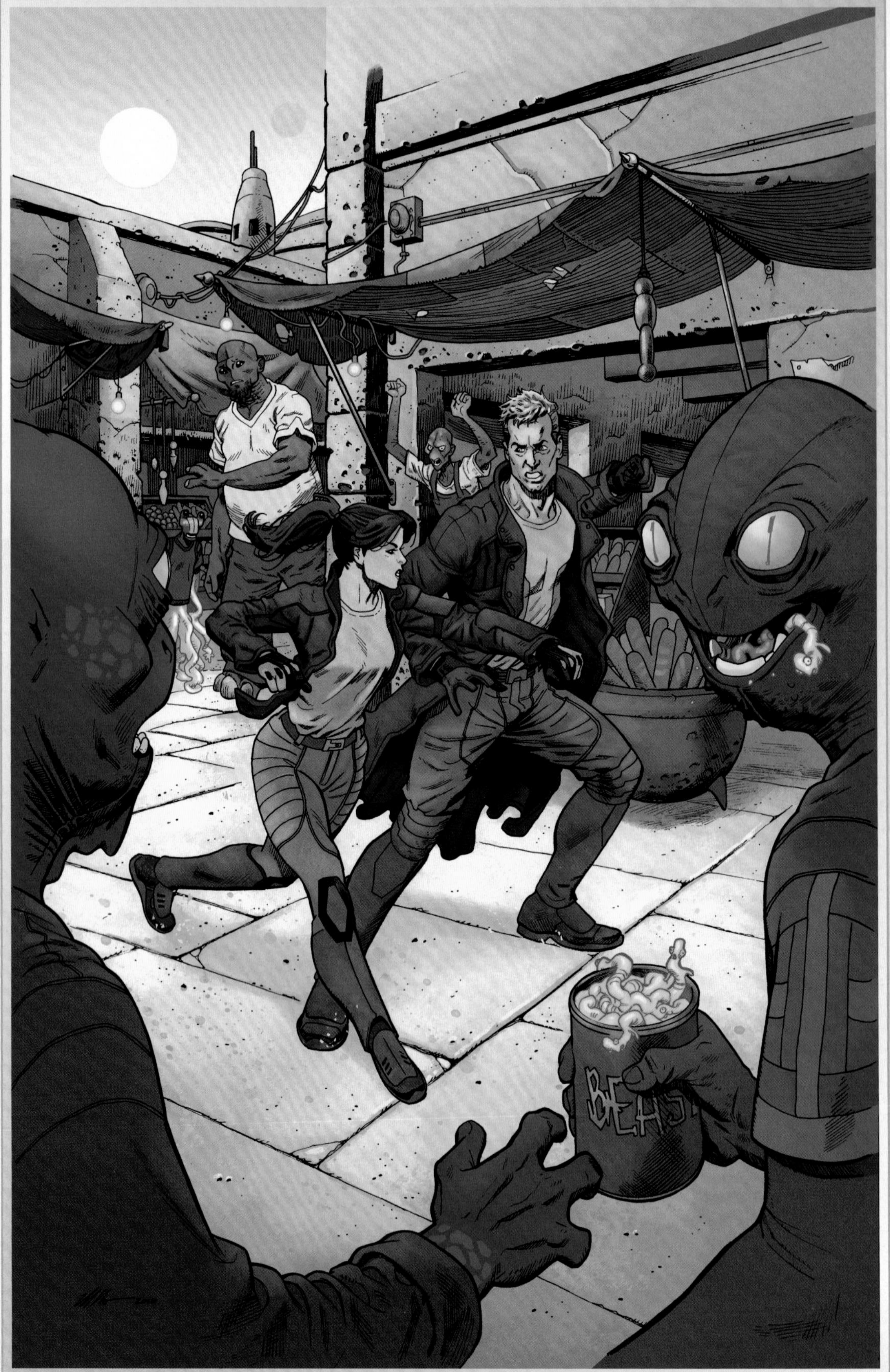

SEVEN
WE ARE NEVER EVER EVER GETTING BACK TOGETHER

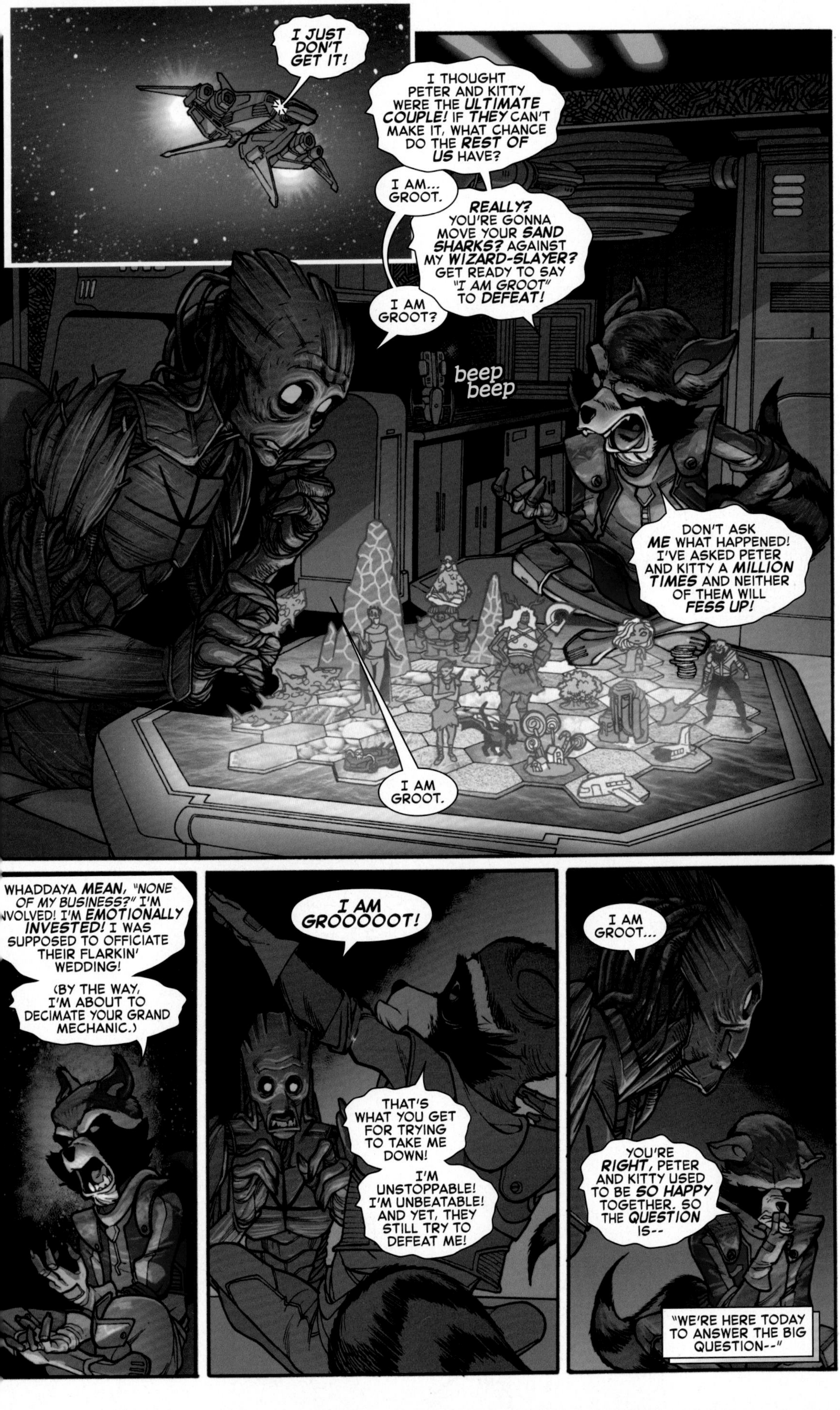
I JUST DON'T GET IT!
I THOUGHT PETER AND KITTY WERE THE ULTIMATE COUPLE! IF THEY CAN'T MAKE IT, WHAT CHANCE DO THE REST OF US HAVE?
I AM... GROOT.
REALLY? YOU'RE GONNA MOVE YOUR SAND SHARKS? AGAINST MY WIZARD-SLAYER? GET READY TO SAY "I AM GROOT" TO DEFEAT!
I AM GROOT?
beep beep
DON'T ASK ME WHAT HAPPENED! I'VE ASKED PETER AND KITTY A MILLION TIMES AND NEITHER OF THEM WILL FESS UP!
I AM GROOT.
WHADDAYA MEAN, "NONE OF MY BUSINESS?" I'M INVOLVED! I'M EMOTIONALLY INVESTED! I WAS SUPPOSED TO OFFICIATE THEIR FLARKIN' WEDDING!
(BY THE WAY, I'M ABOUT TO DECIMATE YOUR GRAND MECHANIC.)
I AM GROOOOOT!
THAT'S WHAT YOU GET FOR TRYING TO TAKE ME DOWN!
I'M UNSTOPPABLE! I'M UNBEATABLE! AND YET, THEY STILL TRY TO DEFEAT ME!
I AM GROOT...
YOU'RE RIGHT, PETER AND KITTY USED TO BE SO HAPPY TOGETHER. SO THE QUESTION IS--
"WE'RE HERE TODAY TO ANSWER THE BIG QUESTION--"

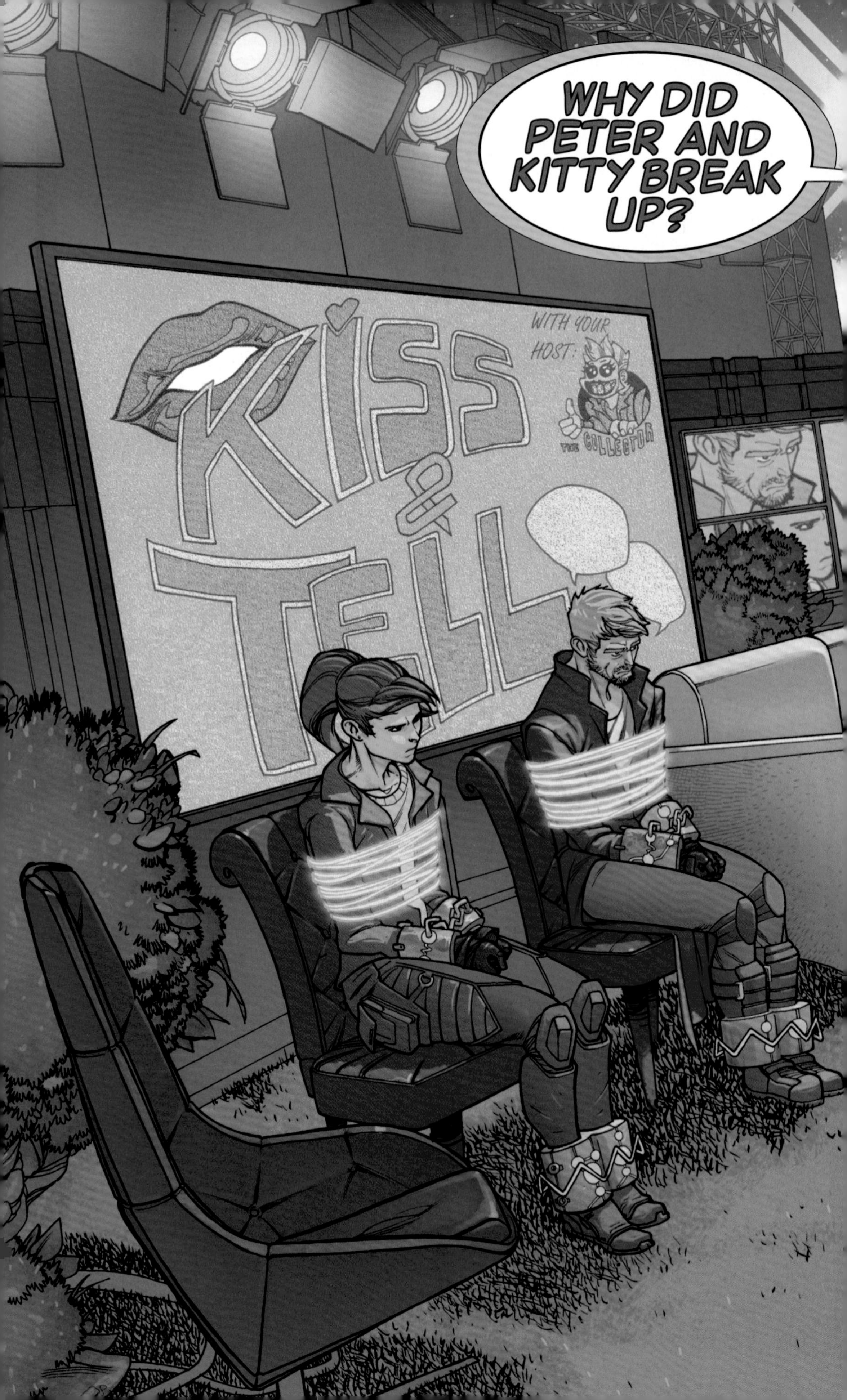
WHY DID PETER AND KITTY BREAK UP?
KISS & TELL
WITH YOUR HOST:
THE COLLECTOR

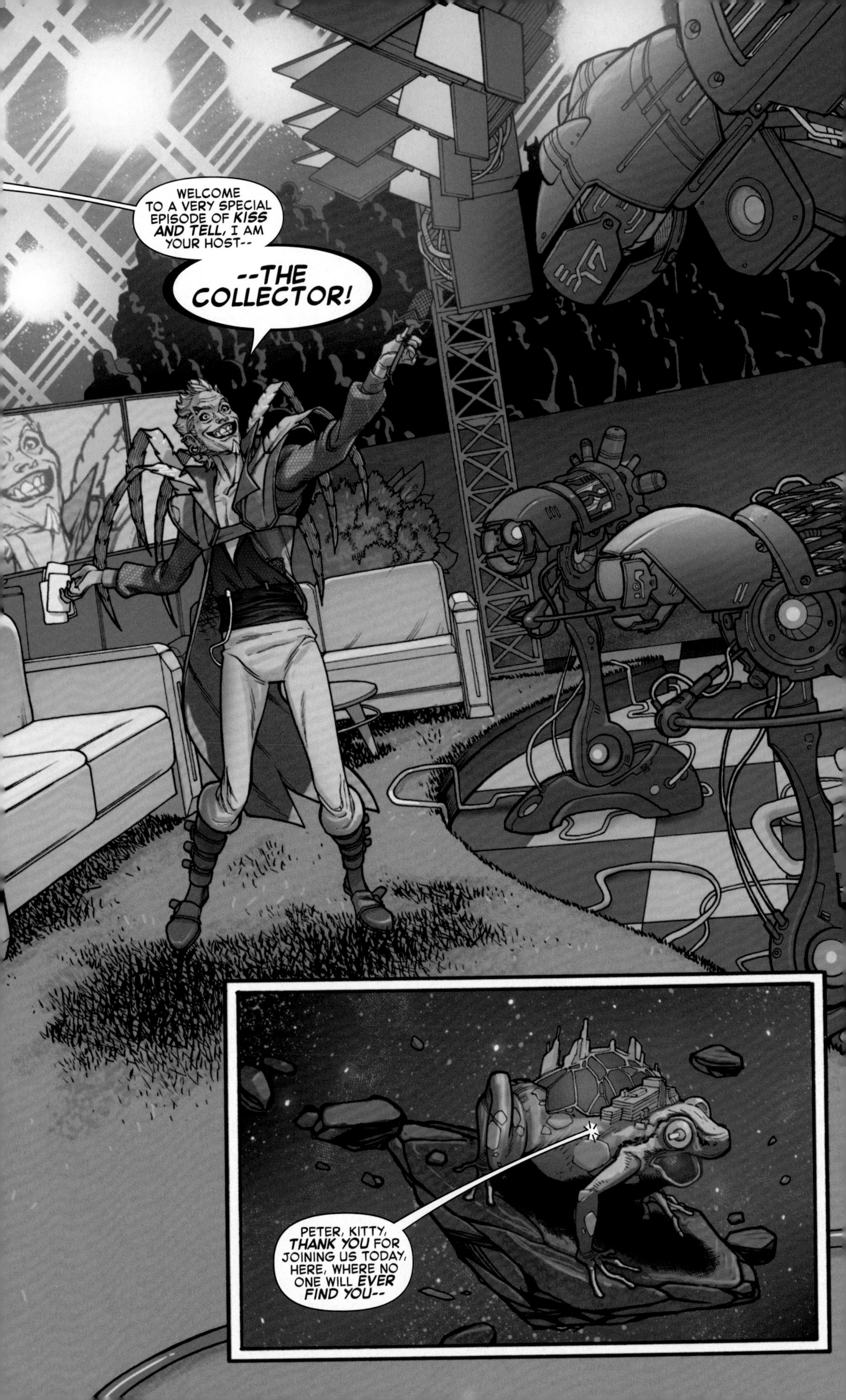
WELCOME TO A VERY SPECIAL EPISODE OF KISS AND TELL, I AM YOUR HOST--
--THE COLLECTOR!
PETER, KITTY, THANK YOU FOR JOINING US TODAY, HERE, WHERE NO ONE WILL EVER FIND YOU--

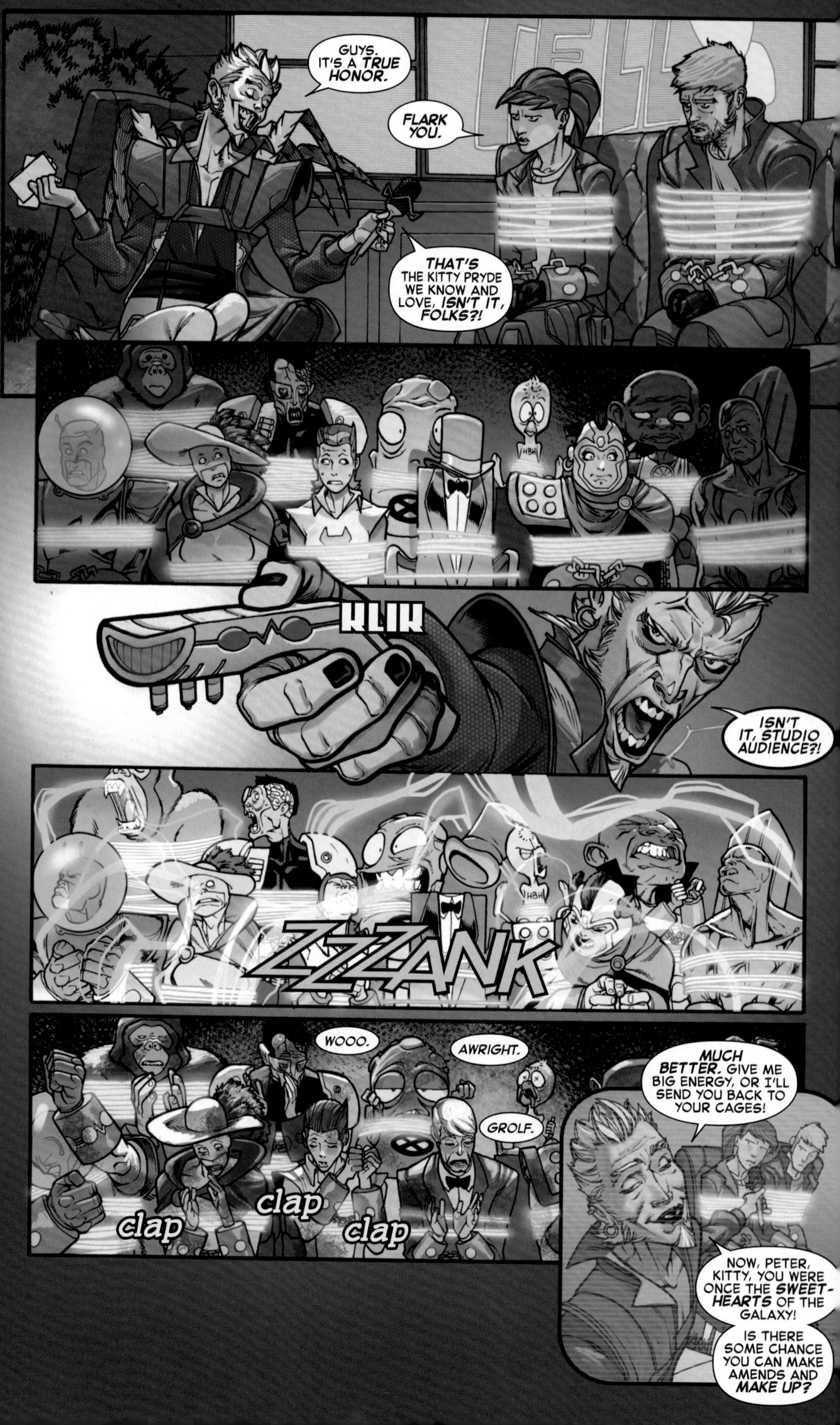
GUYS. IT'S A TRUE HONOR.
FLARK YOU.
THAT'S THE KITTY PRYDE WE KNOW AND LOVE, ISN'T IT, FOLKS?!
KLIK
ISN'T IT, STUDIO AUDIENCE?!
ZZZANK
WOOO.
AWRIGHT.
GROLF.
clap
clap
clap
MUCH BETTER. GIVE ME BIG ENERGY, OR I'LL SEND YOU BACK TO YOUR CAGES!
NOW, PETER, KITTY, YOU WERE ONCE THE SWEET-HEARTS OF THE GALAXY!
IS THERE SOME CHANCE YOU CAN MAKE AMENDS AND MAKE UP?

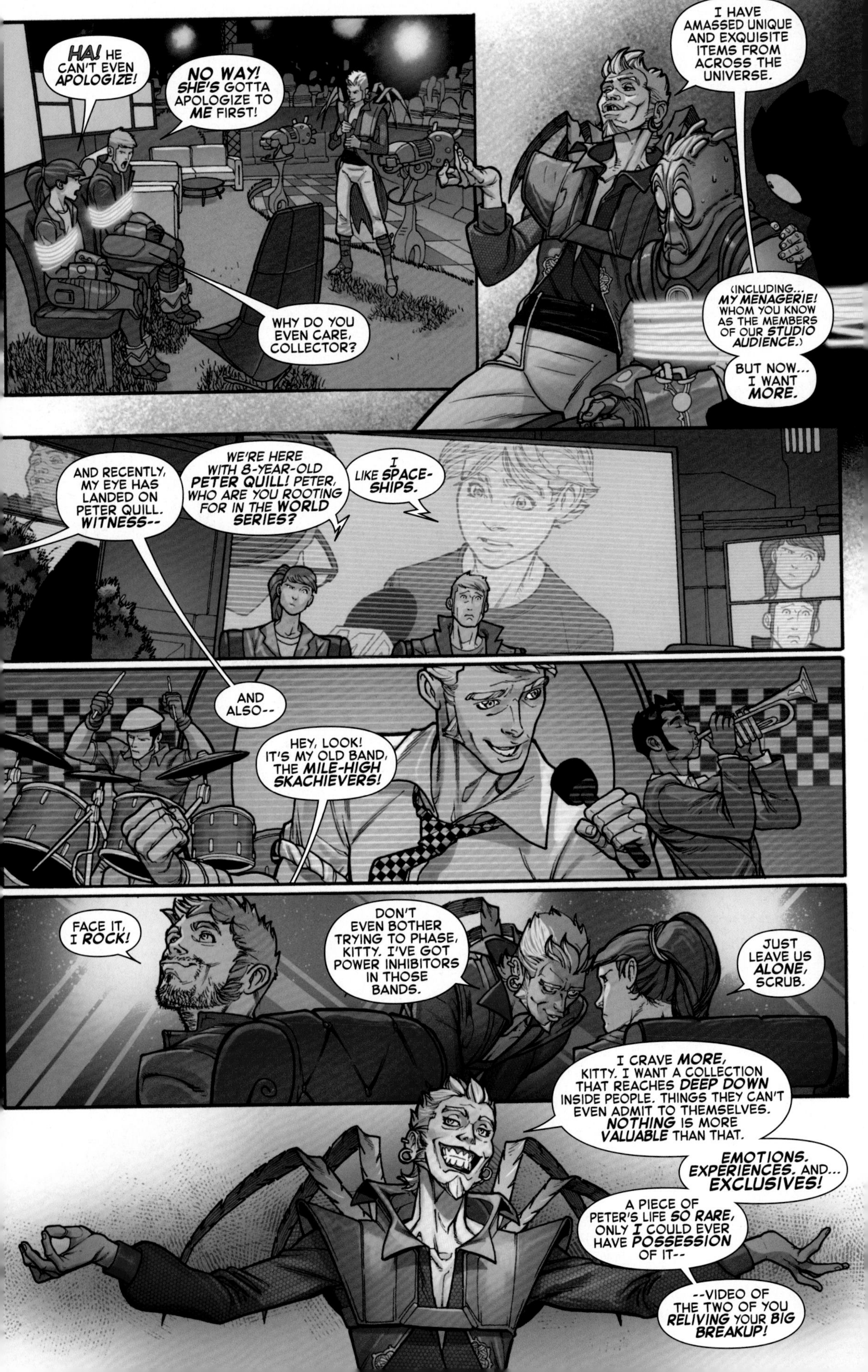
HA! HE CAN'T EVEN APOLOGIZE!
NO WAY! SHE'S GOTTA APOLOGIZE TO ME FIRST!
WHY DO YOU EVEN CARE, COLLECTOR?
I HAVE AMASSED UNIQUE AND EXQUISITE ITEMS FROM ACROSS THE UNIVERSE.
(INCLUDING... MY MENAGERIE! WHOM YOU KNOW AS THE MEMBERS OF OUR STUDIO AUDIENCE.)
BUT NOW... I WANT MORE.
AND RECENTLY, MY EYE HAS LANDED ON PETER QUILL. WITNESS--
WE'RE HERE WITH 8-YEAR-OLD PETER QUILL! PETER, WHO ARE YOU ROOTING FOR IN THE WORLD SERIES?
I LIKE SPACE-SHIPS.
AND ALSO--
HEY, LOOK! IT'S MY OLD BAND, THE MILE-HIGH SKACHIEVERS!
FACE IT, I ROCK!
DON'T EVEN BOTHER TRYING TO PHASE, KITTY. I'VE GOT POWER INHIBITORS IN THOSE BANDS.
JUST LEAVE US ALONE, SCRUB.
I CRAVE MORE, KITTY. I WANT A COLLECTION THAT REACHES DEEP DOWN INSIDE PEOPLE. THINGS THEY CAN'T EVEN ADMIT TO THEMSELVES. NOTHING IS MORE VALUABLE THAN THAT.
EMOTIONS. EXPERIENCES. AND... EXCLUSIVES!
A PIECE OF PETER'S LIFE SO RARE, ONLY I COULD EVER HAVE POSSESSION OF IT--
--VIDEO OF THE TWO OF YOU RELIVING YOUR BIG BREAKUP!

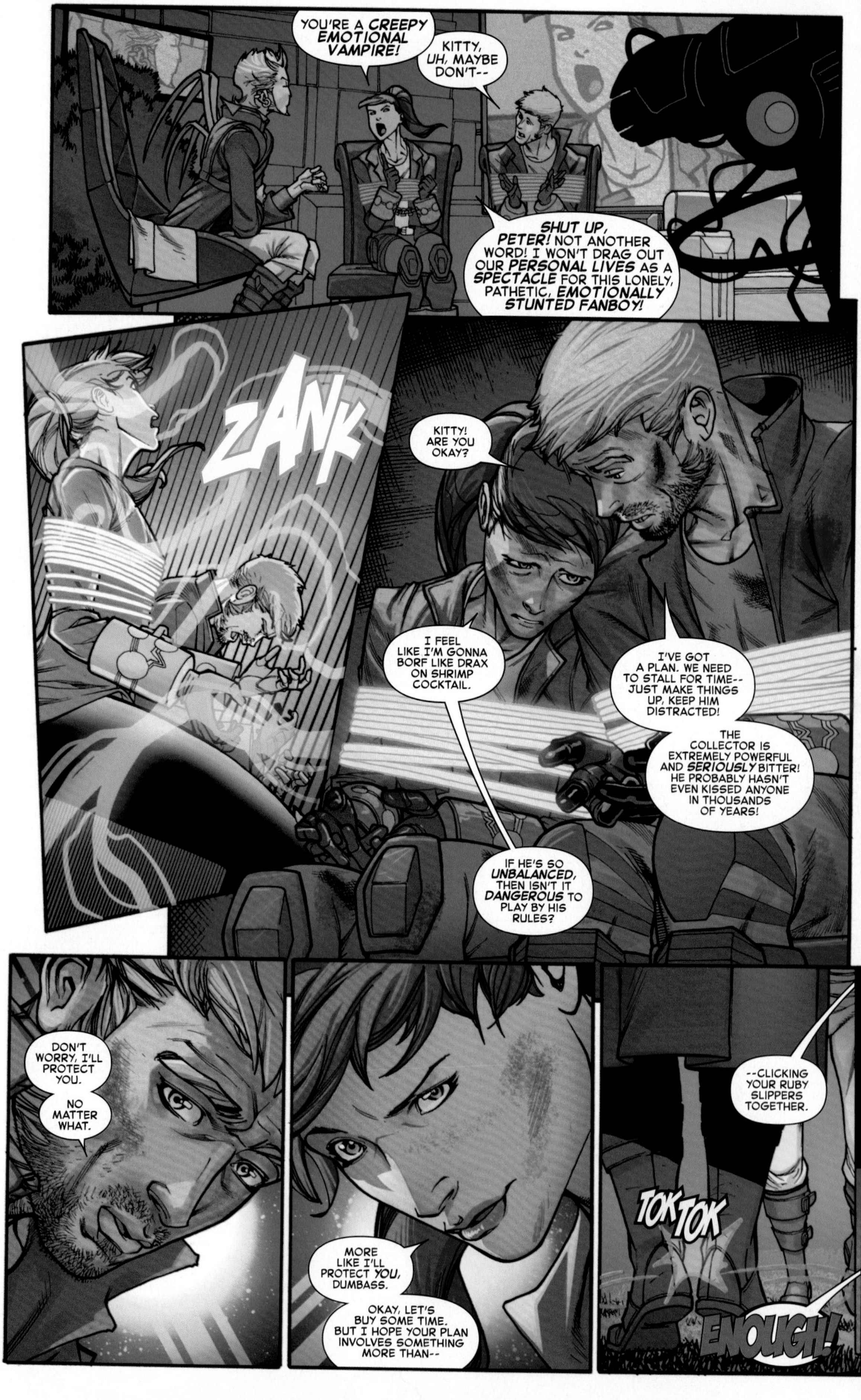
YOU'RE A CREEPY EMOTIONAL VAMPIRE!
KITTY, UH, MAYBE DON'T--
SHUT UP, PETER! NOT ANOTHER WORD! I WON'T DRAG OUT OUR PERSONAL LIVES AS A SPECTACLE FOR THIS LONELY, PATHETIC, EMOTIONALLY STUNTED FANBOY!
ZANK
KITTY! ARE YOU OKAY?
I FEEL LIKE I'M GONNA BORF LIKE DRAX ON SHRIMP COCKTAIL.
I'VE GOT A PLAN. WE NEED TO STALL FOR TIME-- JUST MAKE THINGS UP, KEEP HIM DISTRACTED!
THE COLLECTOR IS EXTREMELY POWERFUL AND SERIOUSLY BITTER! HE PROBABLY HASN'T EVEN KISSED ANYONE IN THOUSANDS OF YEARS!
IF HE'S SO UNBALANCED, THEN ISN'T IT DANGEROUS TO PLAY BY HIS RULES?
DON'T WORRY, I'LL PROTECT YOU.
NO MATTER WHAT.
MORE LIKE I'LL PROTECT YOU, DUMBASS.
OKAY, LET'S BUY SOME TIME. BUT I HOPE YOUR PLAN INVOLVES SOMETHING MORE THAN--
--CLICKING YOUR RUBY SLIPPERS TOGETHER.
TOK TOK
ENOUGH!

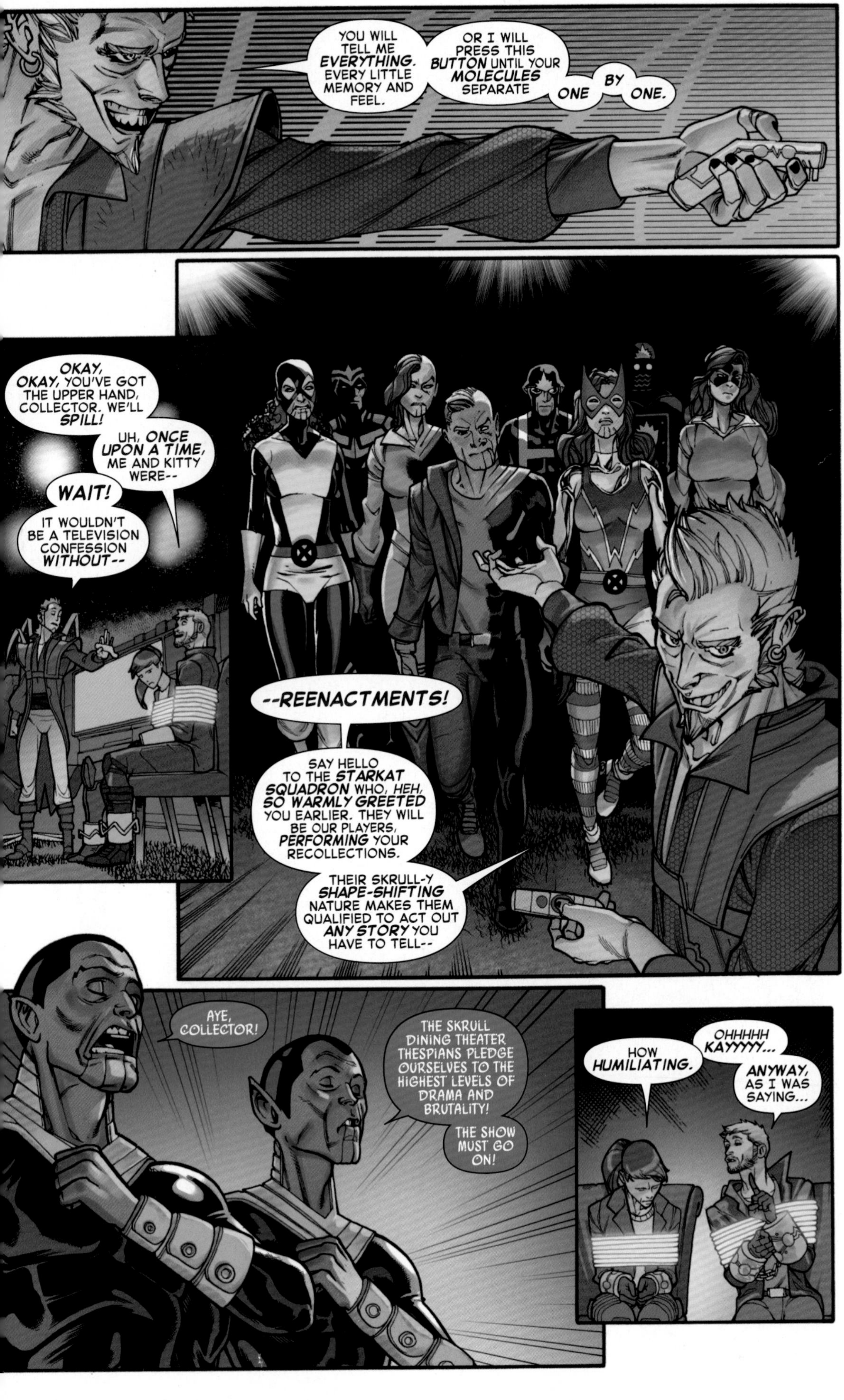
YOU WILL TELL ME EVERYTHING. EVERY LITTLE MEMORY AND FEEL.
OR I WILL PRESS THIS BUTTON UNTIL YOUR MOLECULES SEPARATE
ONE BY ONE.
OKAY, OKAY, YOU'VE GOT THE UPPER HAND, COLLECTOR. WE'LL SPILL!
UH, ONCE UPON A TIME, ME AND KITTY WERE--
WAIT!
IT WOULDN'T BE A TELEVISION CONFESSION WITHOUT--
--REENACTMENTS!
SAY HELLO TO THE STARKAT SQUADRON WHO, HEH, SO WARMLY GREETED YOU EARLIER. THEY WILL BE OUR PLAYERS, PERFORMING YOUR RECOLLECTIONS.
THEIR SKRULL-Y SHAPE-SHIFTING NATURE MAKES THEM QUALIFIED TO ACT OUT ANY STORY YOU HAVE TO TELL--
AYE, COLLECTOR!
THE SKRULL DINING THEATER THESPIANS PLEDGE OURSELVES TO THE HIGHEST LEVELS OF DRAMA AND BRUTALITY!
THE SHOW MUST GO ON!
HOW HUMILIATING.
OHHHHH KAYYYYY...
ANYWAY, AS I WAS SAYING...

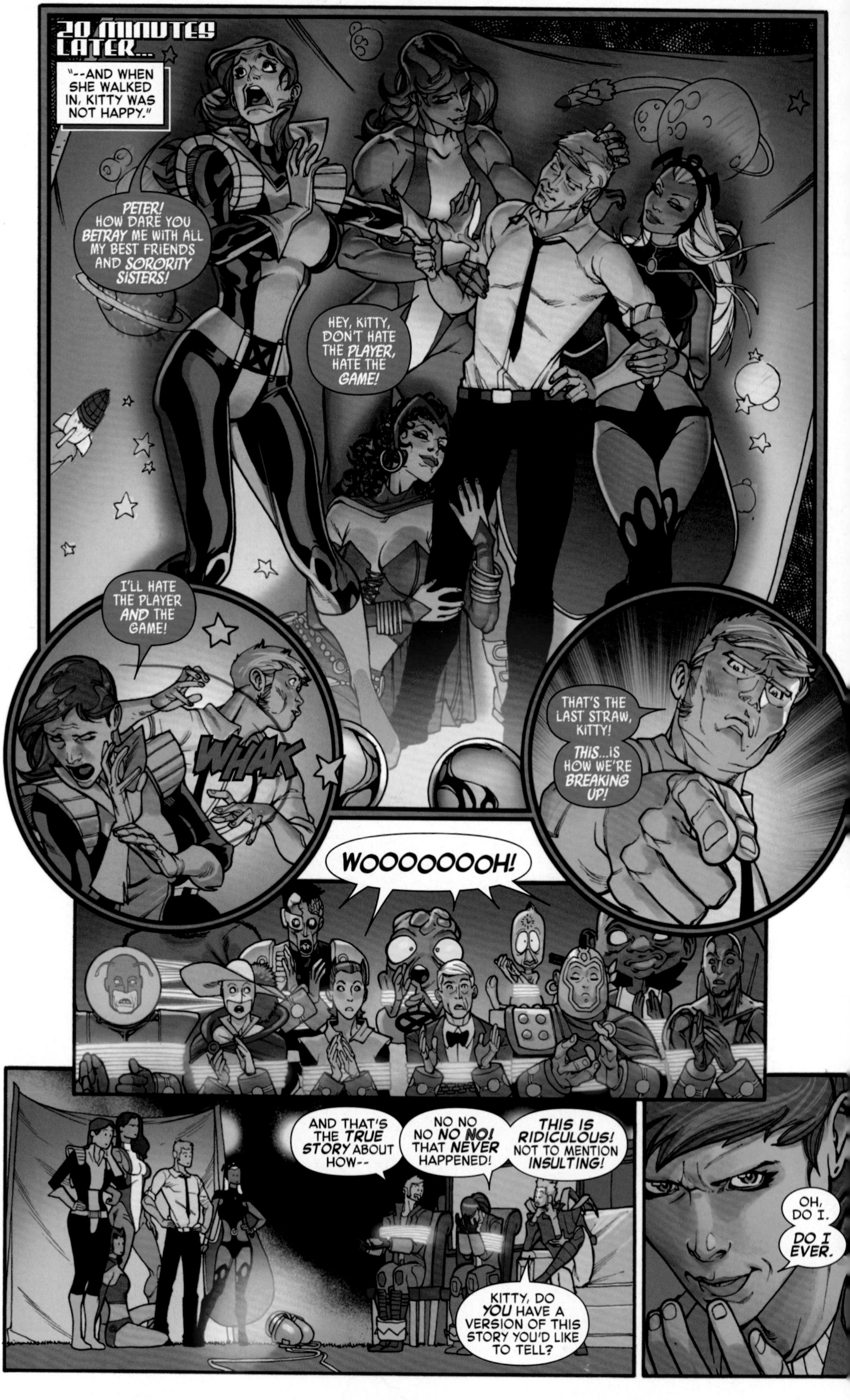
20 MINUTES LATER...
"--AND WHEN SHE WALKED IN, KITTY WAS NOT HAPPY."
PETER! HOW DARE YOU BETRAY ME WITH ALL MY BEST FRIENDS AND SORORITY SISTERS!
HEY, KITTY, DON'T HATE THE PLAYER, HATE THE GAME!
I'LL HATE THE PLAYER AND THE GAME!
WHAK
THAT'S THE LAST STRAW, KITTY! THIS...IS HOW WE'RE BREAKING UP!
WOOOOOOOH!
AND THAT'S THE TRUE STORY ABOUT HOW--
NO NO NO NO NO! THAT NEVER HAPPENED!
THIS IS RIDICULOUS! NOT TO MENTION INSULTING!
KITTY, DO YOU HAVE A VERSION OF THIS STORY YOU'D LIKE TO TELL?
OH, DO I.
DO I EVER.

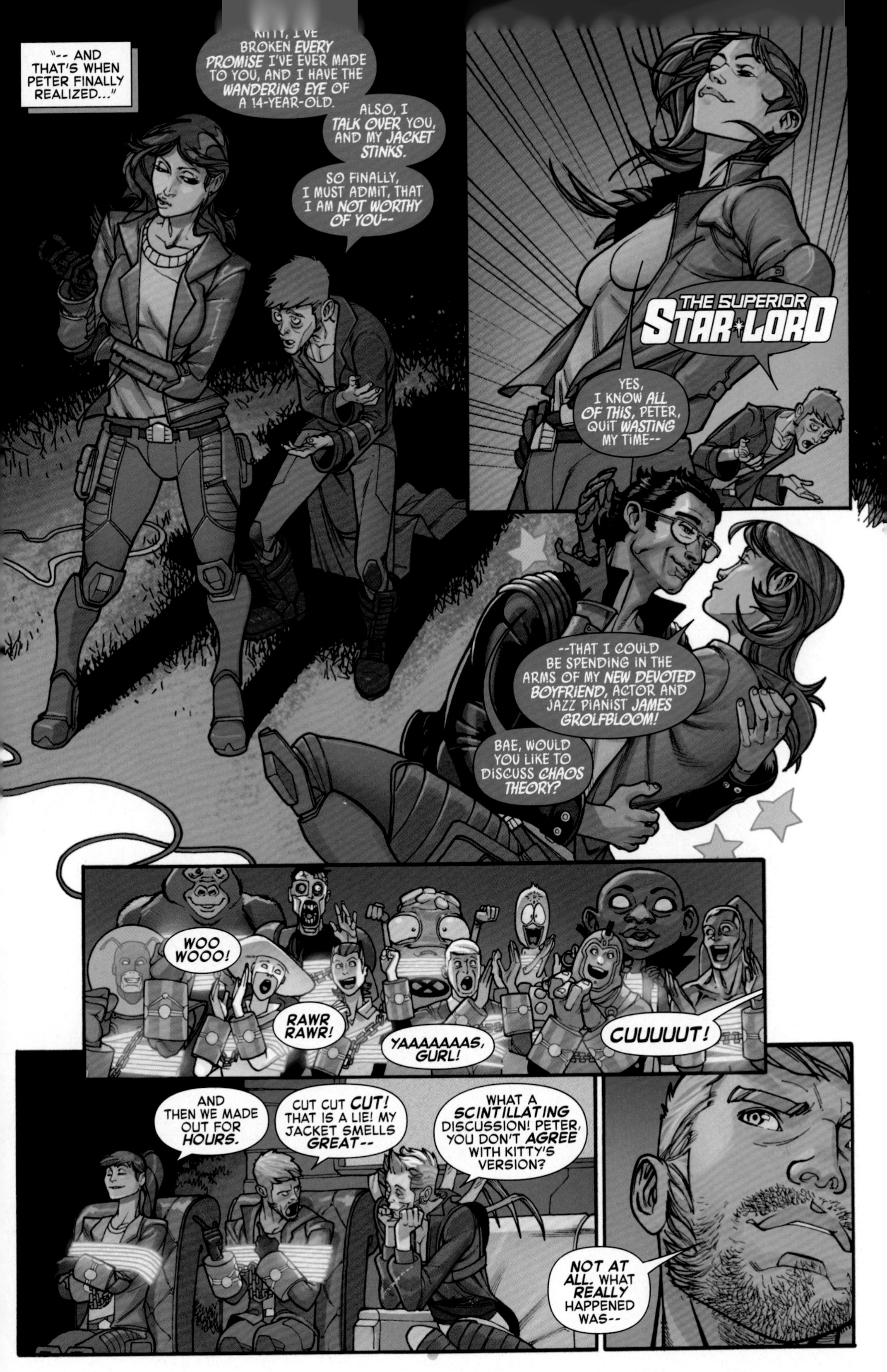
"-- AND THAT'S WHEN PETER FINALLY REALIZED..."
KITTY, I'VE BROKEN EVERY PROMISE I'VE EVER MADE TO YOU, AND I HAVE THE WANDERING EYE OF A 14-YEAR-OLD.
ALSO, I TALK OVER YOU, AND MY JACKET STINKS.
SO FINALLY, I MUST ADMIT, THAT I AM NOT WORTHY OF YOU--
THE SUPERIOR STAR-LORD
YES, I KNOW ALL OF THIS, PETER, QUIT WASTING MY TIME--
--THAT I COULD BE SPENDING IN THE ARMS OF MY NEW DEVOTED BOYFRIEND, ACTOR AND JAZZ PIANIST JAMES GROLFBLOOM!
BAE, WOULD YOU LIKE TO DISCUSS CHAOS THEORY?
WOO WOOO!
RAWR RAWR!
YAAAAAAAS, GURL!
CUUUUUT!
AND THEN WE MADE OUT FOR HOURS.
CUT CUT CUT! THAT IS A LIE! MY JACKET SMELLS GREAT--
WHAT A SCINTILLATING DISCUSSION! PETER, YOU DON'T AGREE WITH KITTY'S VERSION?
NOT AT ALL. WHAT REALLY HAPPENED WAS--

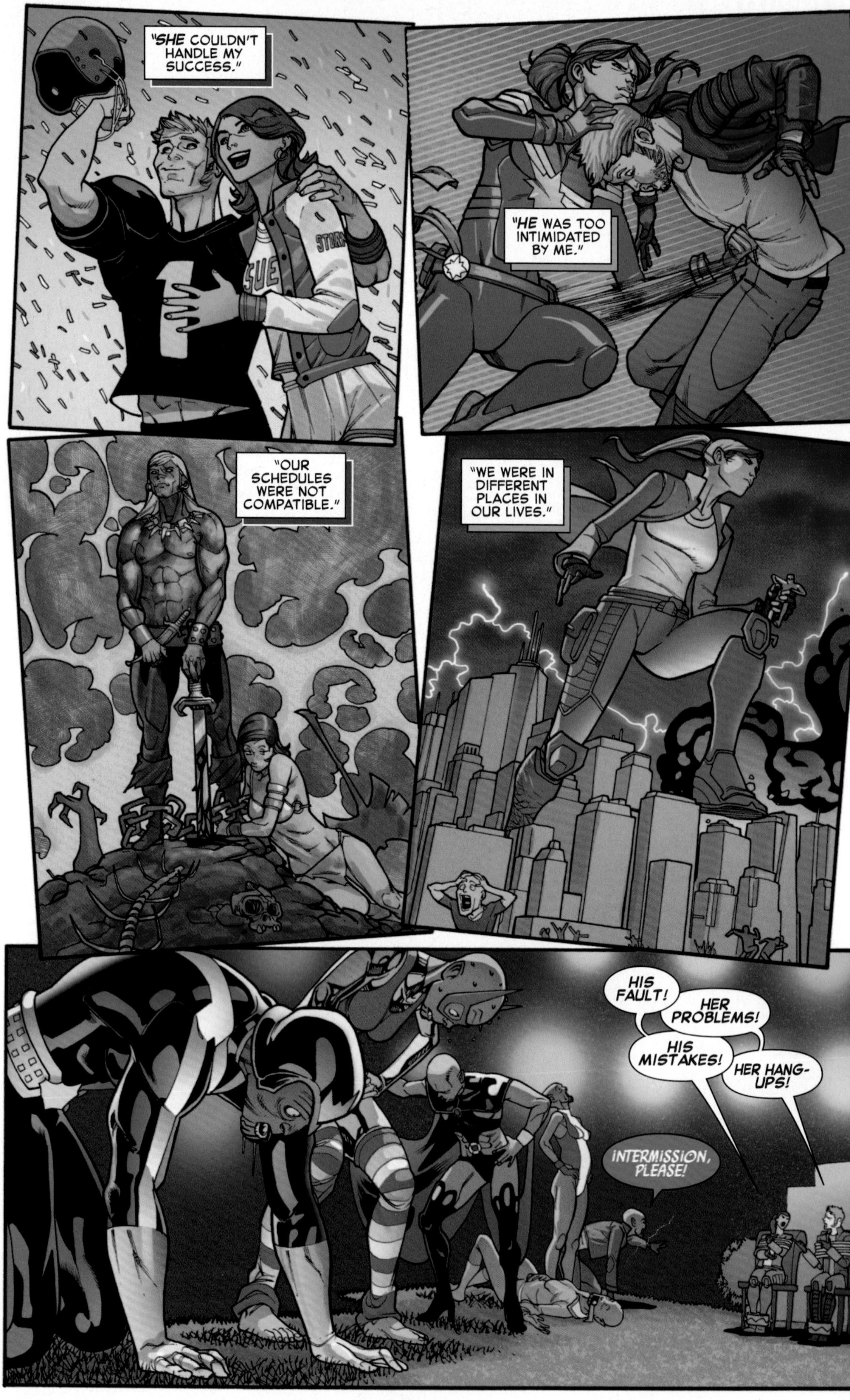
"SHE COULDN'T HANDLE MY SUCCESS."
"HE WAS TOO INTIMIDATED BY ME."
"OUR SCHEDULES WERE NOT COMPATIBLE."
"WE WERE IN DIFFERENT PLACES IN OUR LIVES."
HIS FAULT!
HER PROBLEMS!
HIS MISTAKES!
HER HANG-UPS!
INTERMISSION, PLEASE!

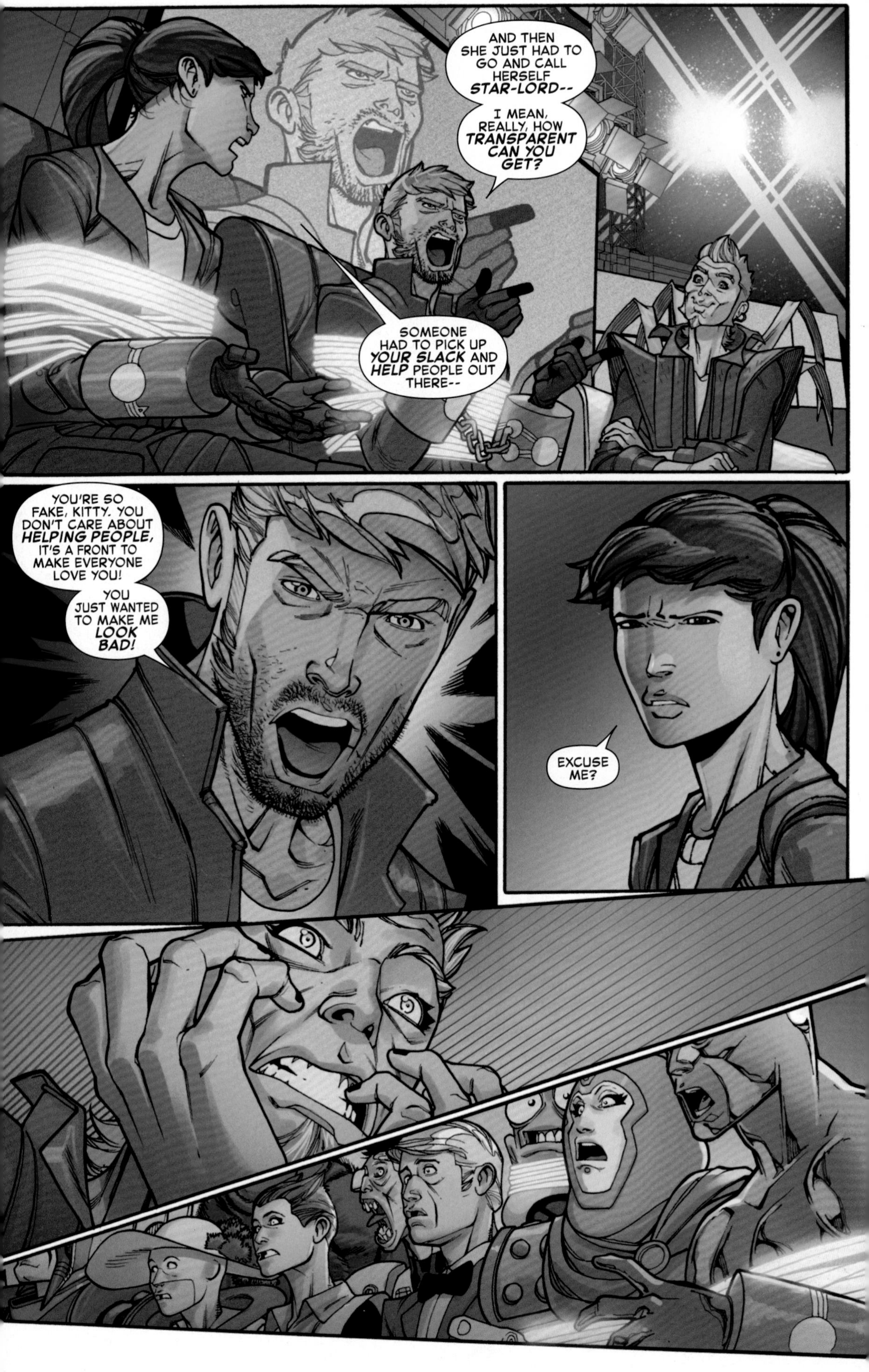
AND THEN SHE JUST HAD TO GO AND CALL HERSELF STAR-LORD--
I MEAN, REALLY, HOW TRANSPARENT CAN YOU GET?
SOMEONE HAD TO PICK UP YOUR SLACK AND HELP PEOPLE OUT THERE--
YOU'RE SO FAKE, KITTY. YOU DON'T CARE ABOUT HELPING PEOPLE, IT'S A FRONT TO MAKE EVERYONE LOVE YOU!
YOU JUST WANTED TO MAKE ME LOOK BAD!
EXCUSE ME?

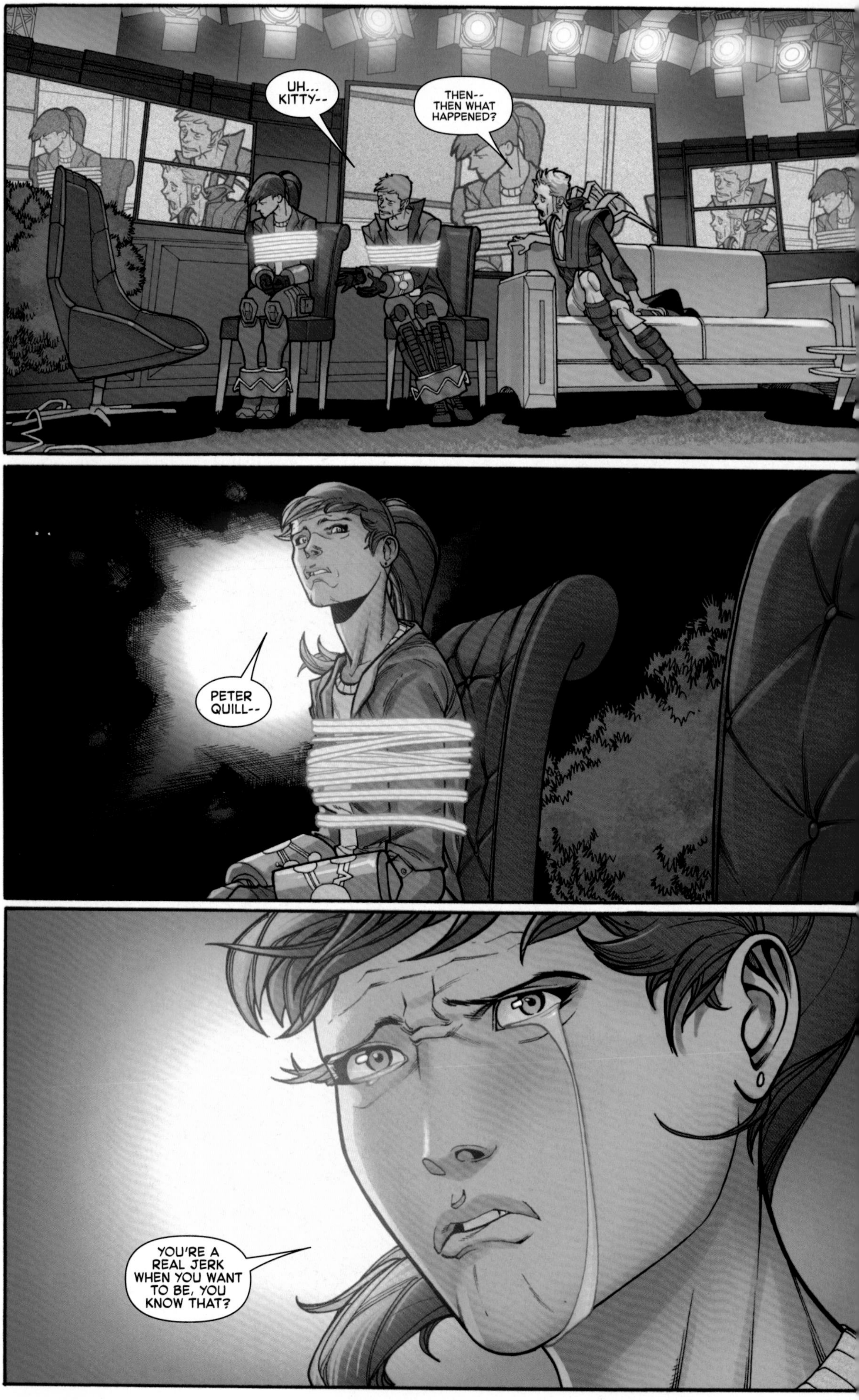
UH... KITTY--
THEN-- THEN WHAT HAPPENED?
PETER QUILL--
YOU'RE A REAL JERK WHEN YOU WANT TO BE, YOU KNOW THAT?

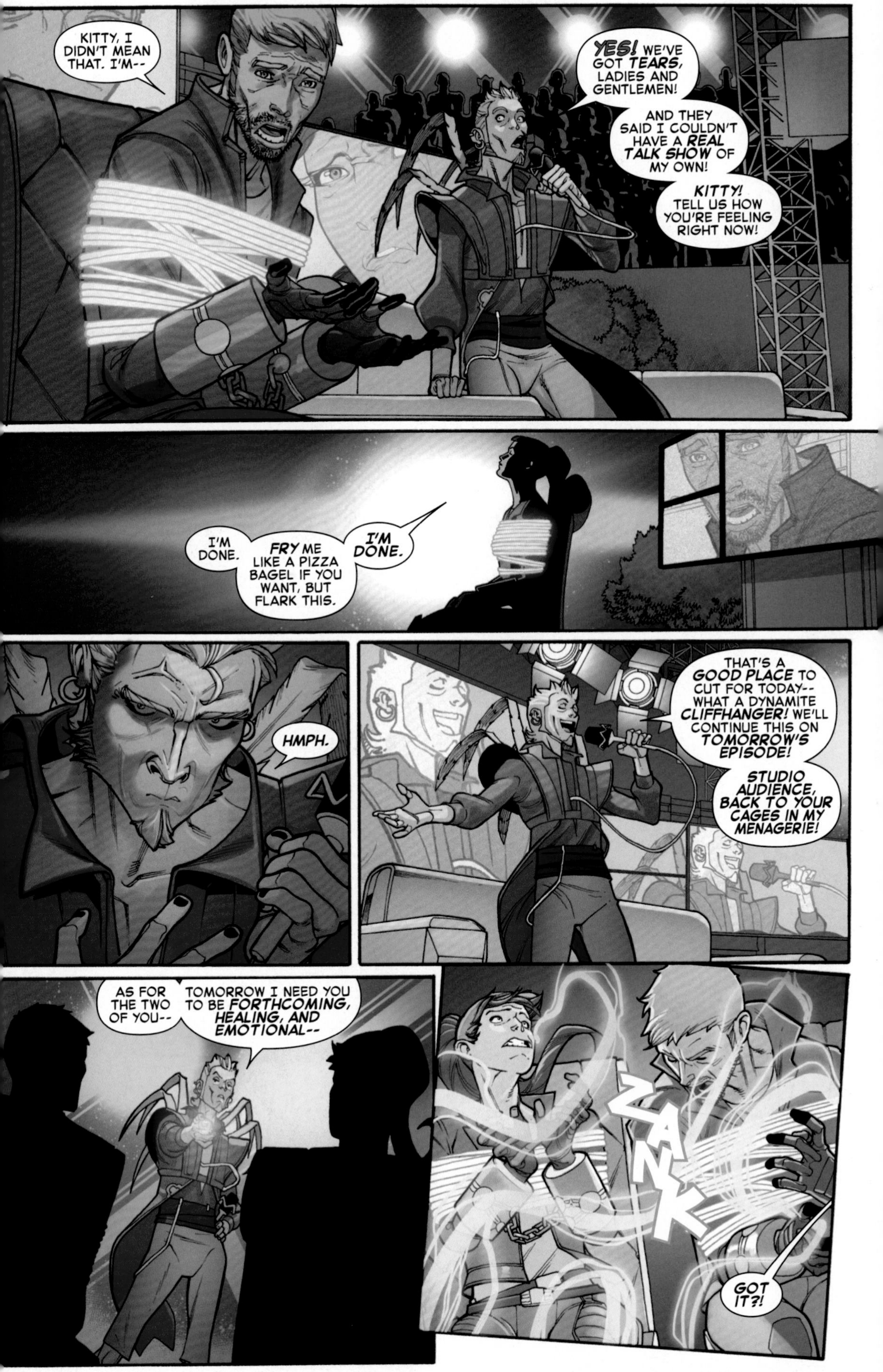
KITTY, I DIDN'T MEAN THAT. I'M--
YES! WE'VE GOT TEARS, LADIES AND GENTLEMEN!
AND THEY SAID I COULDN'T HAVE A REAL TALK SHOW OF MY OWN!
KITTY! TELL US HOW YOU'RE FEELING RIGHT NOW!
I'M DONE.
FRY ME LIKE A PIZZA BAGEL IF YOU WANT, BUT FLARK THIS.
I'M DONE.
HMPH.
THAT'S A GOOD PLACE TO CUT FOR TODAY-- WHAT A DYNAMITE CLIFFHANGER! WE'LL CONTINUE THIS ON TOMORROW'S EPISODE!
STUDIO AUDIENCE, BACK TO YOUR CAGES IN MY MENAGERIE!
AS FOR THE TWO OF YOU--
TOMORROW I NEED YOU TO BE FORTHCOMING, HEALING, AND EMOTIONAL--
ZZAK
GOT IT?!

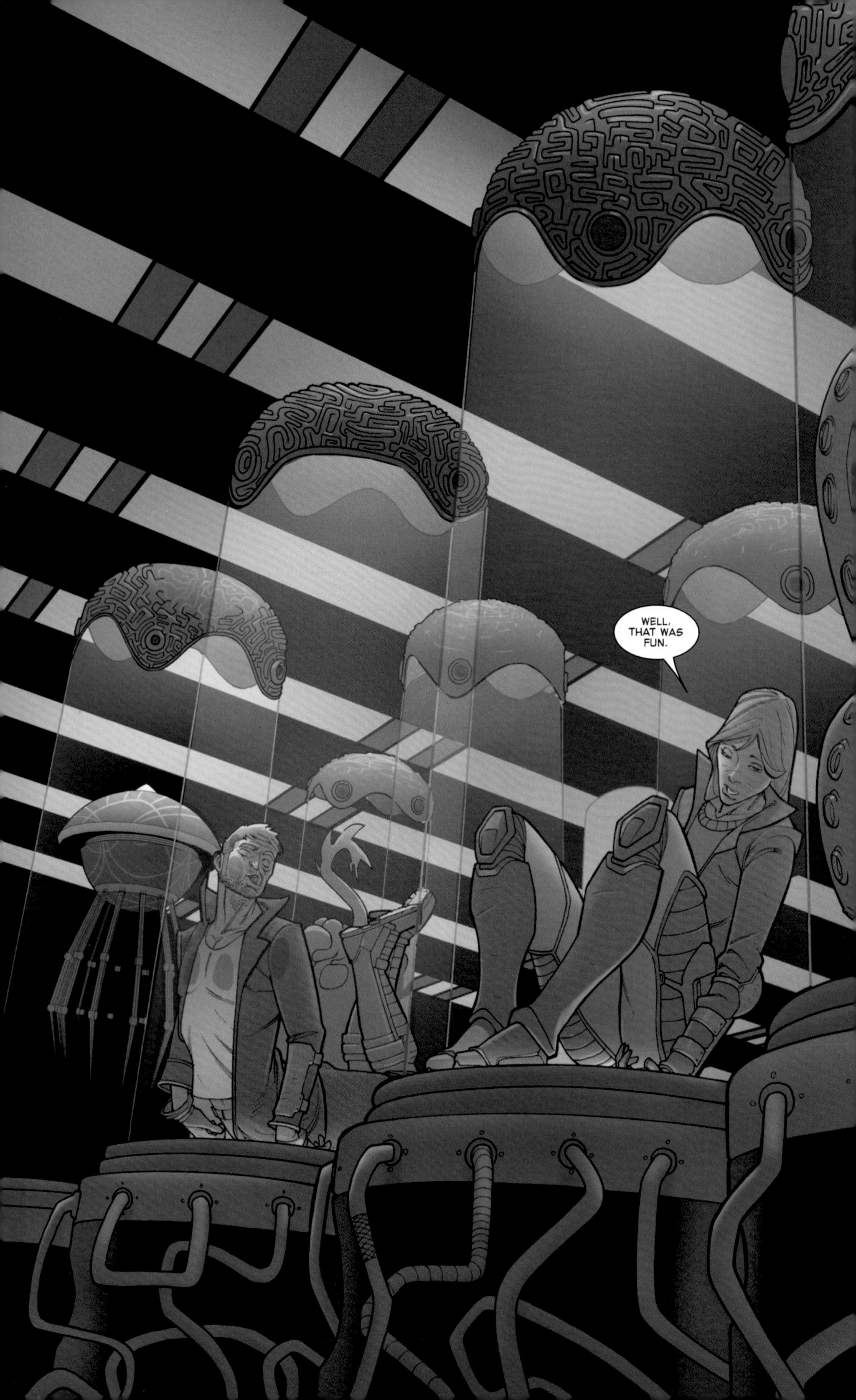
WELL, THAT WAS FUN.

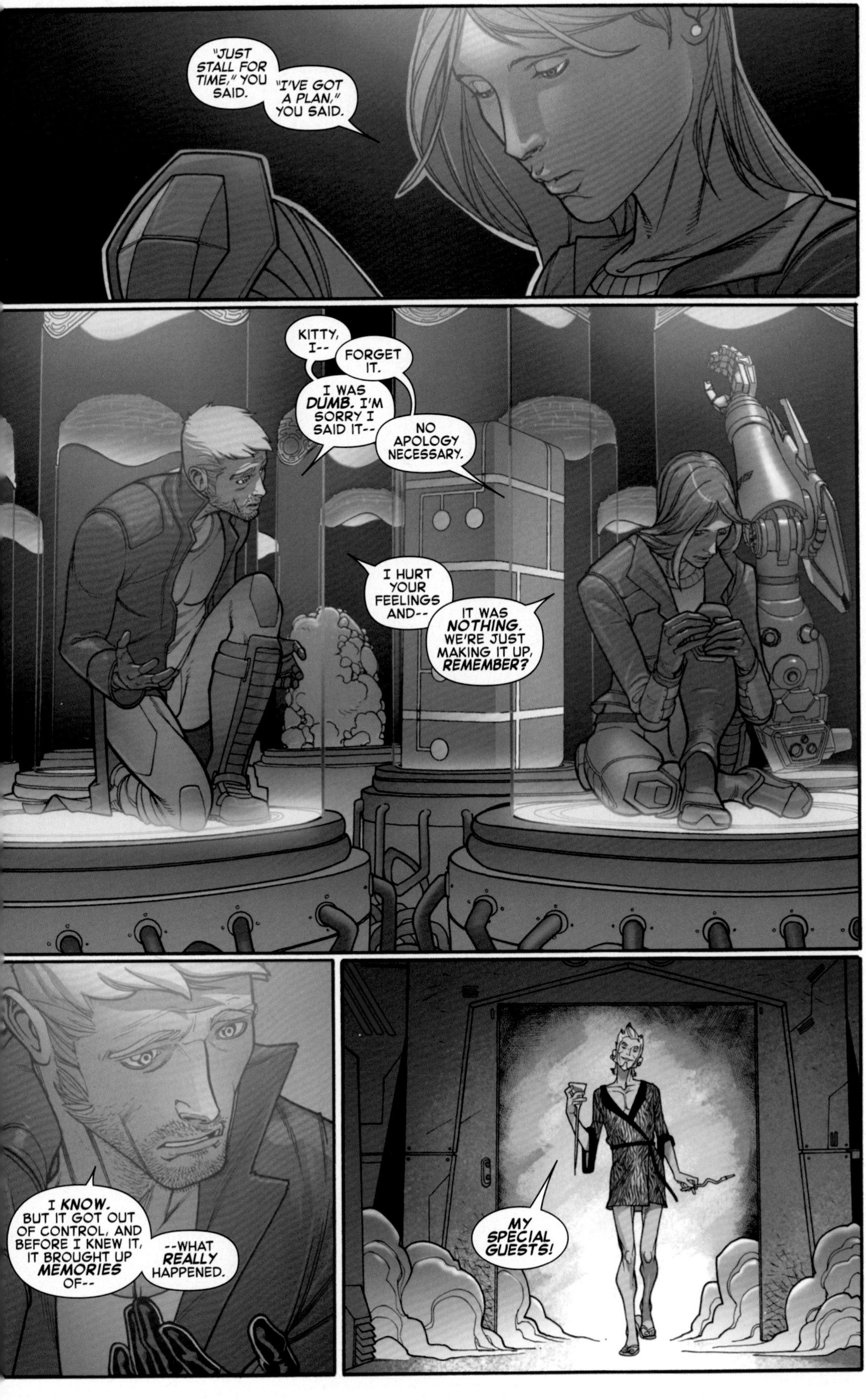
"JUST STALL FOR TIME," YOU SAID.
"I'VE GOT A PLAN," YOU SAID.
KITTY, I--
FORGET IT.
I WAS DUMB. I'M SORRY I SAID IT--
NO APOLOGY NECESSARY.
I HURT YOUR FEELINGS AND--
IT WAS NOTHING. WE'RE JUST MAKING IT UP, REMEMBER?
I KNOW. BUT IT GOT OUT OF CONTROL, AND BEFORE I KNEW IT, IT BROUGHT UP MEMORIES OF--
--WHAT REALLY HAPPENED.
MY SPECIAL GUESTS!

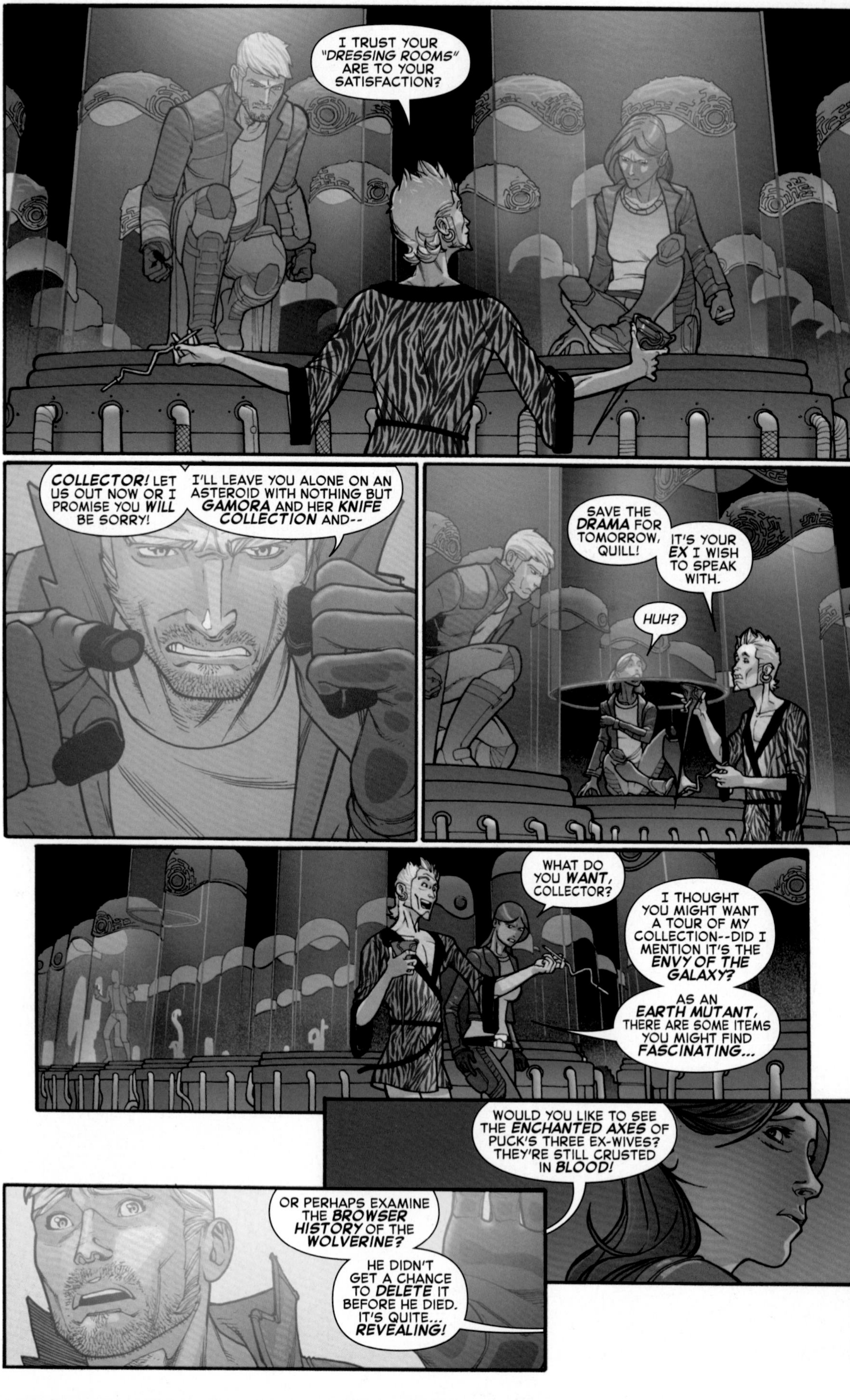
I TRUST YOUR "DRESSING ROOMS" ARE TO YOUR SATISFACTION?
COLLECTOR! LET US OUT NOW OR I PROMISE YOU WILL BE SORRY!
I'LL LEAVE YOU ALONE ON AN ASTEROID WITH NOTHING BUT GAMORA AND HER KNIFE COLLECTION AND--
SAVE THE DRAMA FOR TOMORROW, QUILL!
IT'S YOUR EX I WISH TO SPEAK WITH.
HUH?
WHAT DO YOU WANT, COLLECTOR?
I THOUGHT YOU MIGHT WANT A TOUR OF MY COLLECTION--DID I MENTION IT'S THE ENVY OF THE GALAXY?
AS AN EARTH MUTANT, THERE ARE SOME ITEMS YOU MIGHT FIND FASCINATING...
WOULD YOU LIKE TO SEE THE ENCHANTED AXES OF PUCK'S THREE EX-WIVES? THEY'RE STILL CRUSTED IN BLOOD!
OR PERHAPS EXAMINE THE BROWSER HISTORY OF THE WOLVERINE?
HE DIDN'T GET A CHANCE TO DELETE IT BEFORE HE DIED. IT'S QUITE... REVEALING!

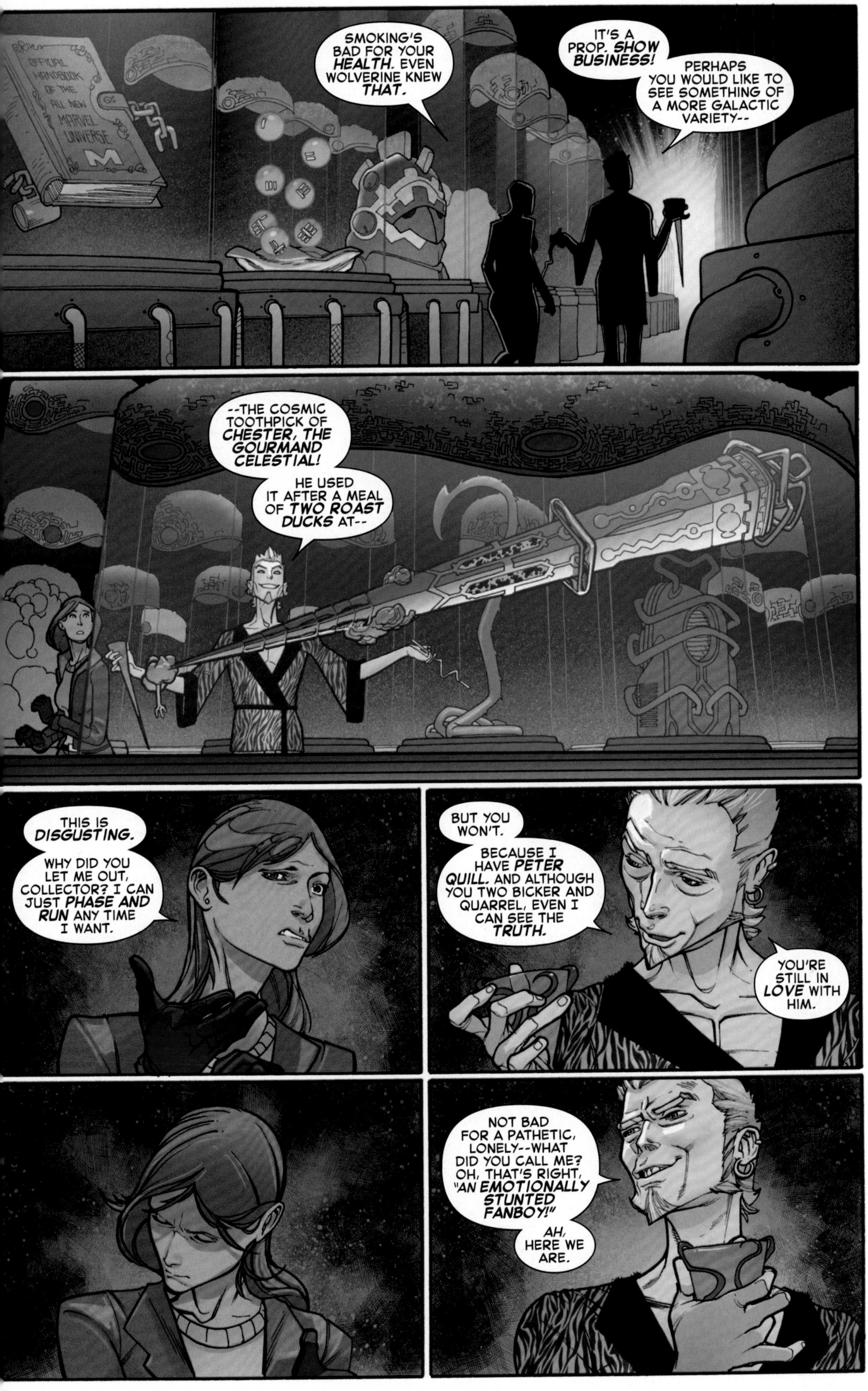
OFFICIAL HANDBOOK OF THE ALL NEW MARVEL UNIVERSE
SMOKING'S BAD FOR YOUR **HEALTH.** EVEN WOLVERINE KNEW **THAT.**
IT'S A PROP. **SHOW BUSINESS!**
PERHAPS YOU WOULD LIKE TO SEE SOMETHING OF A MORE GALACTIC VARIETY--
--THE COSMIC TOOTHPICK OF **CHESTER, THE GOURMAND CELESTIAL!**
HE USED IT AFTER A MEAL OF **TWO ROAST DUCKS** AT--
THIS IS **DISGUSTING.**
WHY DID YOU LET ME OUT, COLLECTOR? I CAN JUST **PHASE AND RUN** ANY TIME I WANT.
BUT YOU WON'T.
BECAUSE I HAVE **PETER QUILL**. AND ALTHOUGH YOU TWO BICKER AND QUARREL, EVEN I CAN SEE THE **TRUTH.**
YOU'RE STILL IN **LOVE** WITH HIM.
NOT BAD FOR A PATHETIC, LONELY--WHAT DID YOU CALL ME? OH, THAT'S RIGHT, *"AN **EMOTIONALLY STUNTED FANBOY!**"*
AH, HERE WE ARE.

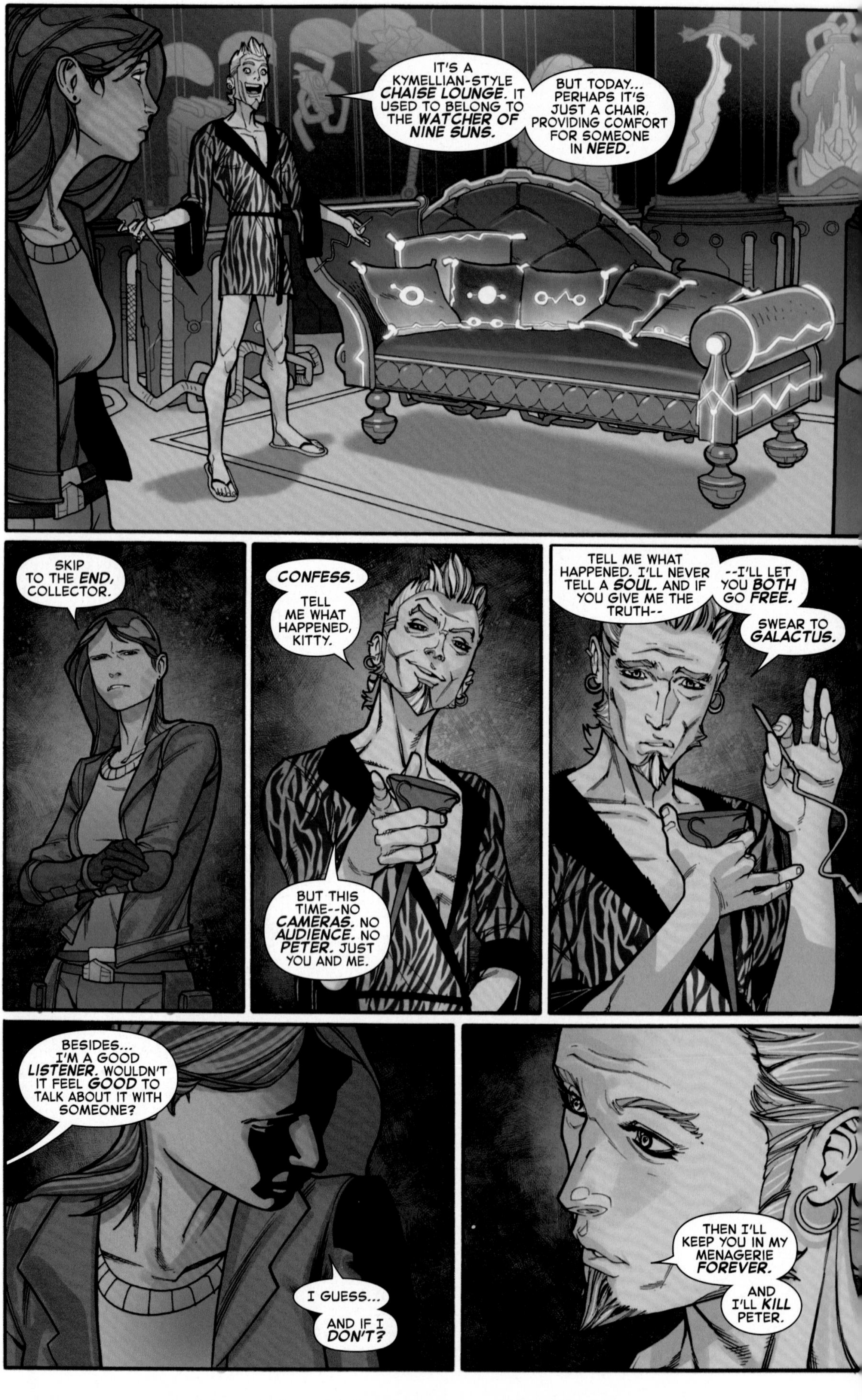
IT'S A KYMELLIAN-STYLE *CHAISE LOUNGE.* IT USED TO BELONG TO THE *WATCHER OF NINE SUNS.*
BUT TODAY... PERHAPS IT'S JUST A CHAIR, PROVIDING COMFORT FOR SOMEONE IN *NEED.*
SKIP TO THE *END,* COLLECTOR.
CONFESS.
TELL ME WHAT HAPPENED, KITTY.
BUT THIS TIME--NO *CAMERAS.* NO *AUDIENCE.* NO *PETER.* JUST YOU AND ME.
TELL ME WHAT HAPPENED. I'LL NEVER TELL A *SOUL.* AND IF YOU GIVE ME THE TRUTH--
--I'LL LET YOU *BOTH* GO *FREE.*
SWEAR TO *GALACTUS.*
BESIDES... I'M A GOOD *LISTENER.* WOULDN'T IT FEEL *GOOD* TO TALK ABOUT IT WITH SOMEONE?
I GUESS...
AND IF I *DON'T?*
THEN I'LL KEEP YOU IN MY MENAGERIE *FOREVER.*
AND I'LL *KILL* PETER.

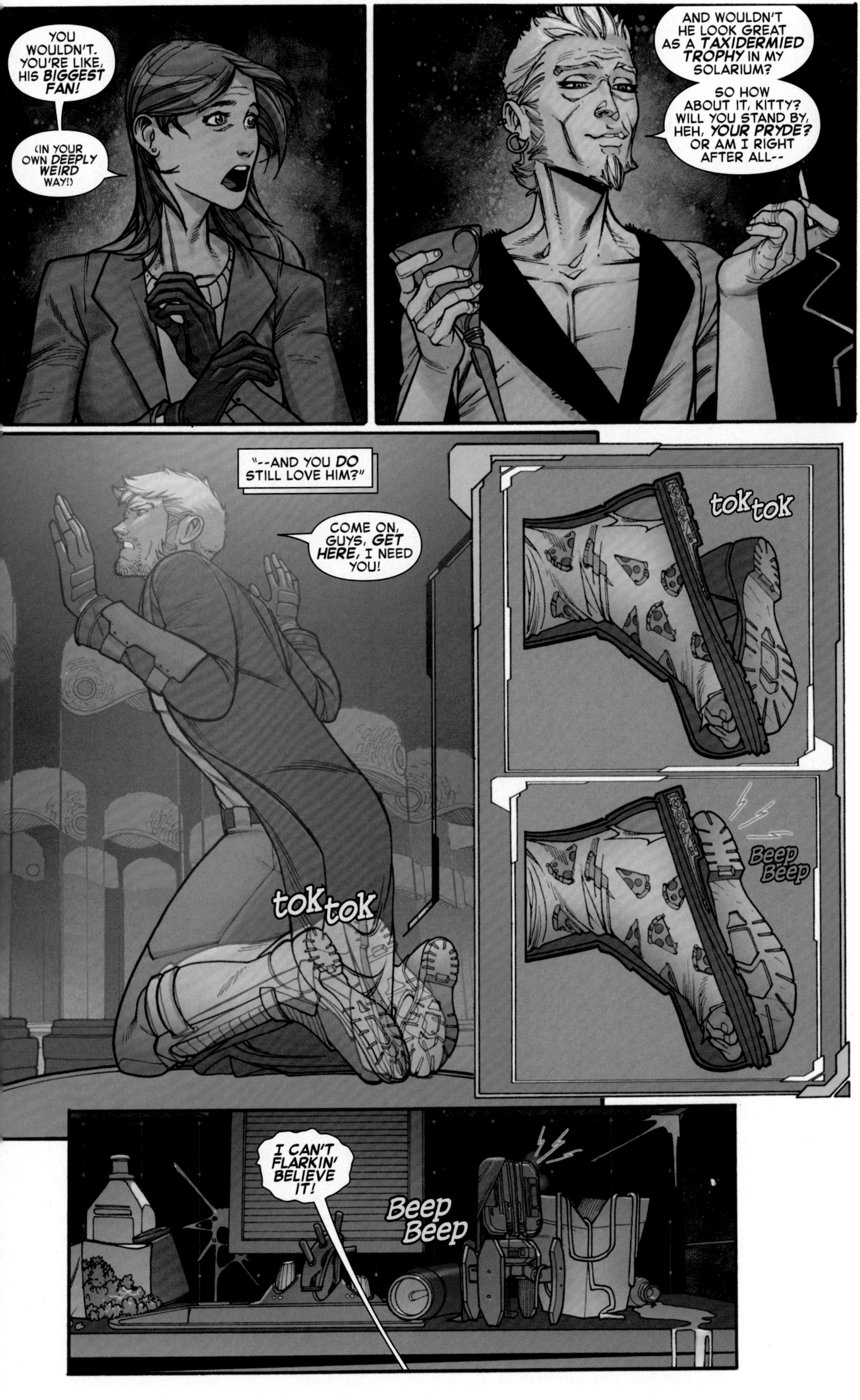
YOU WOULDN'T. YOU'RE LIKE, HIS *BIGGEST FAN!*
(IN YOUR OWN *DEEPLY WEIRD* WAY!)
AND WOULDN'T HE LOOK GREAT AS A *TAXIDERMIED TROPHY* IN MY SOLARIUM?
SO HOW ABOUT IT, KITTY? WILL YOU STAND BY, HEH, *YOUR PRYDE?* OR AM I RIGHT AFTER ALL--
"--AND YOU *DO* STILL LOVE HIM?"
COME ON, GUYS, *GET HERE,* I NEED YOU!
tok tok
tok tok
Beep Beep
I CAN'T FLARKIN' BELIEVE IT!
Beep Beep

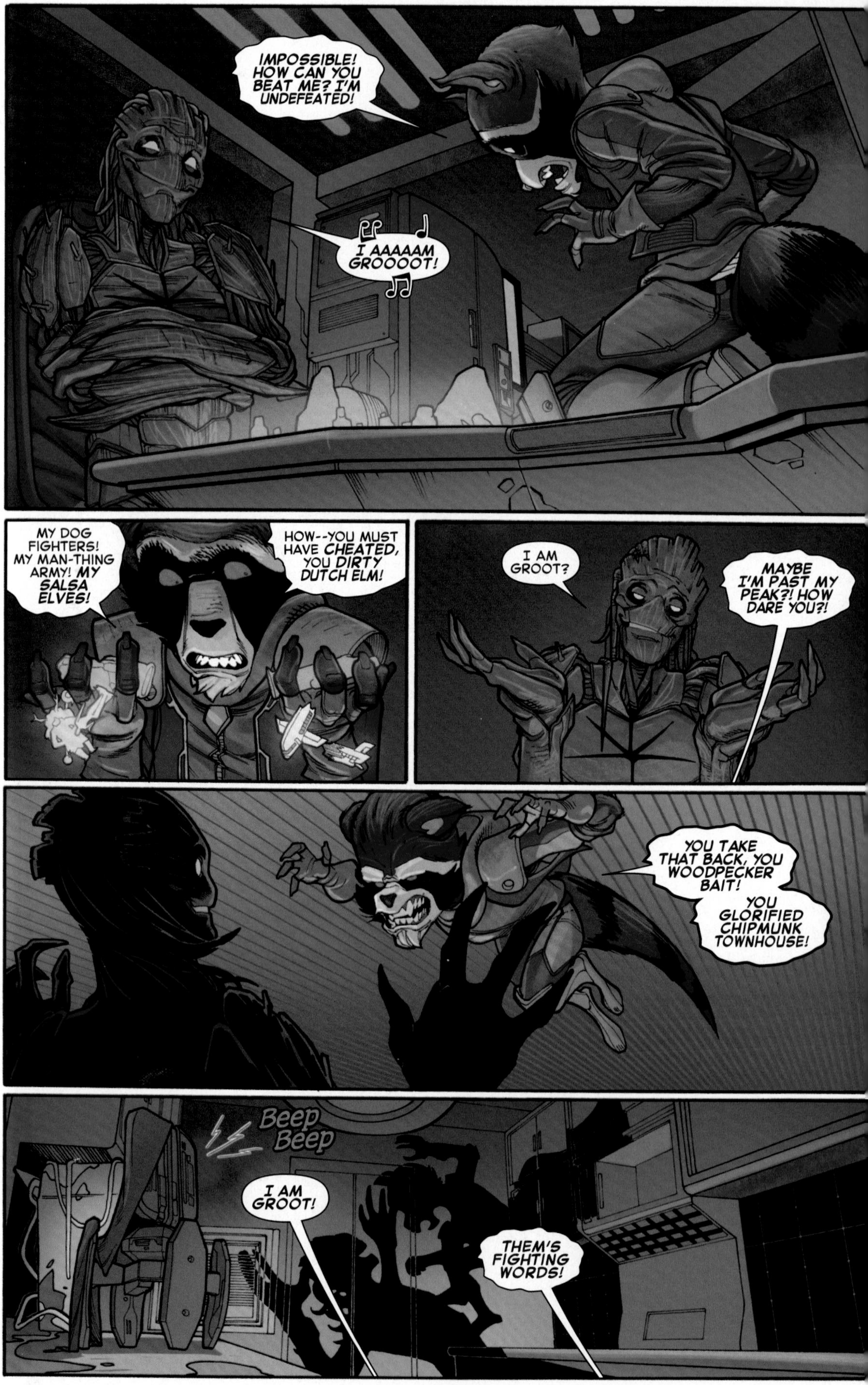
IMPOSSIBLE! HOW CAN YOU BEAT ME? I'M UNDEFEATED!
I AAAAAM GROOOOT!
MY DOG FIGHTERS! MY MAN-THING ARMY! MY SALSA ELVES!
HOW--YOU MUST HAVE CHEATED, YOU DIRTY DUTCH ELM!
I AM GROOT?
MAYBE I'M PAST MY PEAK?! HOW DARE YOU?!
YOU TAKE THAT BACK, YOU WOODPECKER BAIT!
YOU GLORIFIED CHIPMUNK TOWNHOUSE!
Beep Beep
I AM GROOT!
THEM'S FIGHTING WORDS!

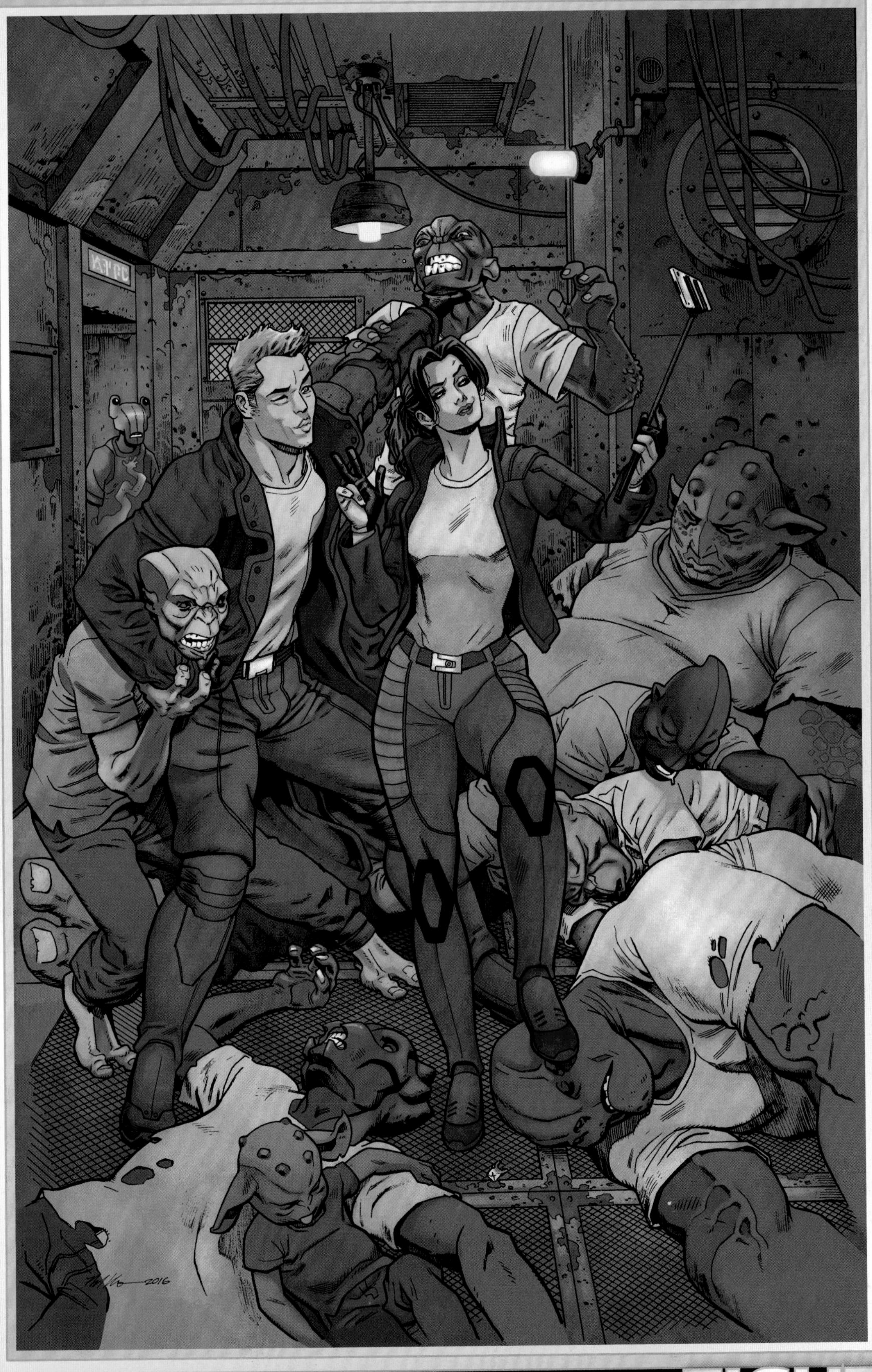

YOU'RE GONNA CARRY THAT WEIGHT

EIGHT

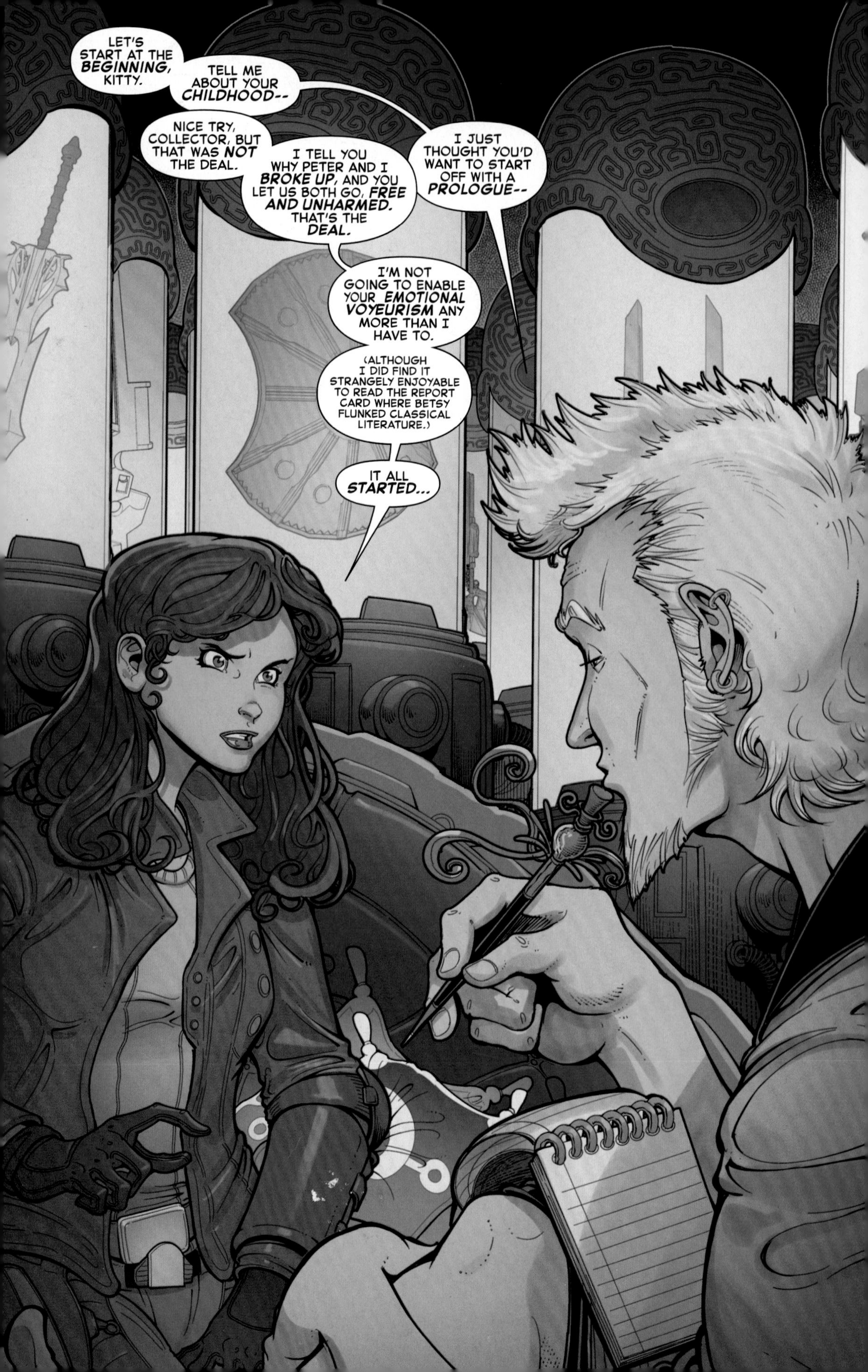
LET'S START AT THE **BEGINNING,** KITTY.
TELL ME ABOUT YOUR **CHILDHOOD--**
NICE TRY, COLLECTOR, BUT THAT WAS **NOT** THE DEAL.
I TELL YOU WHY PETER AND I **BROKE UP,** AND YOU LET US BOTH GO, **FREE AND UNHARMED.** THAT'S THE **DEAL.**
I JUST THOUGHT YOU'D WANT TO START OFF WITH A **PROLOGUE--**
I'M NOT GOING TO ENABLE YOUR **EMOTIONAL VOYEURISM** ANY MORE THAN I HAVE TO.
(ALTHOUGH I DID FIND IT STRANGELY ENJOYABLE TO READ THE REPORT CARD WHERE BETSY FLUNKED CLASSICAL LITERATURE.)
IT ALL **STARTED...**

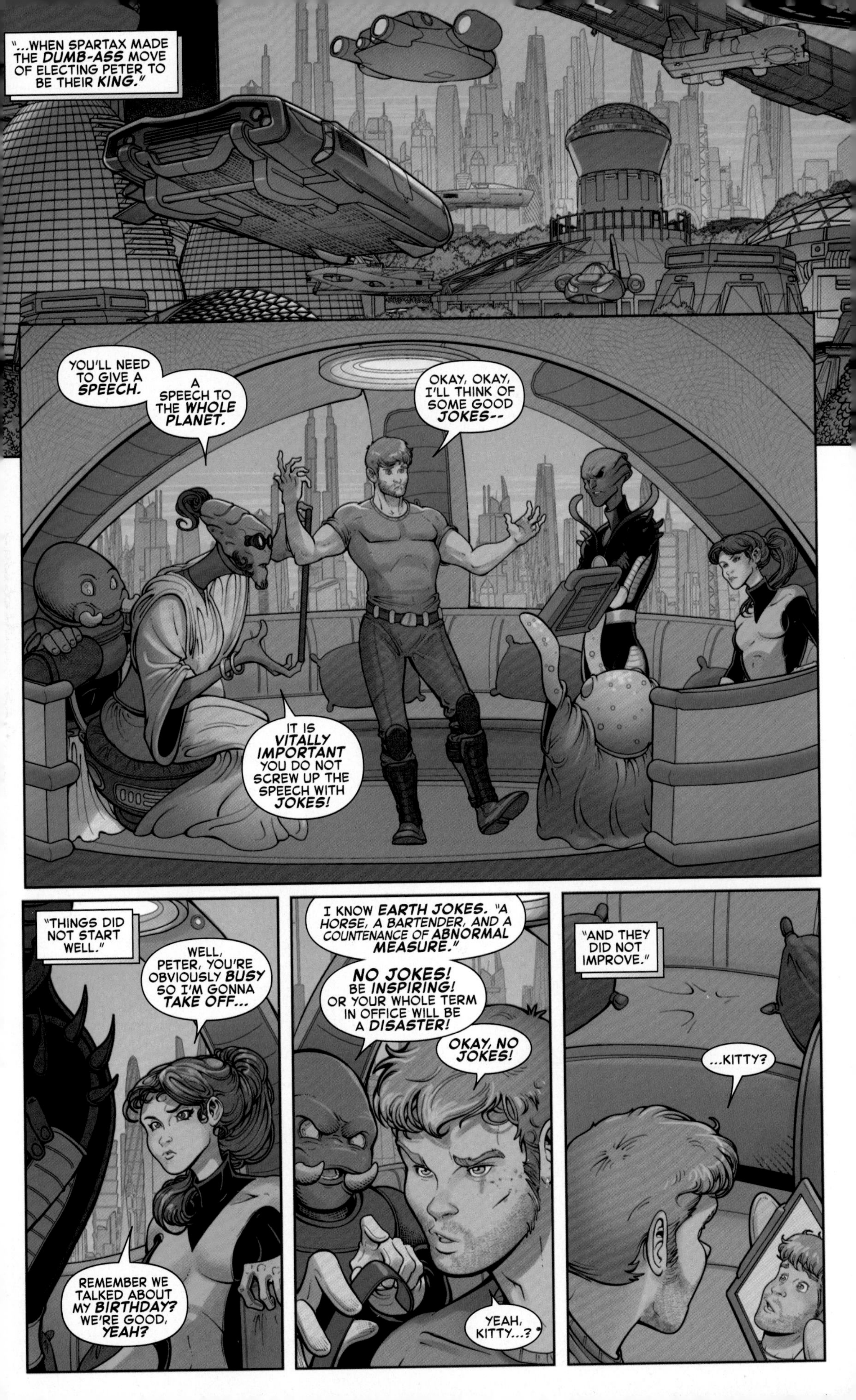
"...WHEN SPARTAX MADE THE DUMB-ASS MOVE OF ELECTING PETER TO BE THEIR KING."
YOU'LL NEED TO GIVE A SPEECH.
A SPEECH TO THE WHOLE PLANET.
OKAY, OKAY, I'LL THINK OF SOME GOOD JOKES--
IT IS VITALLY IMPORTANT YOU DO NOT SCREW UP THE SPEECH WITH JOKES!
"THINGS DID NOT START WELL."
WELL, PETER, YOU'RE OBVIOUSLY BUSY SO I'M GONNA TAKE OFF...
REMEMBER WE TALKED ABOUT MY BIRTHDAY? WE'RE GOOD, YEAH?
I KNOW EARTH JOKES. "A HORSE, A BARTENDER, AND A COUNTENANCE OF ABNORMAL MEASURE."
NO JOKES! BE INSPIRING! OR YOUR WHOLE TERM IN OFFICE WILL BE A DISASTER!
OKAY, NO JOKES!
YEAH, KITTY...?
"AND THEY DID NOT IMPROVE."
...KITTY?

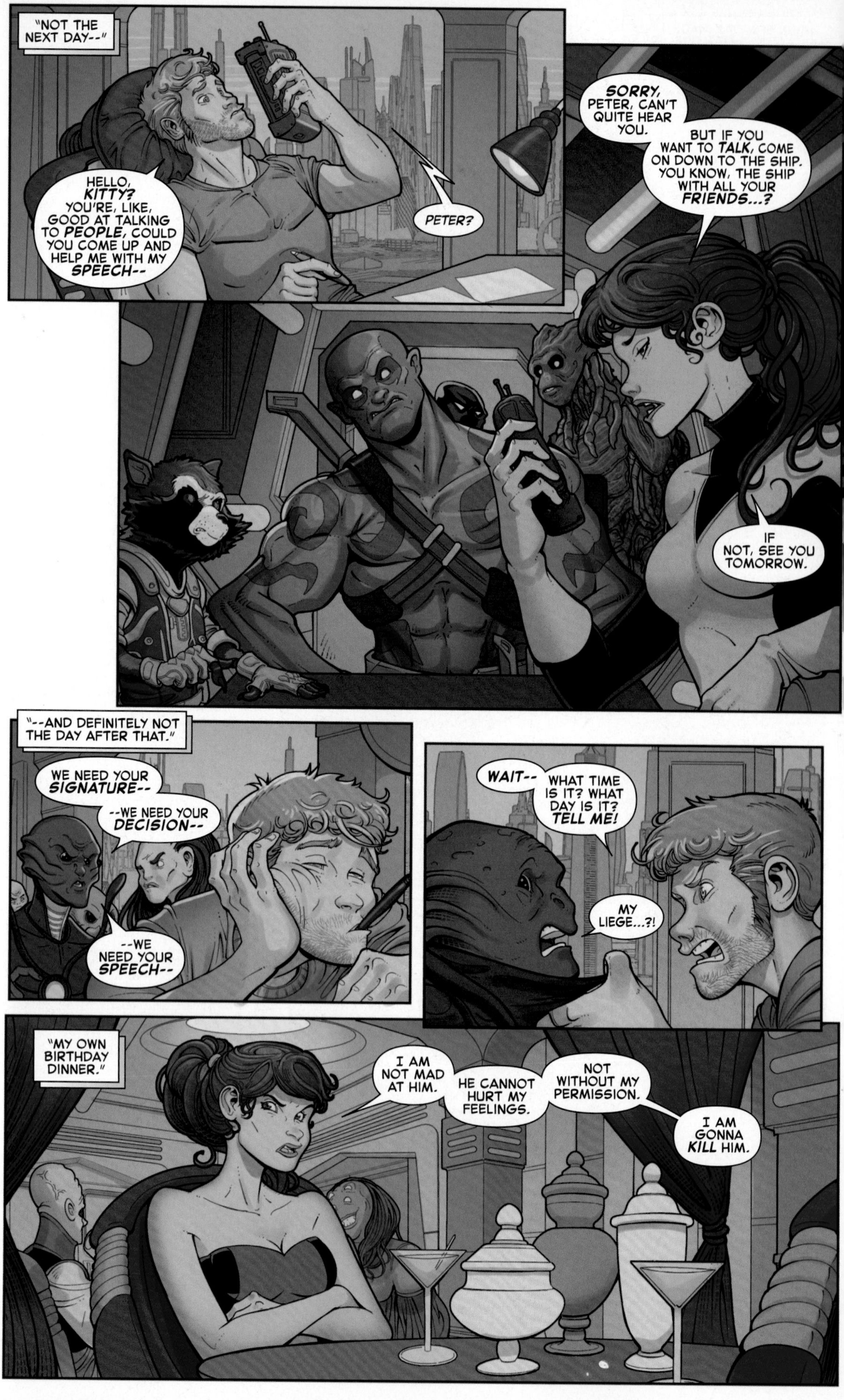
"NOT THE NEXT DAY--"
HELLO, KITTY? YOU'RE, LIKE, GOOD AT TALKING TO PEOPLE, COULD YOU COME UP AND HELP ME WITH MY SPEECH--
PETER?
SORRY, PETER, CAN'T QUITE HEAR YOU.
BUT IF YOU WANT TO TALK, COME ON DOWN TO THE SHIP. YOU KNOW, THE SHIP WITH ALL YOUR FRIENDS...?
IF NOT, SEE YOU TOMORROW.
"--AND DEFINITELY NOT THE DAY AFTER THAT."
WE NEED YOUR SIGNATURE--
--WE NEED YOUR DECISION--
--WE NEED YOUR SPEECH--
WAIT--
WHAT TIME IS IT? WHAT DAY IS IT? TELL ME!
MY LIEGE...?!
"MY OWN BIRTHDAY DINNER."
I AM NOT MAD AT HIM.
HE CANNOT HURT MY FEELINGS.
NOT WITHOUT MY PERMISSION.
I AM GONNA KILL HIM.

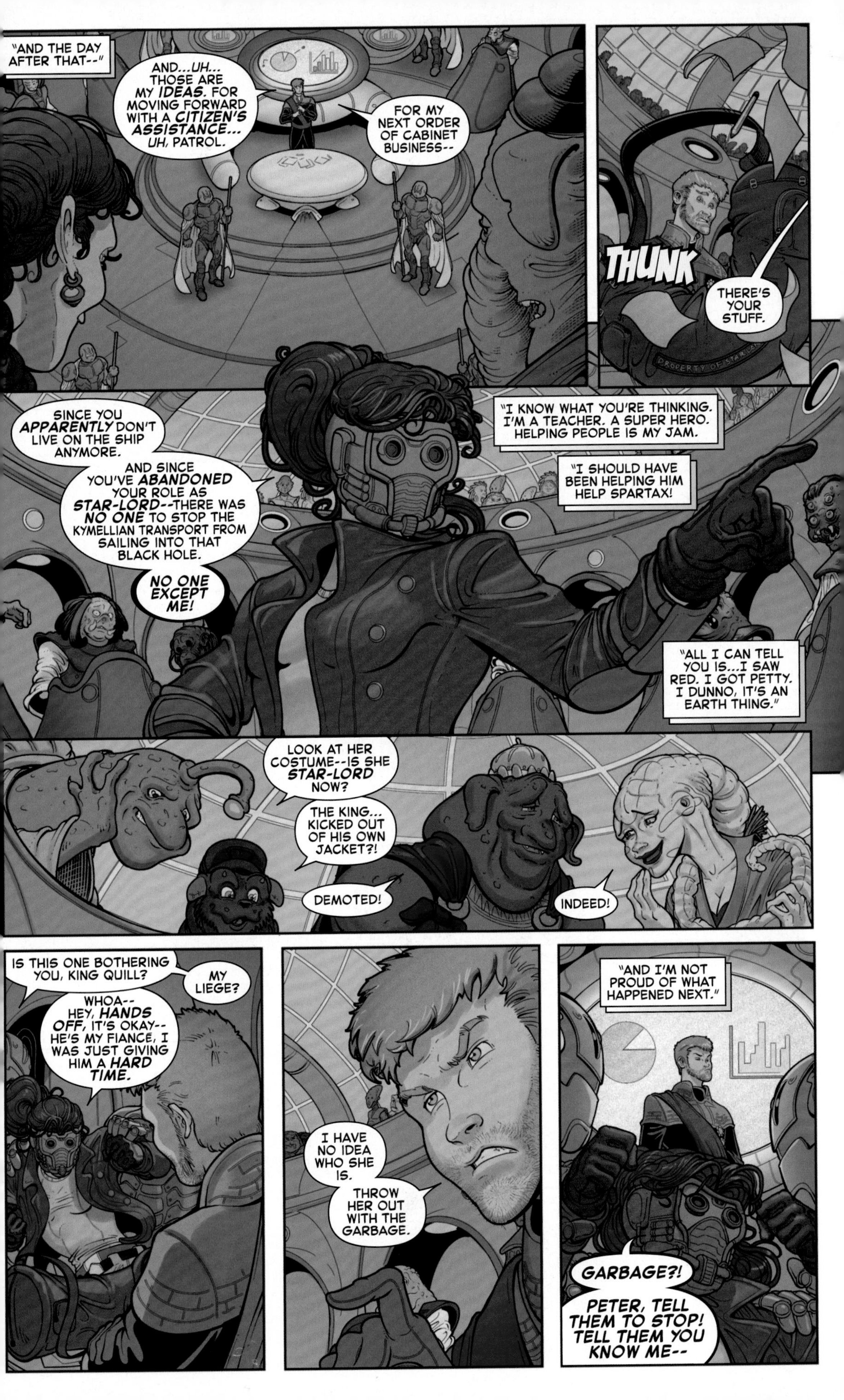
"AND THE DAY AFTER THAT--"
AND...UH... THOSE ARE MY IDEAS. FOR MOVING FORWARD WITH A CITIZEN'S ASSISTANCE... UH, PATROL.
FOR MY NEXT ORDER OF CABINET BUSINESS--
THUNK
THERE'S YOUR STUFF.
PROPERTY OF STAR-LORD
SINCE YOU APPARENTLY DON'T LIVE ON THE SHIP ANYMORE.
AND SINCE YOU'VE ABANDONED YOUR ROLE AS STAR-LORD--THERE WAS NO ONE TO STOP THE KYMELLIAN TRANSPORT FROM SAILING INTO THAT BLACK HOLE.
NO ONE EXCEPT ME!
"I KNOW WHAT YOU'RE THINKING. I'M A TEACHER. A SUPER HERO. HELPING PEOPLE IS MY JAM.
"I SHOULD HAVE BEEN HELPING HIM HELP SPARTAX!
"ALL I CAN TELL YOU IS...I SAW RED. I GOT PETTY. I DUNNO, IT'S AN EARTH THING."
LOOK AT HER COSTUME--IS SHE STAR-LORD NOW?
THE KING... KICKED OUT OF HIS OWN JACKET?!
DEMOTED!
INDEED!
IS THIS ONE BOTHERING YOU, KING QUILL?
MY LIEGE?
WHOA-- HEY, HANDS OFF, IT'S OKAY-- HE'S MY FIANCE, I WAS JUST GIVING HIM A HARD TIME.
I HAVE NO IDEA WHO SHE IS.
THROW HER OUT WITH THE GARBAGE.
"AND I'M NOT PROUD OF WHAT HAPPENED NEXT."
GARBAGE?!
PETER, TELL THEM TO STOP! TELL THEM YOU KNOW ME--

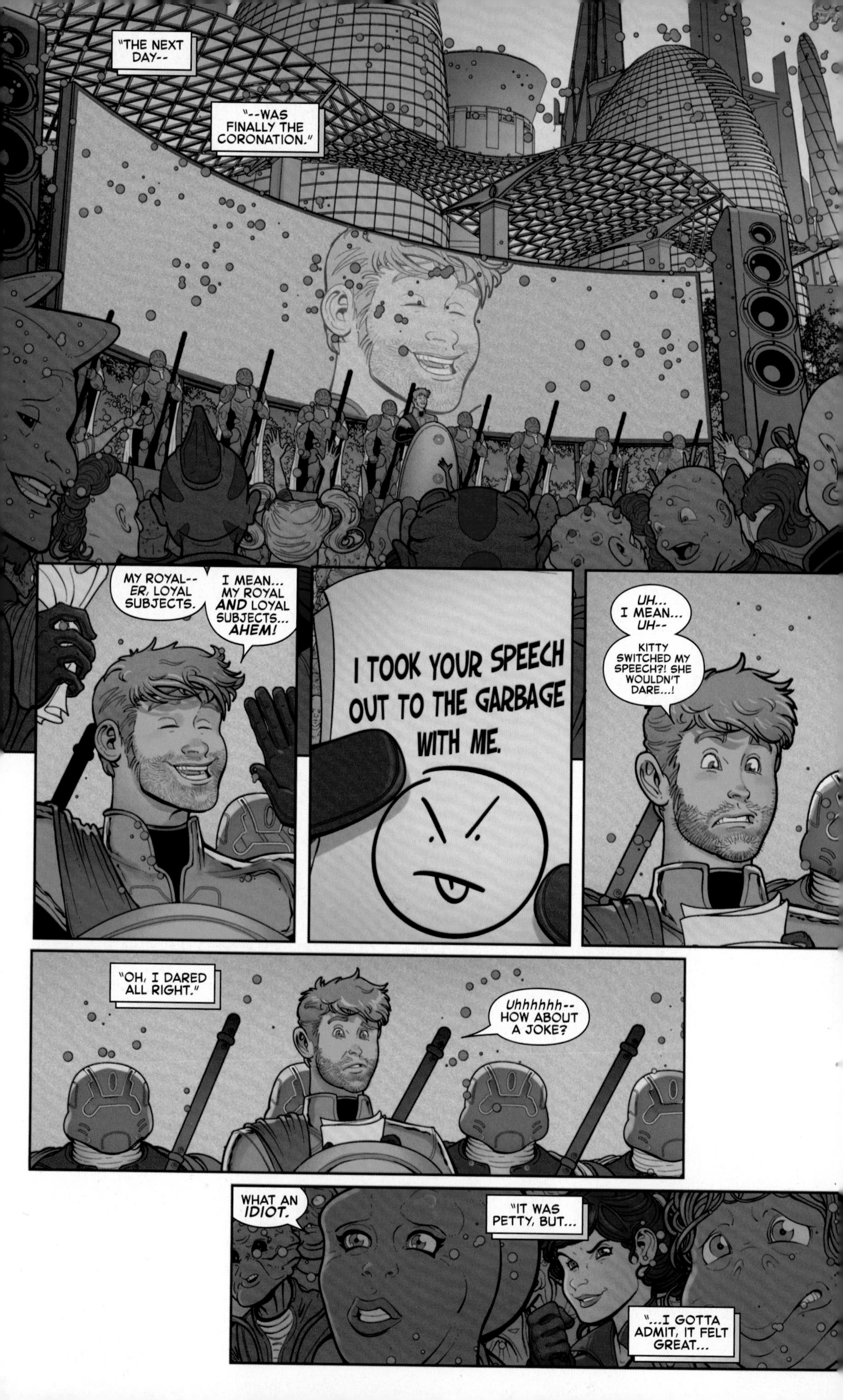
"THE NEXT DAY--
"--WAS FINALLY THE CORONATION."
MY ROYAL-- *ER*, LOYAL SUBJECTS.
I MEAN... MY ROYAL **AND** LOYAL SUBJECTS... ***AHEM!***
I TOOK YOUR SPEECH OUT TO THE GARBAGE WITH ME.
UH... I MEAN... UH--
KITTY SWITCHED MY SPEECH?! SHE WOULDN'T DARE...!
"OH, I DARED ALL RIGHT."
Uhhhhhh-- HOW ABOUT A JOKE?
WHAT AN *IDIOT.*
"IT WAS PETTY, BUT...
"...I GOTTA ADMIT, IT FELT GREAT...

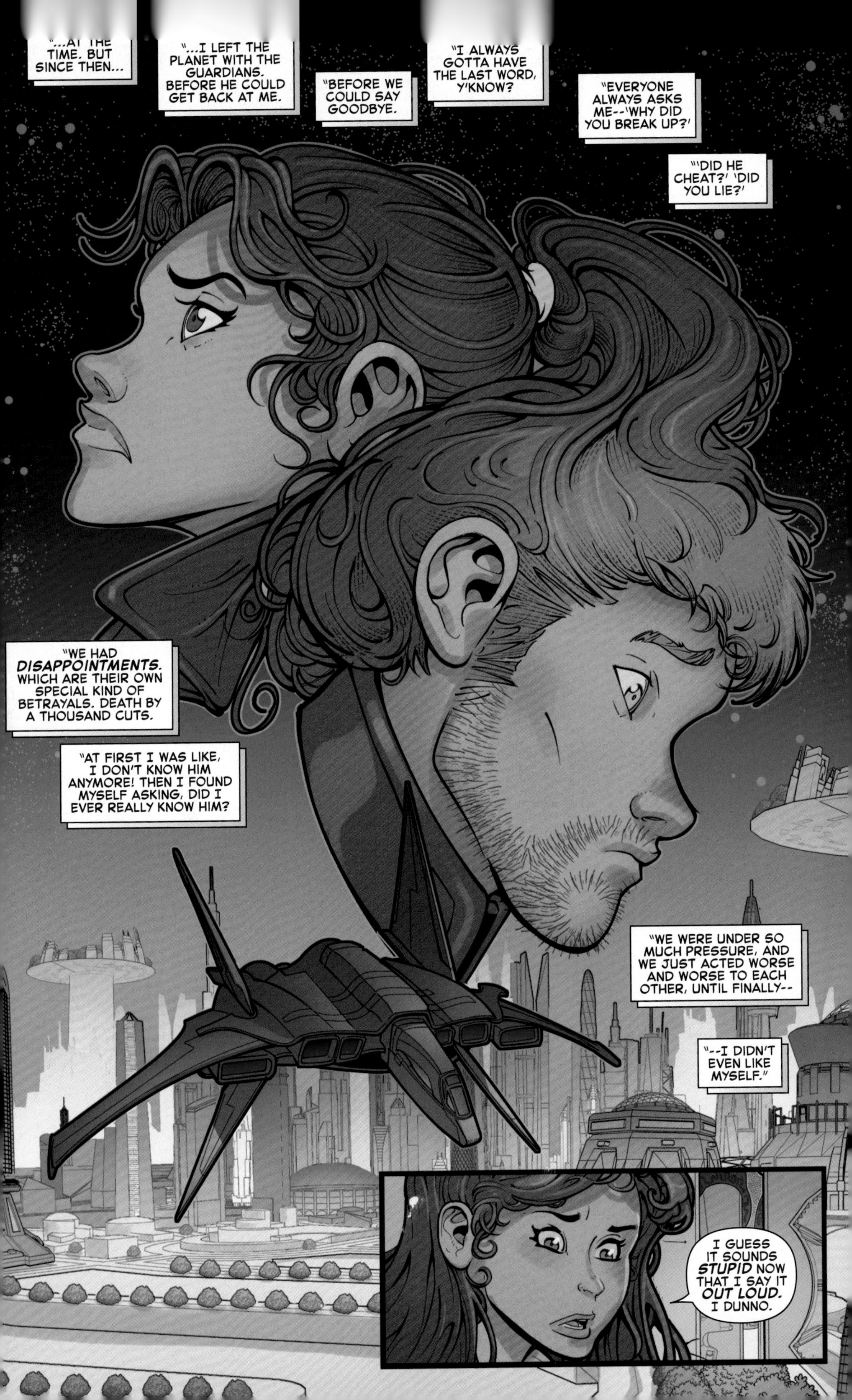
"...AT THE TIME. BUT SINCE THEN...
"...I LEFT THE PLANET WITH THE GUARDIANS. BEFORE HE COULD GET BACK AT ME.
"BEFORE WE COULD SAY GOODBYE.
"I ALWAYS GOTTA HAVE THE LAST WORD, Y'KNOW?
"EVERYONE ALWAYS ASKS ME--'WHY DID YOU BREAK UP?'
"'DID HE CHEAT?' 'DID YOU LIE?'
"WE HAD DISAPPOINTMENTS. WHICH ARE THEIR OWN SPECIAL KIND OF BETRAYALS. DEATH BY A THOUSAND CUTS.
"AT FIRST I WAS LIKE, I DON'T KNOW HIM ANYMORE! THEN I FOUND MYSELF ASKING, DID I EVER REALLY KNOW HIM?
"WE WERE UNDER SO MUCH PRESSURE, AND WE JUST ACTED WORSE AND WORSE TO EACH OTHER, UNTIL FINALLY--
"--I DIDN'T EVEN LIKE MYSELF."
I GUESS IT SOUNDS STUPID NOW THAT I SAY IT OUT LOUD. I DUNNO.

WHAT?! WHERE HAVE YOU GONE--?!

--FOR YOUR SORROW AND CANDOR--

--ONE OF THE SADDEST TEARS IN MY ENTIRE COLLECTION. THANK YOU, KITTY PRYDE--

THAT IS--

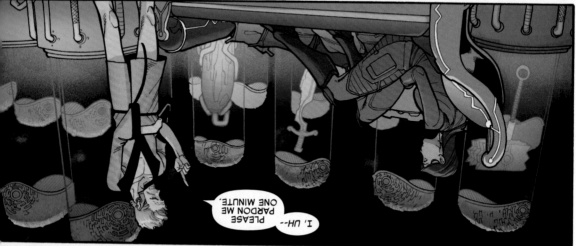

I, UH-- PLEASE PARDON ME ONE MINUTE.

SO...."TRAGIC...."

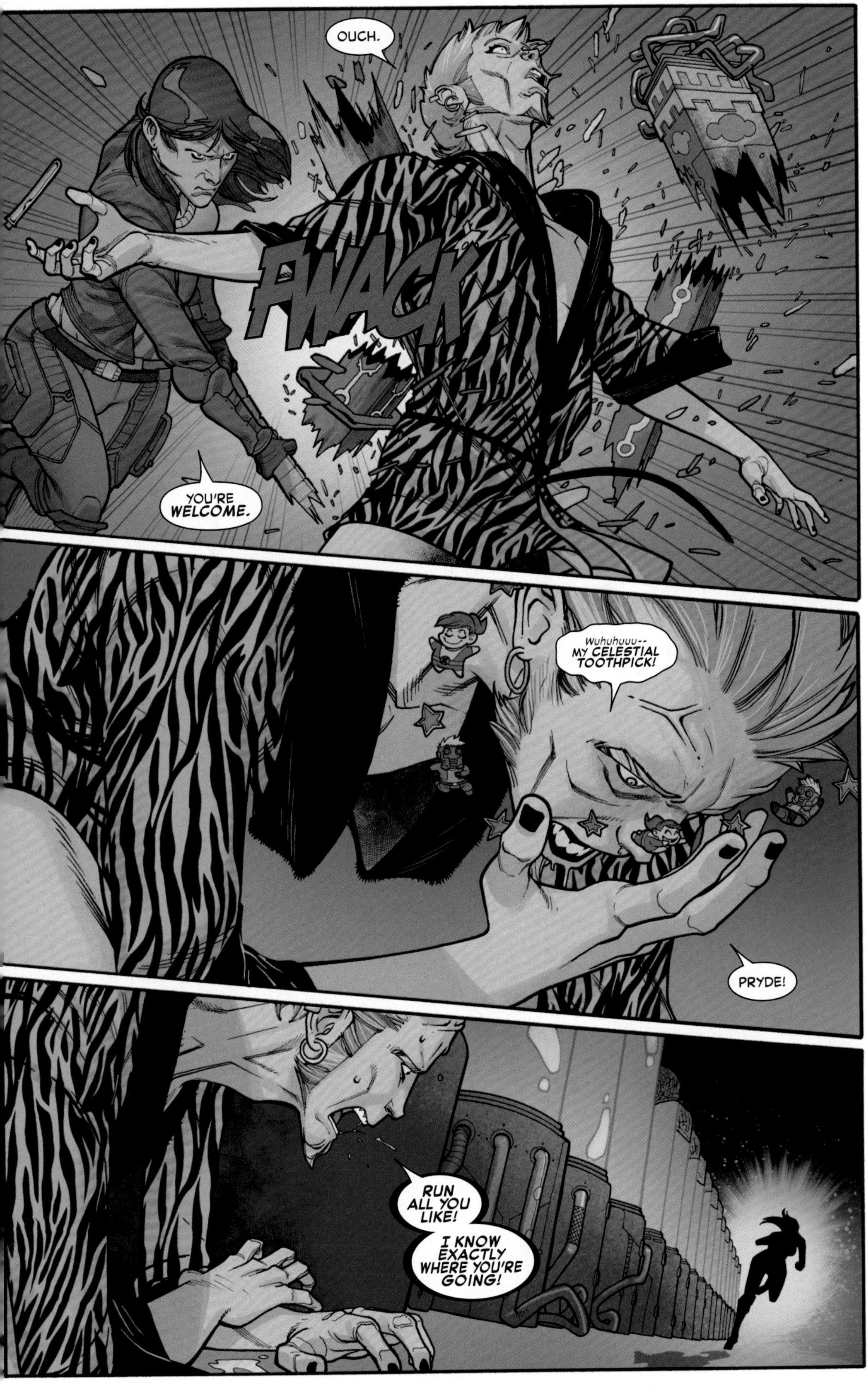
OUCH.
FWACK
YOU'RE WELCOME.
Wuhuhuuu-- MY CELESTIAL TOOTHPICK!
PRYDE!
RUN ALL YOU LIKE!
I KNOW EXACTLY WHERE YOU'RE GOING!

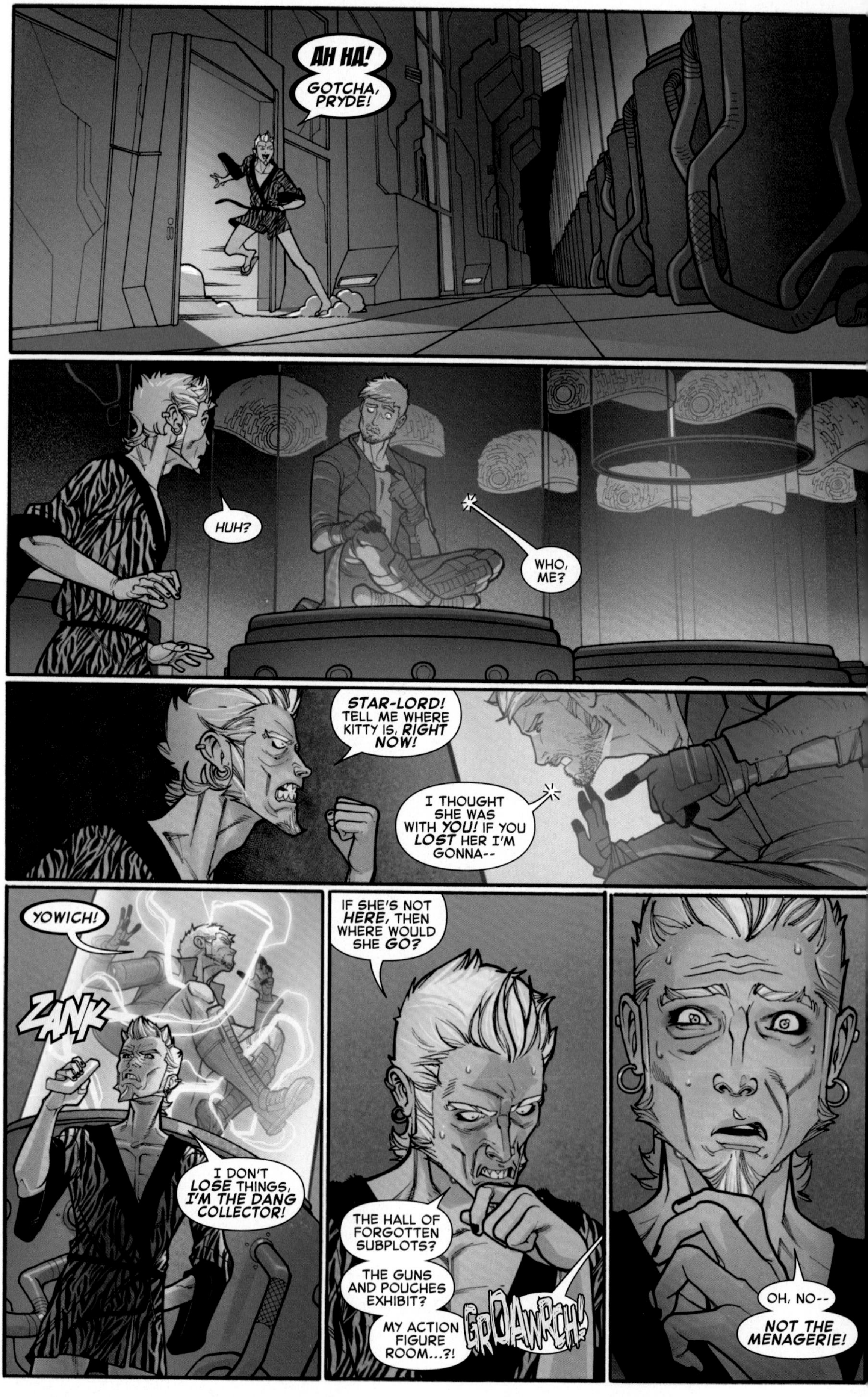
AH HA!
GOTCHA, PRYDE!
HUH?
WHO, ME?
STAR-LORD! TELL ME WHERE KITTY IS, RIGHT NOW!
I THOUGHT SHE WAS WITH YOU! IF YOU LOST HER I'M GONNA--
YOWICH!
ZANK
I DON'T LOSE THINGS, I'M THE DANG COLLECTOR!
IF SHE'S NOT HERE, THEN WHERE WOULD SHE GO?
THE HALL OF FORGOTTEN SUBPLOTS?
THE GUNS AND POUCHES EXHIBIT?
MY ACTION FIGURE ROOM...?!
GROAWRCH!
OH, NO--
NOT THE MENAGERIE!

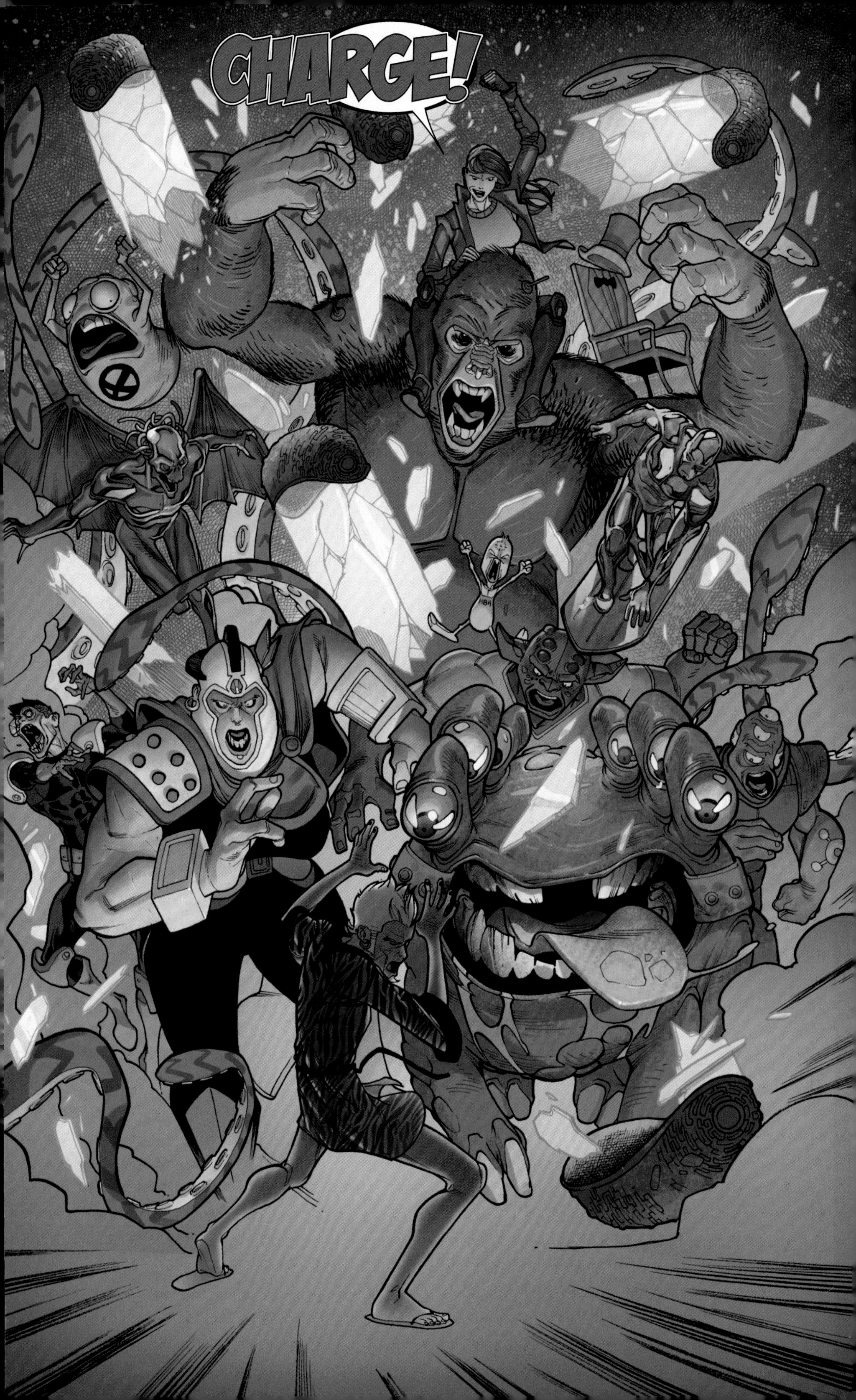
CHARGE!

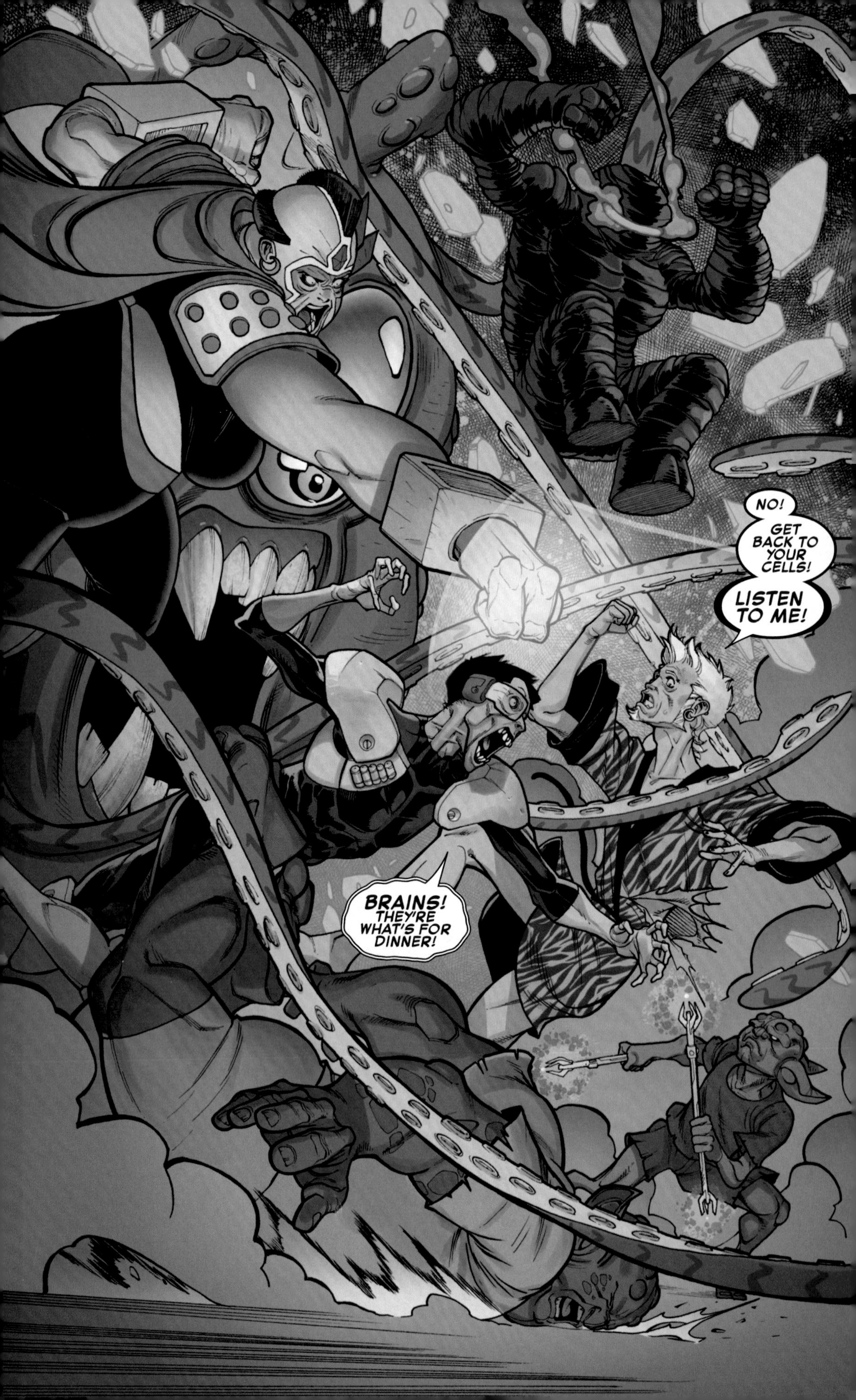
NO!
GET BACK TO YOUR CELLS!
LISTEN TO ME!
BRAINS! THEY'RE WHAT'S FOR DINNER!

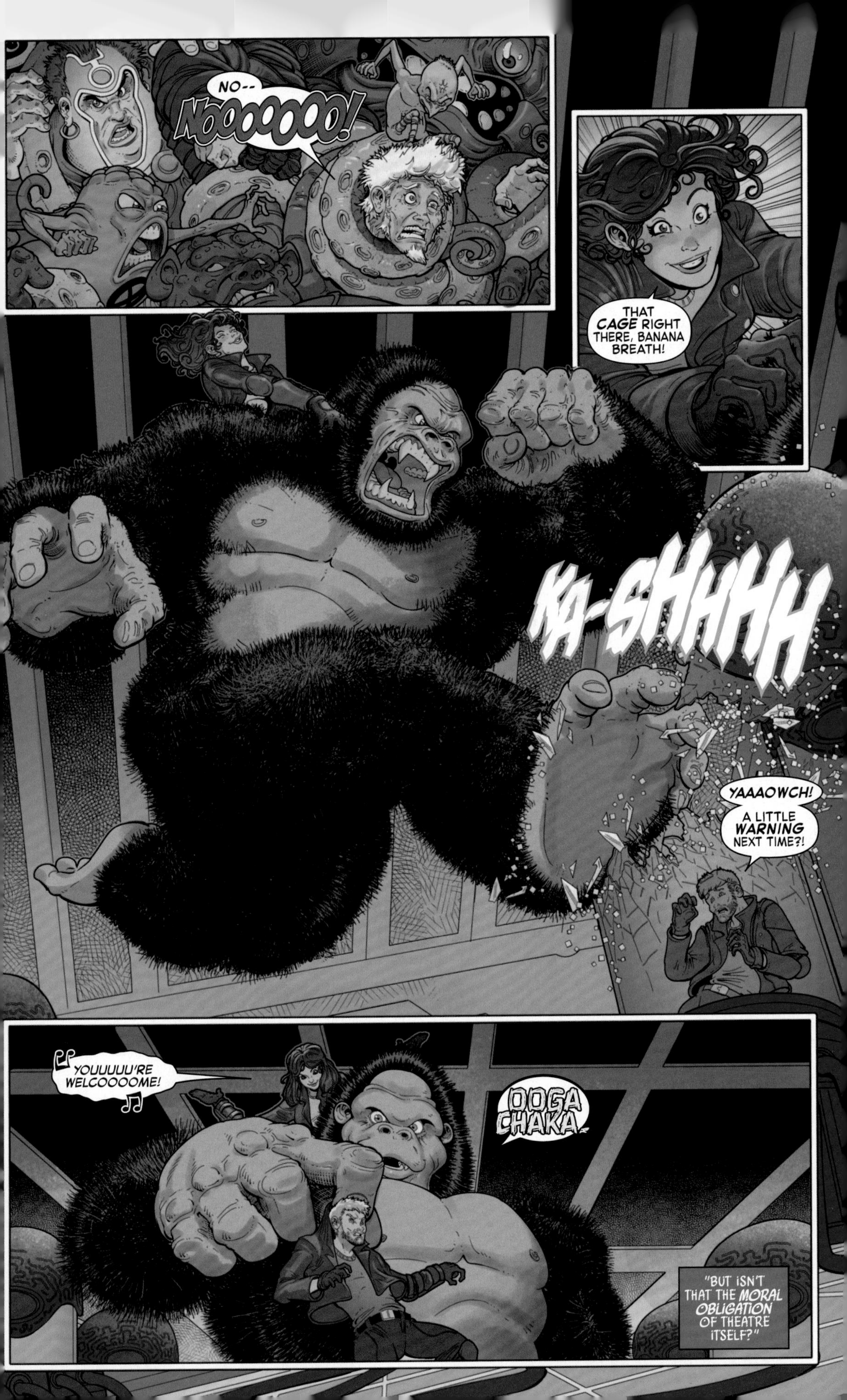
NO--
NOOOOOOO!
THAT CAGE RIGHT THERE, BANANA BREATH!
KA-SHHHH
YAAAOWCH!
A LITTLE WARNING NEXT TIME?!
YOUUUUU'RE WELCOOOOME!
OOGA CHAKA.
"BUT ISN'T THAT THE MORAL OBLIGATION OF THEATRE ITSELF?"

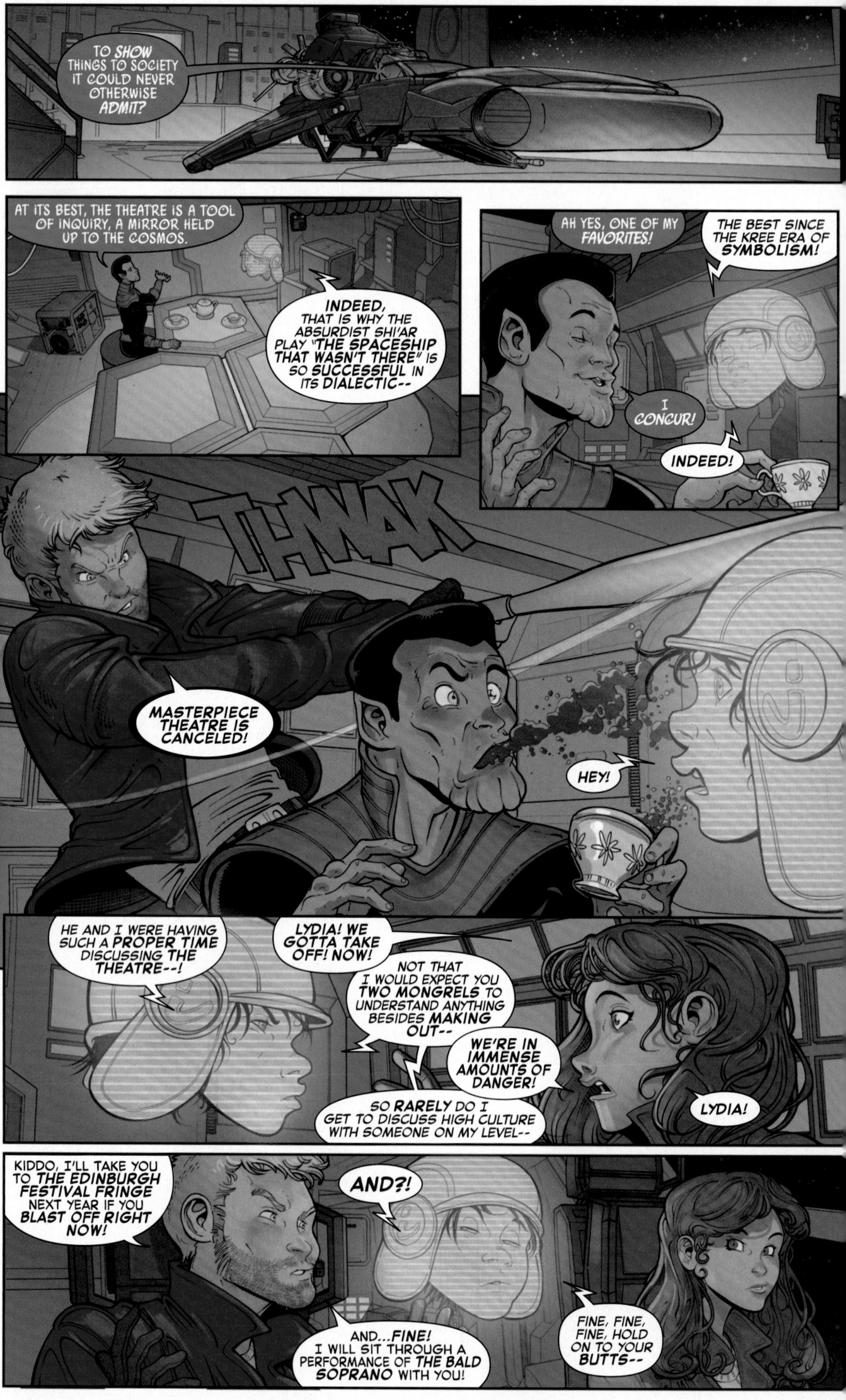
TO SHOW THINGS TO SOCIETY IT COULD NEVER OTHERWISE ADMIT?
AT ITS BEST, THE THEATRE IS A TOOL OF INQUIRY, A MIRROR HELD UP TO THE COSMOS.
INDEED, THAT IS WHY THE ABSURDIST SHI'AR PLAY "THE SPACESHIP THAT WASN'T THERE" IS SO SUCCESSFUL IN ITS DIALECTIC--
AH YES, ONE OF MY FAVORITES!
THE BEST SINCE THE KREE ERA OF SYMBOLISM!
I CONCUR!
INDEED!
THWAK
MASTERPIECE THEATRE IS CANCELED!
HEY!
HE AND I WERE HAVING SUCH A PROPER TIME DISCUSSING THE THEATRE--!
LYDIA! WE GOTTA TAKE OFF! NOW!
NOT THAT I WOULD EXPECT YOU TWO MONGRELS TO UNDERSTAND ANYTHING BESIDES MAKING OUT--
WE'RE IN IMMENSE AMOUNTS OF DANGER!
SO RARELY DO I GET TO DISCUSS HIGH CULTURE WITH SOMEONE ON MY LEVEL--
LYDIA!
KIDDO, I'LL TAKE YOU TO THE EDINBURGH FESTIVAL FRINGE NEXT YEAR IF YOU BLAST OFF RIGHT NOW!
AND?!
AND...FINE! I WILL SIT THROUGH A PERFORMANCE OF THE BALD SOPRANO WITH YOU!
FINE, FINE, FINE, HOLD ON TO YOUR BUTTS--

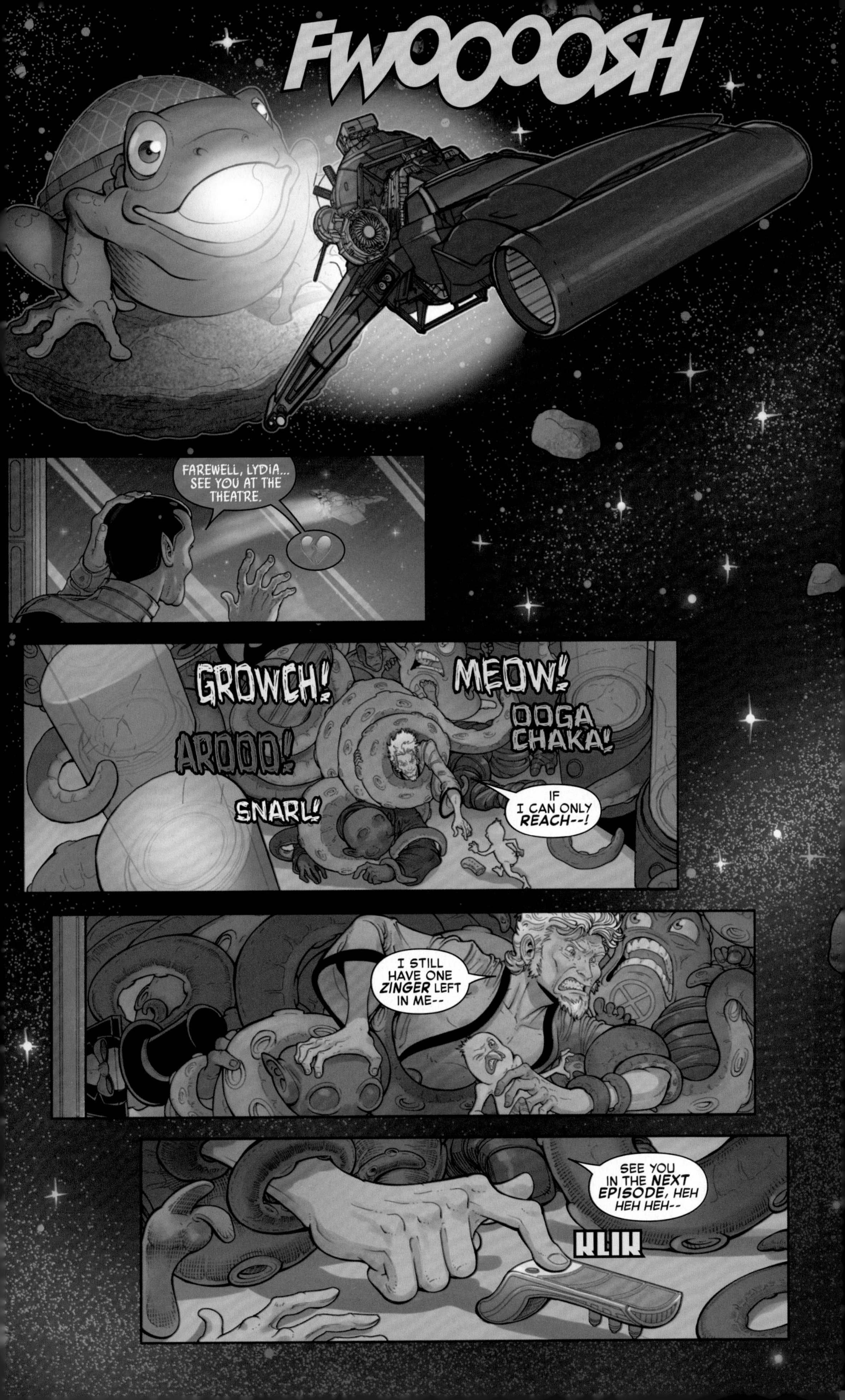
FWOOOOSH
FAREWELL, LYDIA... SEE YOU AT THE THEATRE.
GROWCH!
MEOW!
OOGA CHAKA!
AROOO!
SNARL!
IF I CAN ONLY REACH--!
I STILL HAVE ONE ZINGER LEFT IN ME--
SEE YOU IN THE NEXT EPISODE, HEH HEH HEH--
KLIK

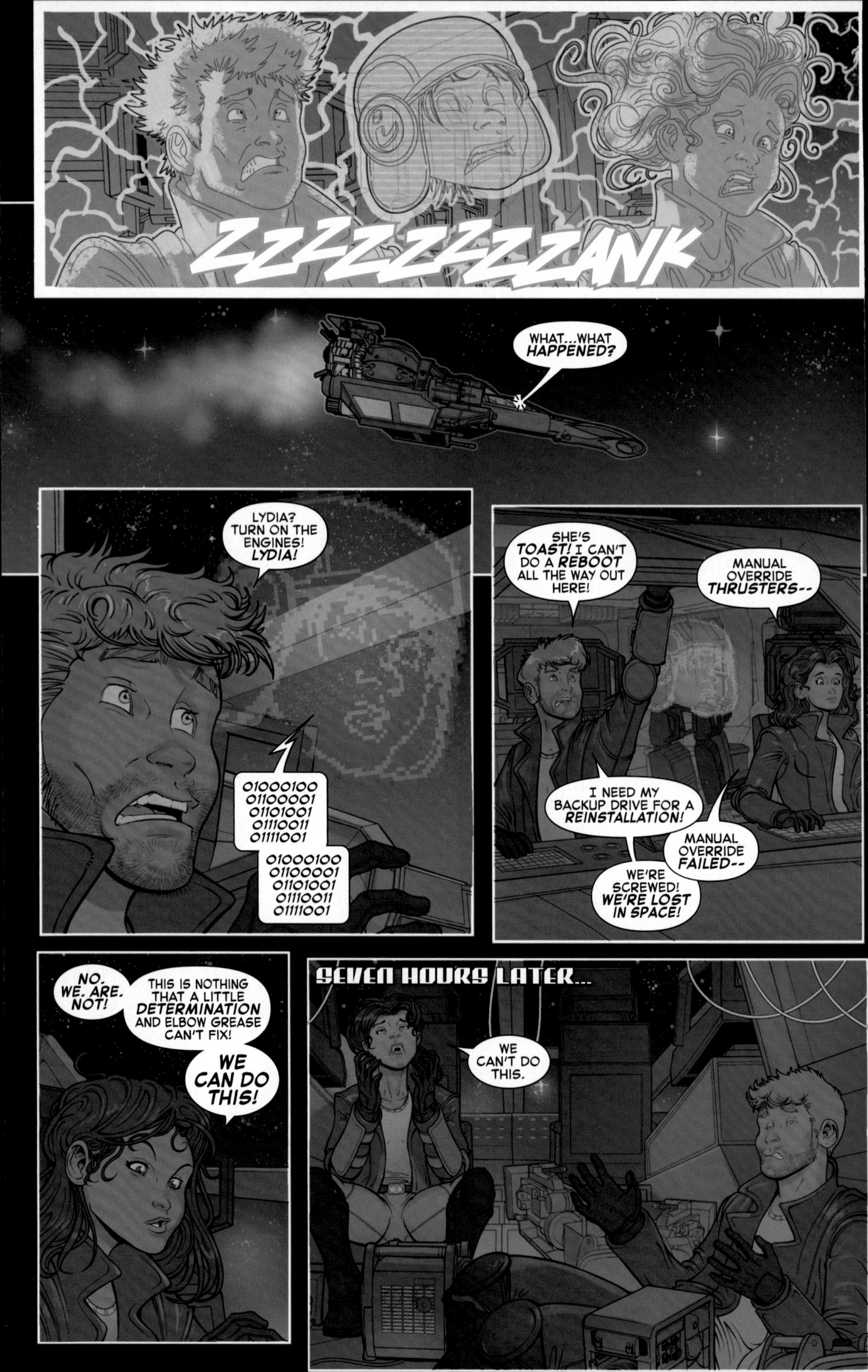
ZZZZZZZZZANK
WHAT...WHAT HAPPENED?
LYDIA? TURN ON THE ENGINES! LYDIA!
01000100 01100001 01101001 01110011 01111001
01000100 01100001 01101001 01110011 01111001
SHE'S TOAST! I CAN'T DO A REBOOT ALL THE WAY OUT HERE!
MANUAL OVERRIDE THRUSTERS--
I NEED MY BACKUP DRIVE FOR A REINSTALLATION!
MANUAL OVERRIDE FAILED--
WE'RE SCREWED! WE'RE LOST IN SPACE!
NO. WE. ARE. NOT!
THIS IS NOTHING THAT A LITTLE DETERMINATION AND ELBOW GREASE CAN'T FIX!
WE CAN DO THIS!
SEVEN HOURS LATER...
WE CAN'T DO THIS.

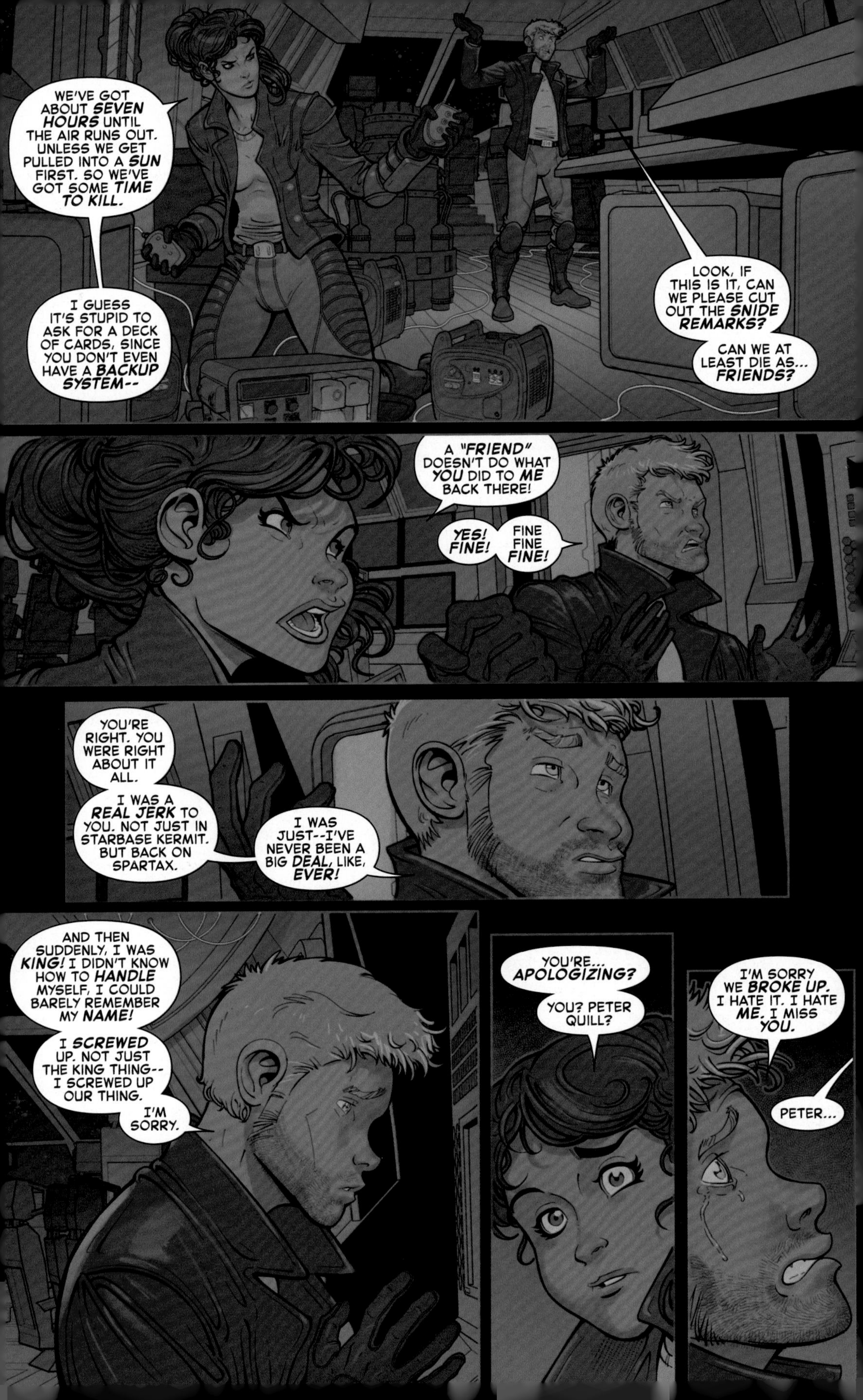

WE'VE GOT ABOUT SEVEN HOURS UNTIL THE AIR RUNS OUT. UNLESS WE GET PULLED INTO A SUN FIRST. SO WE'VE GOT SOME TIME TO KILL.
I GUESS IT'S STUPID TO ASK FOR A DECK OF CARDS, SINCE YOU DON'T EVEN HAVE A BACKUP SYSTEM--
LOOK, IF THIS IS IT, CAN WE PLEASE CUT OUT THE SNIDE REMARKS?
CAN WE AT LEAST DIE AS... FRIENDS?
A "FRIEND" DOESN'T DO WHAT YOU DID TO ME BACK THERE!
YES! FINE!
FINE FINE FINE!
YOU'RE RIGHT. YOU WERE RIGHT ABOUT IT ALL.
I WAS A REAL JERK TO YOU. NOT JUST IN STARBASE KERMIT. BUT BACK ON SPARTAX.
I WAS JUST--I'VE NEVER BEEN A BIG DEAL, LIKE, EVER!
AND THEN SUDDENLY, I WAS KING! I DIDN'T KNOW HOW TO HANDLE MYSELF, I COULD BARELY REMEMBER MY NAME!
I SCREWED UP. NOT JUST THE KING THING-- I SCREWED UP OUR THING.
I'M SORRY.
YOU'RE... APOLOGIZING?
YOU? PETER QUILL?
I'M SORRY WE BROKE UP. I HATE IT. I HATE ME. I MISS YOU.
PETER...

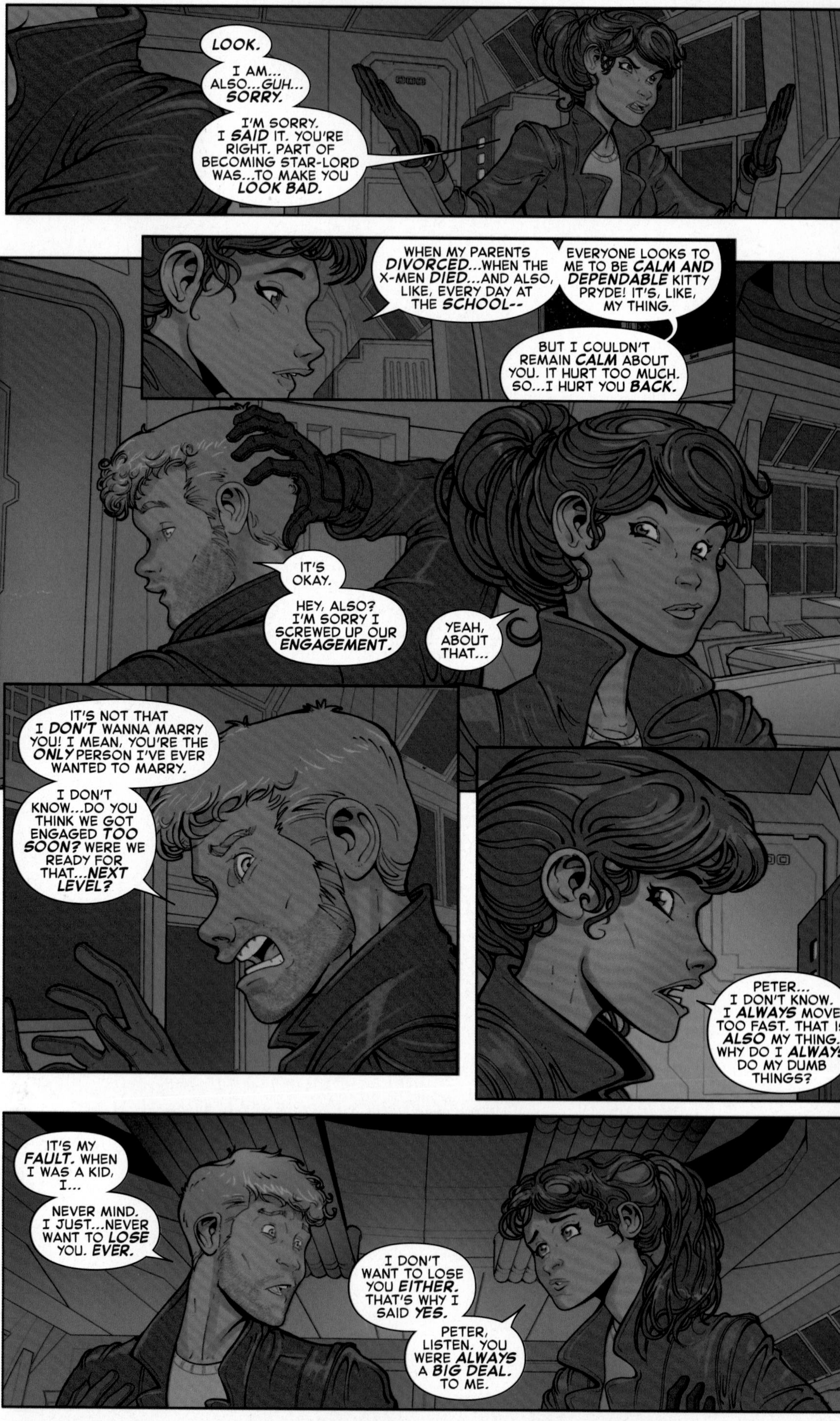
LOOK.
I AM... ALSO...GUH... SORRY.
I'M SORRY. I SAID IT. YOU'RE RIGHT. PART OF BECOMING STAR-LORD WAS...TO MAKE YOU LOOK BAD.
WHEN MY PARENTS DIVORCED...WHEN THE X-MEN DIED...AND ALSO, LIKE, EVERY DAY AT THE SCHOOL--
EVERYONE LOOKS TO ME TO BE CALM AND DEPENDABLE KITTY PRYDE! IT'S, LIKE, MY THING.
BUT I COULDN'T REMAIN CALM ABOUT YOU. IT HURT TOO MUCH. SO...I HURT YOU BACK.
IT'S OKAY.
HEY, ALSO? I'M SORRY I SCREWED UP OUR ENGAGEMENT.
YEAH, ABOUT THAT...
IT'S NOT THAT I DON'T WANNA MARRY YOU! I MEAN, YOU'RE THE ONLY PERSON I'VE EVER WANTED TO MARRY.
I DON'T KNOW...DO YOU THINK WE GOT ENGAGED TOO SOON? WERE WE READY FOR THAT...NEXT LEVEL?
PETER... I DON'T KNOW. I ALWAYS MOVE TOO FAST. THAT IS ALSO MY THING. WHY DO I ALWAYS DO MY DUMB THINGS?
IT'S MY FAULT. WHEN I WAS A KID, I...
NEVER MIND. I JUST...NEVER WANT TO LOSE YOU. EVER.
I DON'T WANT TO LOSE YOU EITHER. THAT'S WHY I SAID YES.
PETER, LISTEN. YOU WERE ALWAYS A BIG DEAL. TO ME.

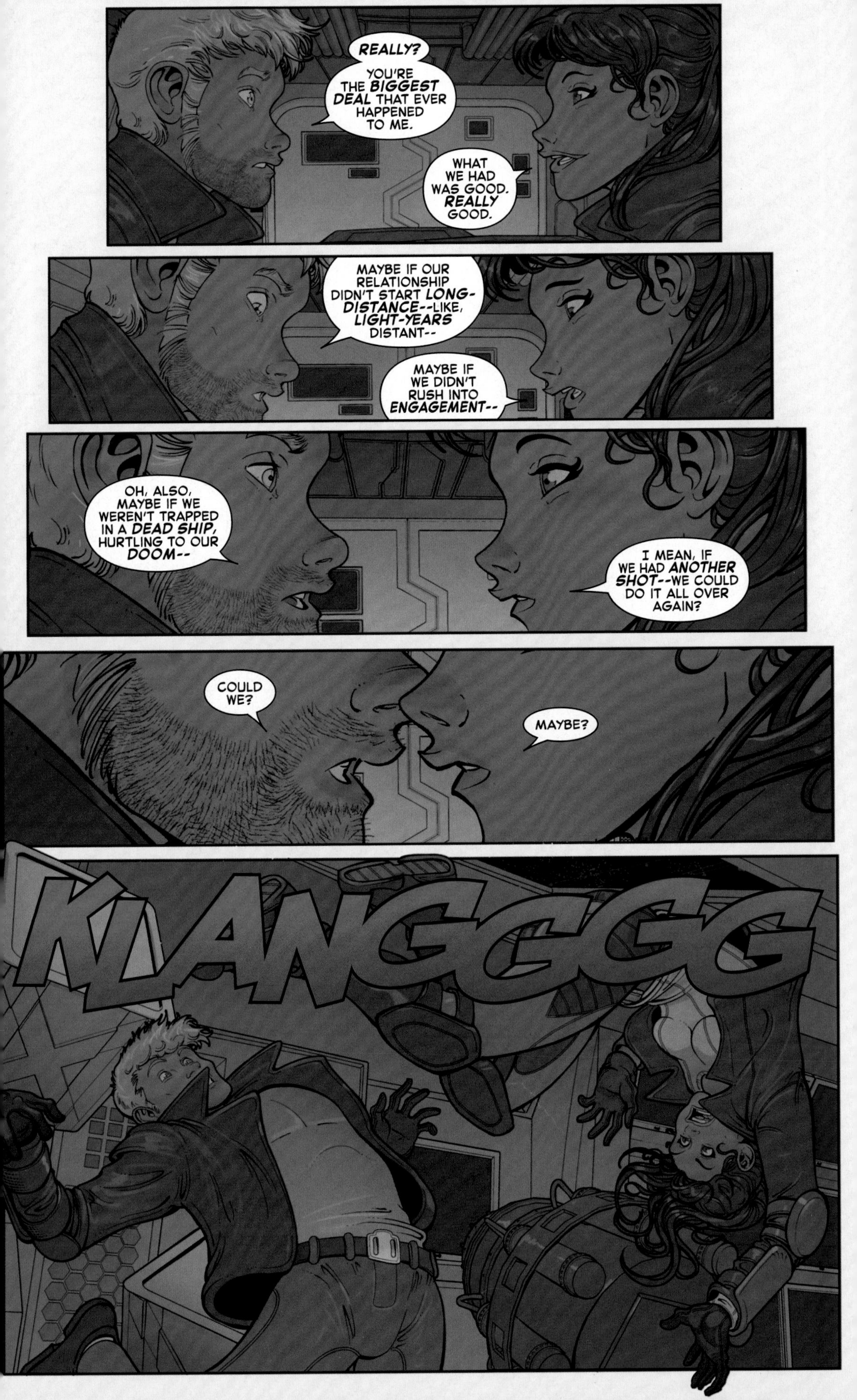
REALLY?
YOU'RE THE BIGGEST DEAL THAT EVER HAPPENED TO ME.
WHAT WE HAD WAS GOOD. REALLY GOOD.
MAYBE IF OUR RELATIONSHIP DIDN'T START LONG-DISTANCE--LIKE, LIGHT-YEARS DISTANT--
MAYBE IF WE DIDN'T RUSH INTO ENGAGEMENT--
OH, ALSO, MAYBE IF WE WEREN'T TRAPPED IN A DEAD SHIP, HURTLING TO OUR DOOM--
I MEAN, IF WE HAD ANOTHER SHOT--WE COULD DO IT ALL OVER AGAIN?
COULD WE?
MAYBE?
KLANGGG

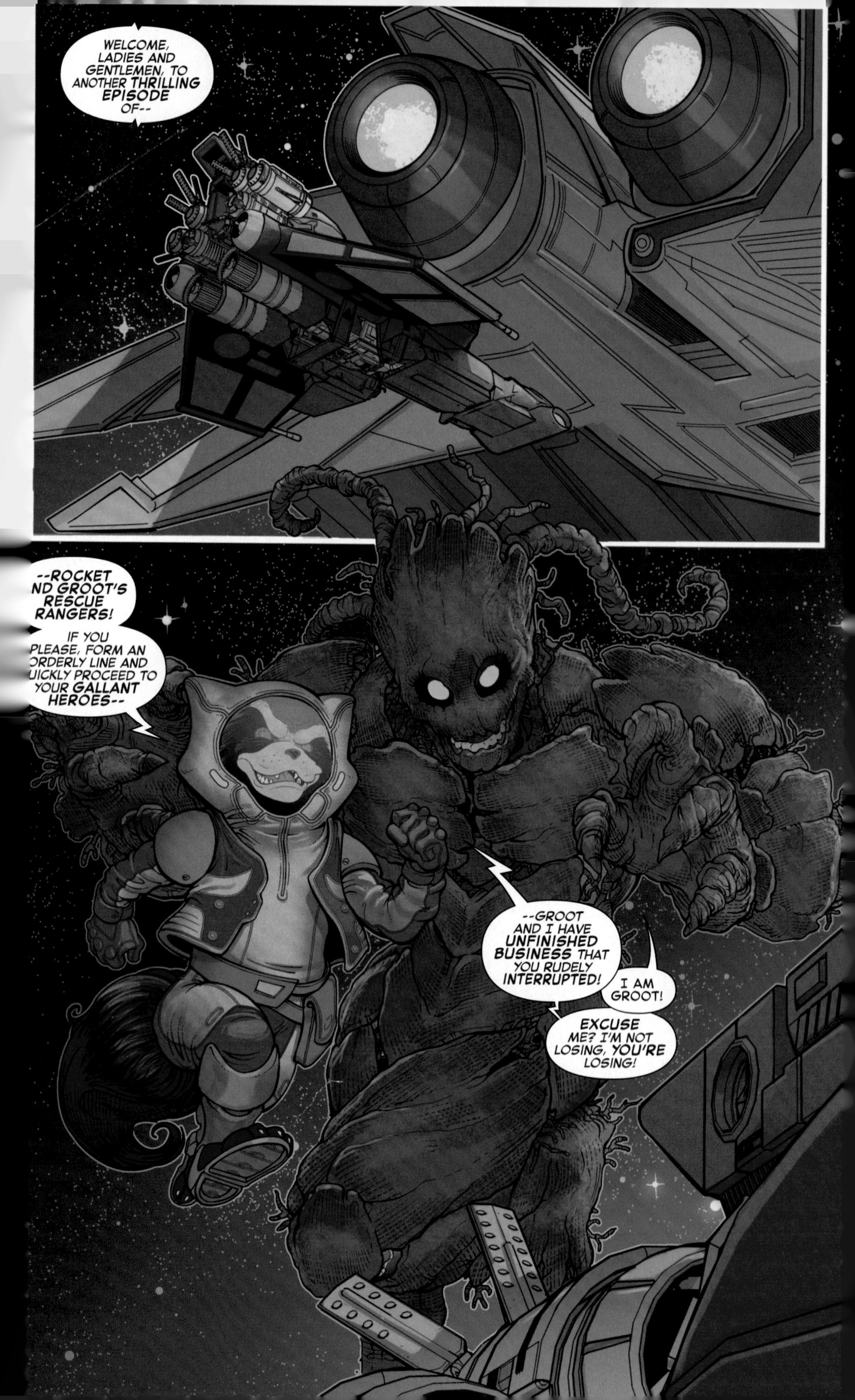
WELCOME, LADIES AND GENTLEMEN, TO ANOTHER THRILLING EPISODE OF--
--ROCKET ND GROOT'S RESCUE RANGERS!
IF YOU PLEASE, FORM AN ORDERLY LINE AND UICKLY PROCEED TO YOUR GALLANT HEROES--
--GROOT AND I HAVE UNFINISHED BUSINESS THAT YOU RUDELY INTERRUPTED!
I AM GROOT!
EXCUSE ME? I'M NOT LOSING, YOU'RE LOSING!

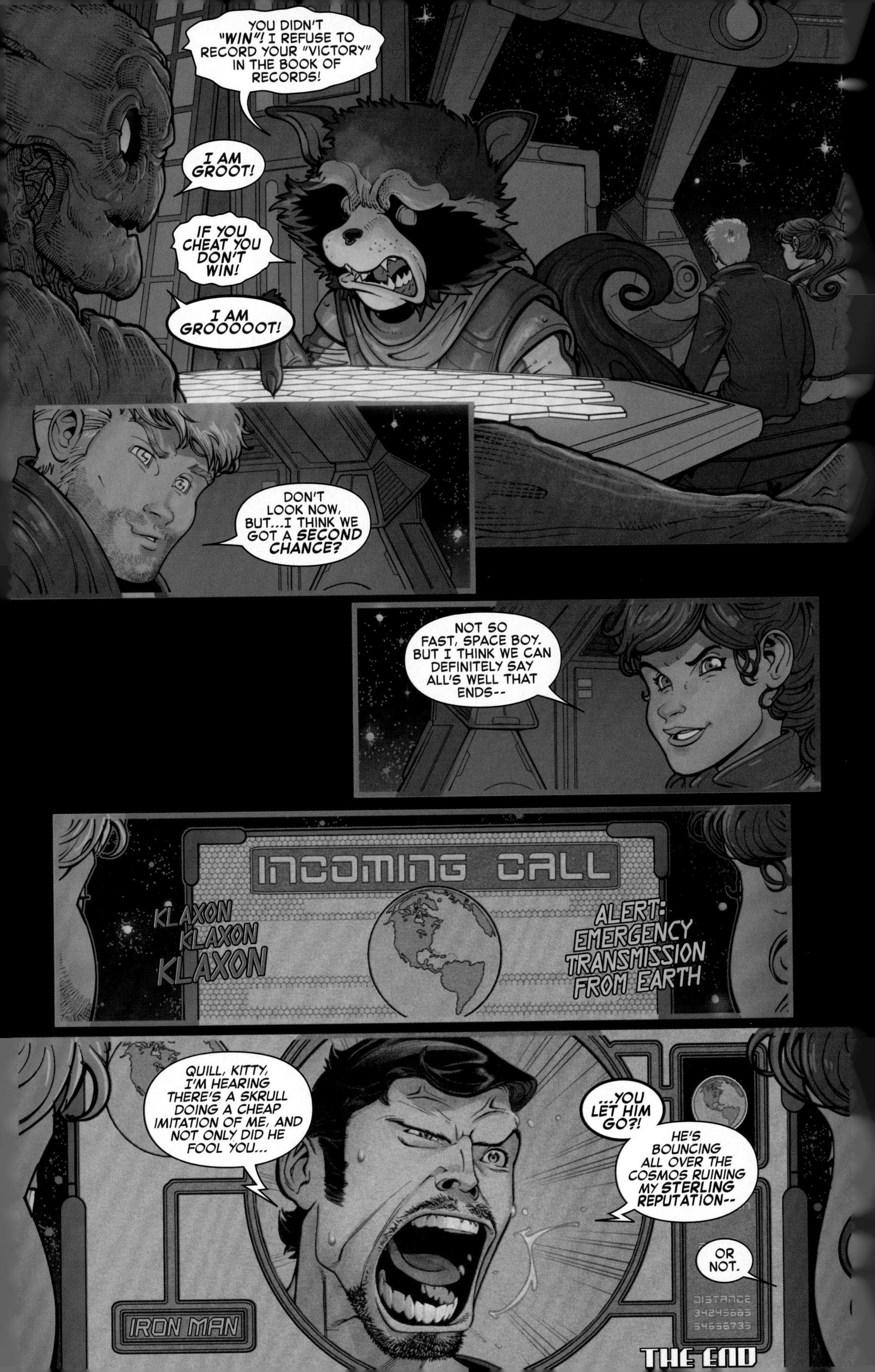
YOU DIDN'T "WIN"! I REFUSE TO RECORD YOUR "VICTORY" IN THE BOOK OF RECORDS!
I AM GROOT!
IF YOU CHEAT YOU DON'T WIN!
I AM GROOOOOT!
DON'T LOOK NOW, BUT...I THINK WE GOT A SECOND CHANCE?
NOT SO FAST, SPACE BOY. BUT I THINK WE CAN DEFINITELY SAY ALL'S WELL THAT ENDS--
INCOMING CALL
KLAXON KLAXON KLAXON
ALERT: EMERGENCY TRANSMISSION FROM EARTH
QUILL, KITTY, I'M HEARING THERE'S A SKRULL DOING A CHEAP IMITATION OF ME, AND NOT ONLY DID HE FOOL YOU...
...YOU LET HIM GO?!
HE'S BOUNCING ALL OVER THE COSMOS RUINING MY STERLING REPUTATION--
OR NOT.
DISTANCE
34245665
34656735
IRON MAN
THE END

THE AVENGERS
APPROVED BY THE COMICS CODE AUTHORITY
28
MAY
IND.
MARVEL COMICS GROUP
12¢
BACK AT LAST! GIANT-MAN!
"AMONG US WALKS...A GOLIATH!"

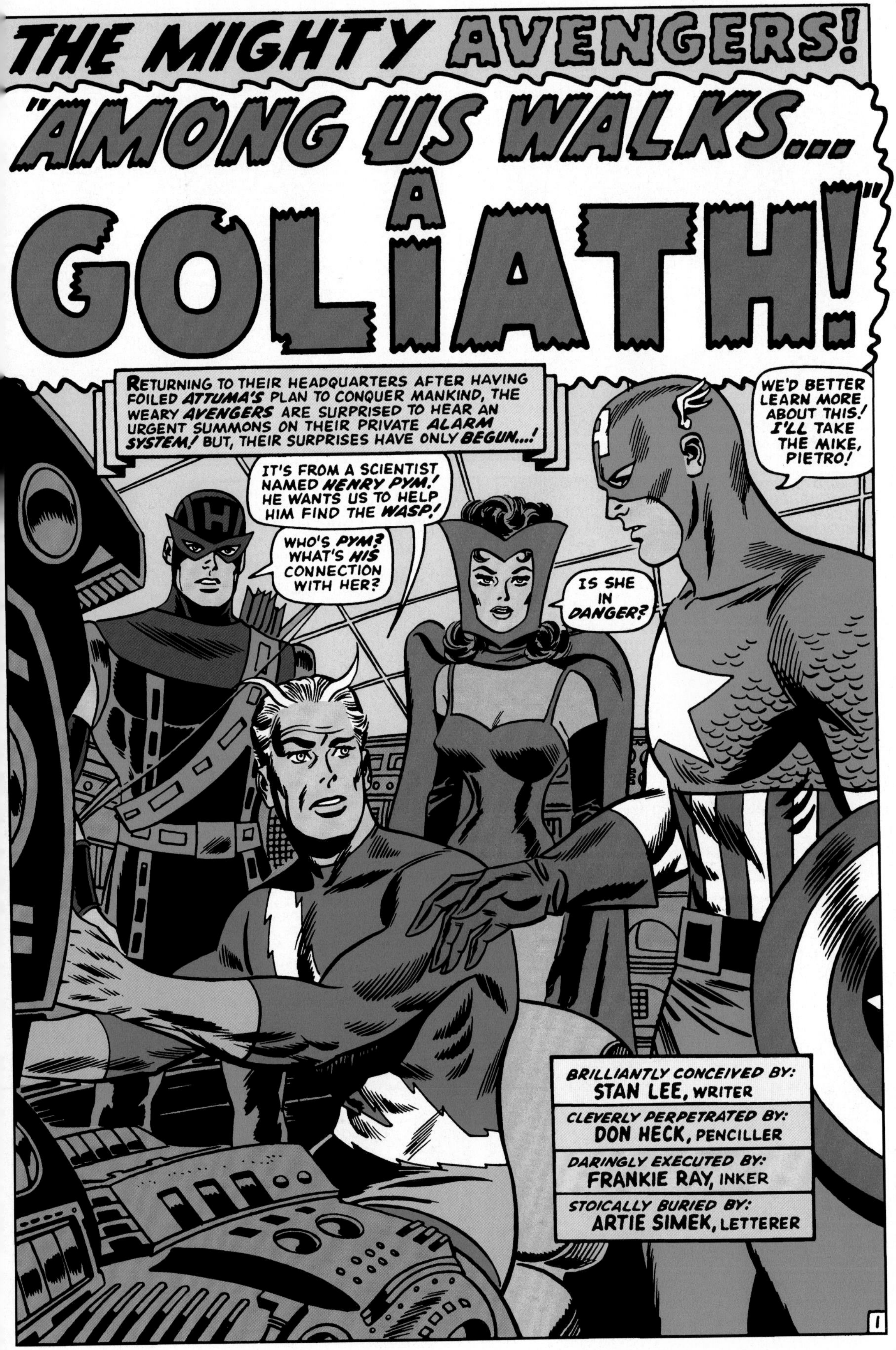
THE MIGHTY AVENGERS!
"AMONG US WALKS... A GOLIATH!"
RETURNING TO THEIR HEADQUARTERS AFTER HAVING FOILED ATTUMA'S PLAN TO CONQUER MANKIND, THE WEARY AVENGERS ARE SURPRISED TO HEAR AN URGENT SUMMONS ON THEIR PRIVATE ALARM SYSTEM! BUT, THEIR SURPRISES HAVE ONLY BEGUN...!
WE'D BETTER LEARN MORE ABOUT THIS! I'LL TAKE THE MIKE, PIETRO!
IT'S FROM A SCIENTIST NAMED HENRY PYM! HE WANTS US TO HELP HIM FIND THE WASP!
WHO'S PYM? WHAT'S HIS CONNECTION WITH HER?
IS SHE IN DANGER?
BRILLIANTLY CONCEIVED BY: STAN LEE, WRITER
CLEVERLY PERPETRATED BY: DON HECK, PENCILLER
DARINGLY EXECUTED BY: FRANKIE RAY, INKER
STOICALLY BURIED BY: ARTIE SIMEK, LETTERER
1

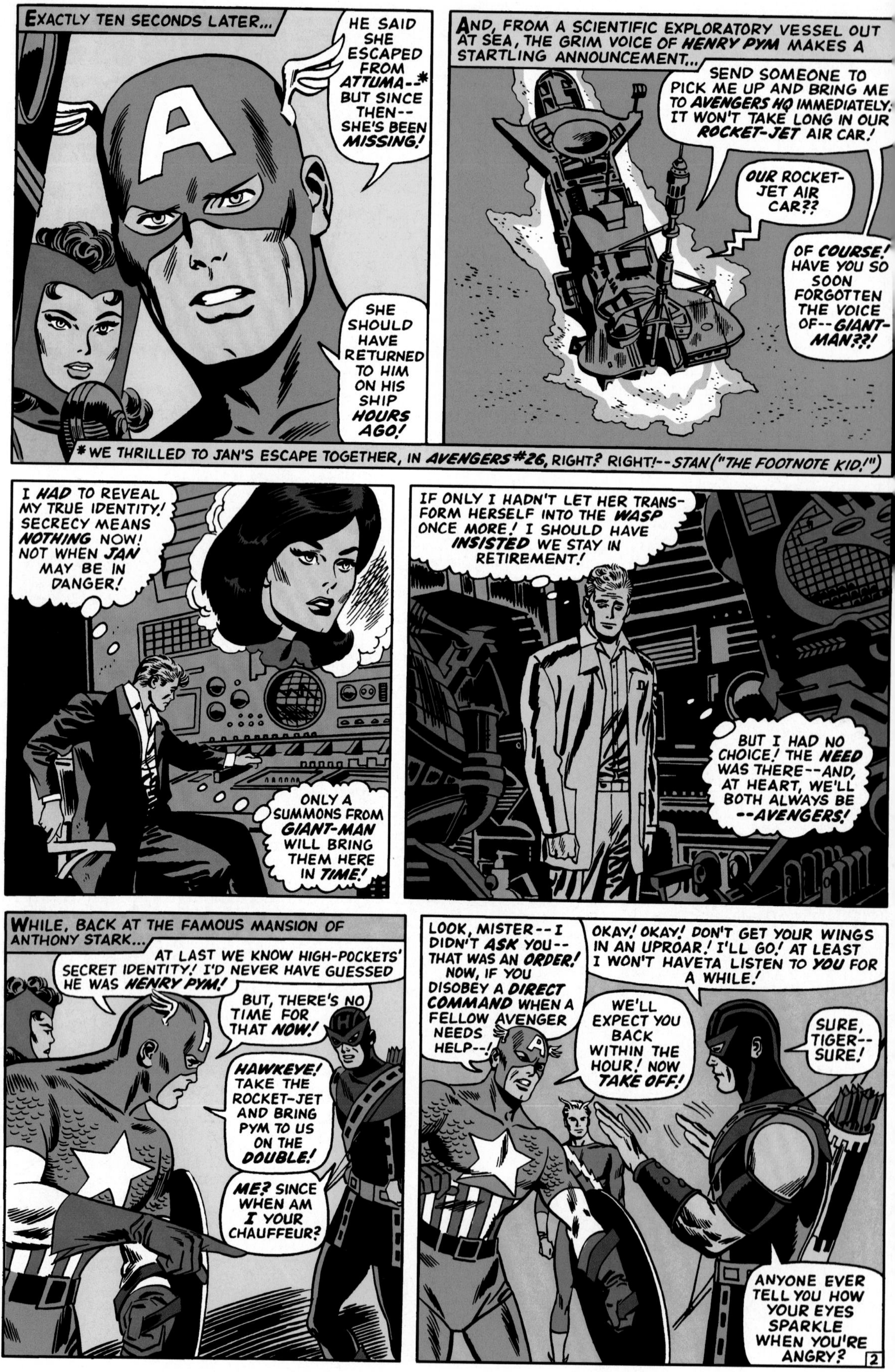
EXACTLY TEN SECONDS LATER...
HE SAID SHE ESCAPED FROM ATTUMA--* BUT SINCE THEN--SHE'S BEEN MISSING!
SHE SHOULD HAVE RETURNED TO HIM ON HIS SHIP HOURS AGO!
AND, FROM A SCIENTIFIC EXPLORATORY VESSEL OUT AT SEA, THE GRIM VOICE OF HENRY PYM MAKES A STARTLING ANNOUNCEMENT...
SEND SOMEONE TO PICK ME UP AND BRING ME TO AVENGERS HQ IMMEDIATELY! IT WON'T TAKE LONG IN OUR ROCKET-JET AIR CAR!
OUR ROCKET-JET AIR CAR??
OF COURSE! HAVE YOU SO SOON FORGOTTEN THE VOICE OF--GIANT-MAN??!
* WE THRILLED TO JAN'S ESCAPE TOGETHER, IN AVENGERS #26, RIGHT? RIGHT!--STAN ("THE FOOTNOTE KID!")
I HAD TO REVEAL MY TRUE IDENTITY! SECRECY MEANS NOTHING NOW! NOT WHEN JAN MAY BE IN DANGER!
ONLY A SUMMONS FROM GIANT-MAN WILL BRING THEM HERE IN TIME!
IF ONLY I HADN'T LET HER TRANS-FORM HERSELF INTO THE WASP ONCE MORE! I SHOULD HAVE INSISTED WE STAY IN RETIREMENT!
BUT I HAD NO CHOICE! THE NEED WAS THERE--AND, AT HEART, WE'LL BOTH ALWAYS BE --AVENGERS!
WHILE, BACK AT THE FAMOUS MANSION OF ANTHONY STARK...
AT LAST WE KNOW HIGH-POCKETS' SECRET IDENTITY! I'D NEVER HAVE GUESSED HE WAS HENRY PYM!
BUT, THERE'S NO TIME FOR THAT NOW!
HAWKEYE! TAKE THE ROCKET-JET AND BRING PYM TO US ON THE DOUBLE!
ME? SINCE WHEN AM I YOUR CHAUFFEUR?
LOOK, MISTER--I DIDN'T ASK YOU--THAT WAS AN ORDER! NOW, IF YOU DISOBEY A DIRECT COMMAND WHEN A FELLOW AVENGER NEEDS HELP--!
OKAY! OKAY! DON'T GET YOUR WINGS IN AN UPROAR! I'LL GO! AT LEAST I WON'T HAVETA LISTEN TO YOU FOR A WHILE!
WE'LL EXPECT YOU BACK WITHIN THE HOUR! NOW TAKE OFF!
SURE, TIGER--SURE!
ANYONE EVER TELL YOU HOW YOUR EYES SPARKLE WHEN YOU'RE ANGRY?
2

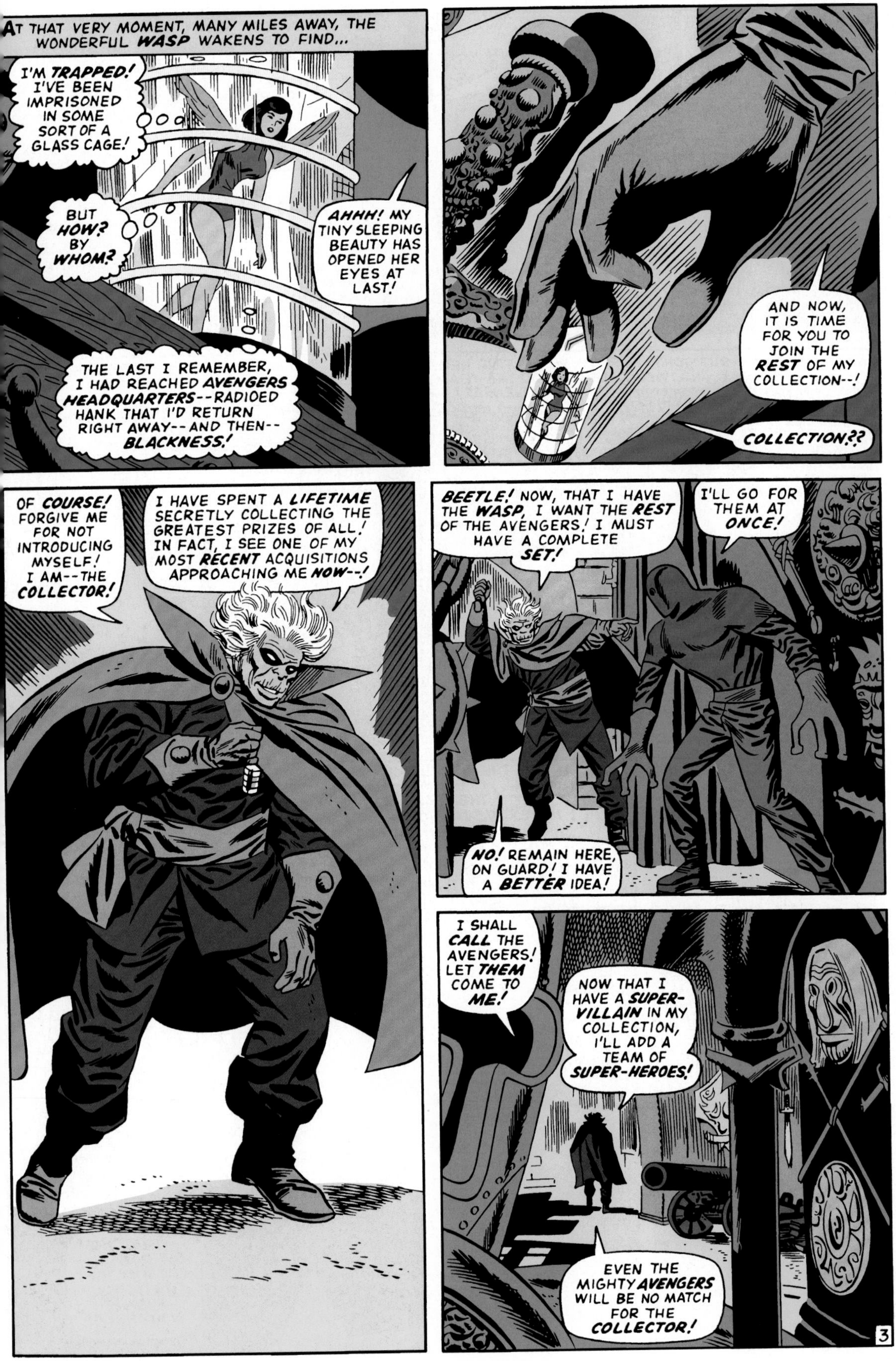
AT THAT VERY MOMENT, MANY MILES AWAY, THE WONDERFUL **WASP** WAKENS TO FIND...
I'M **TRAPPED!** I'VE BEEN IMPRISONED IN SOME SORT OF A GLASS CAGE!
BUT **HOW?** BY **WHOM?**
AHHH! MY TINY SLEEPING BEAUTY HAS OPENED HER EYES AT LAST!
THE LAST I REMEMBER, I HAD REACHED **AVENGERS HEADQUARTERS**--RADIOED HANK THAT I'D RETURN RIGHT AWAY--AND THEN--**BLACKNESS!**
AND NOW, IT IS TIME FOR YOU TO JOIN THE **REST** OF MY COLLECTION--!
COLLECTION??
OF **COURSE!** FORGIVE ME FOR NOT INTRODUCING MYSELF! I AM--THE **COLLECTOR!**
I HAVE SPENT A **LIFETIME** SECRETLY COLLECTING THE GREATEST PRIZES OF ALL! IN FACT, I SEE ONE OF MY MOST **RECENT** ACQUISITIONS APPROACHING ME **NOW**--!
BEETLE! NOW, THAT I HAVE THE **WASP**, I WANT THE **REST** OF THE AVENGERS! I MUST HAVE A COMPLETE **SET!**
I'LL GO FOR THEM AT **ONCE!**
NO! REMAIN HERE, ON GUARD! I HAVE A **BETTER** IDEA!
I SHALL **CALL** THE AVENGERS! LET **THEM** COME TO **ME!**
NOW THAT I HAVE A **SUPER-VILLAIN** IN MY COLLECTION, I'LL ADD A TEAM OF **SUPER-HEROES!**
EVEN THE MIGHTY **AVENGERS** WILL BE NO MATCH FOR THE **COLLECTOR!**

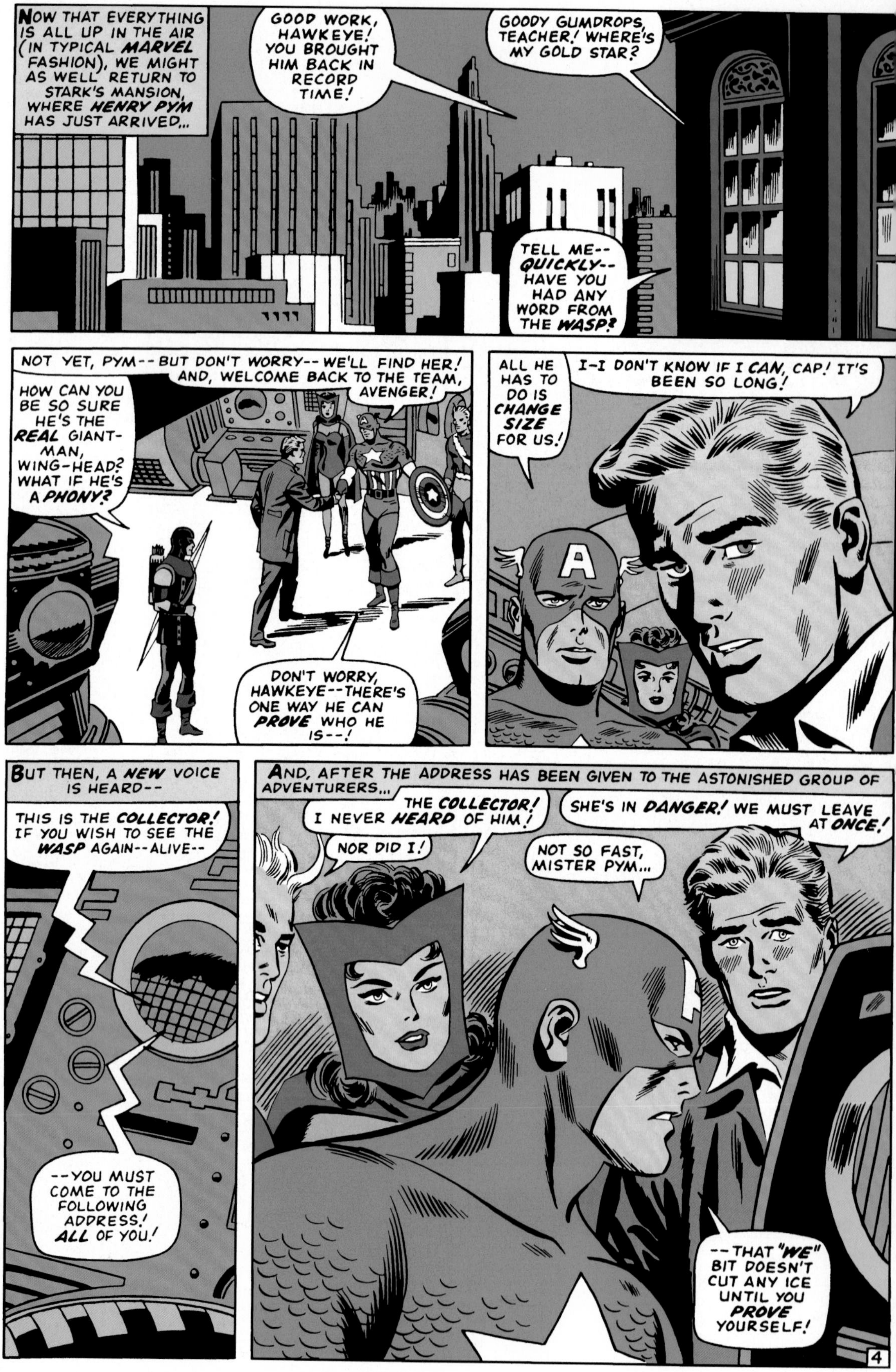
NOW THAT EVERYTHING IS ALL UP IN THE AIR (IN TYPICAL MARVEL FASHION), WE MIGHT AS WELL RETURN TO STARK'S MANSION, WHERE HENRY PYM HAS JUST ARRIVED...
GOOD WORK, HAWKEYE! YOU BROUGHT HIM BACK IN RECORD TIME!
GOODY GUMDROPS, TEACHER! WHERE'S MY GOLD STAR?
TELL ME-- QUICKLY-- HAVE YOU HAD ANY WORD FROM THE WASP?
NOT YET, PYM-- BUT DON'T WORRY-- WE'LL FIND HER! AND, WELCOME BACK TO THE TEAM, AVENGER!
HOW CAN YOU BE SO SURE HE'S THE REAL GIANT-MAN, WING-HEAD? WHAT IF HE'S A PHONY?
DON'T WORRY, HAWKEYE--THERE'S ONE WAY HE CAN PROVE WHO HE IS--!
ALL HE HAS TO DO IS CHANGE SIZE FOR US!
I-I DON'T KNOW IF I CAN, CAP! IT'S BEEN SO LONG!
BUT THEN, A NEW VOICE IS HEARD--
THIS IS THE COLLECTOR! IF YOU WISH TO SEE THE WASP AGAIN--ALIVE--
--YOU MUST COME TO THE FOLLOWING ADDRESS! ALL OF YOU!
AND, AFTER THE ADDRESS HAS BEEN GIVEN TO THE ASTONISHED GROUP OF ADVENTURERS...
THE COLLECTOR! I NEVER HEARD OF HIM!
NOR DID I!
SHE'S IN DANGER! WE MUST LEAVE AT ONCE!
NOT SO FAST, MISTER PYM...
--THAT "WE" BIT DOESN'T CUT ANY ICE UNTIL YOU PROVE YOURSELF!
4

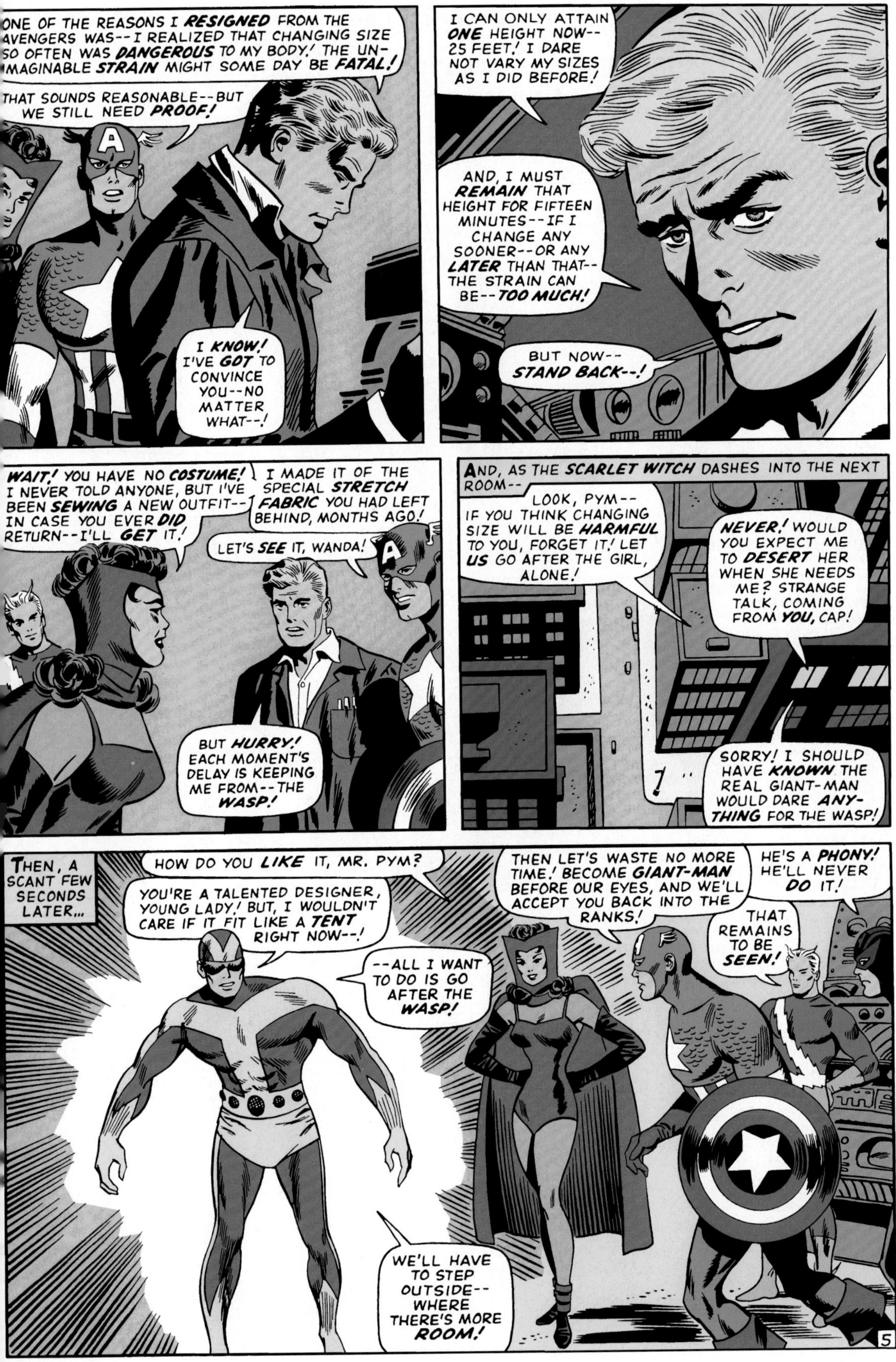
ONE OF THE REASONS I RESIGNED FROM THE AVENGERS WAS--I REALIZED THAT CHANGING SIZE SO OFTEN WAS DANGEROUS TO MY BODY! THE UN-IMAGINABLE STRAIN MIGHT SOME DAY BE FATAL!
THAT SOUNDS REASONABLE--BUT WE STILL NEED PROOF!
I KNOW! I'VE GOT TO CONVINCE YOU--NO MATTER WHAT--!
I CAN ONLY ATTAIN ONE HEIGHT NOW--25 FEET! I DARE NOT VARY MY SIZES AS I DID BEFORE!
AND, I MUST REMAIN THAT HEIGHT FOR FIFTEEN MINUTES--IF I CHANGE ANY SOONER--OR ANY LATER THAN THAT--THE STRAIN CAN BE--TOO MUCH!
BUT NOW--STAND BACK--!
WAIT! YOU HAVE NO COSTUME! I NEVER TOLD ANYONE, BUT I'VE BEEN SEWING A NEW OUTFIT--IN CASE YOU EVER DID RETURN--I'LL GET IT!
I MADE IT OF THE SPECIAL STRETCH FABRIC YOU HAD LEFT BEHIND, MONTHS AGO!
LET'S SEE IT, WANDA!
BUT HURRY! EACH MOMENT'S DELAY IS KEEPING ME FROM--THE WASP!
AND, AS THE SCARLET WITCH DASHES INTO THE NEXT ROOM--
LOOK, PYM--IF YOU THINK CHANGING SIZE WILL BE HARMFUL TO YOU, FORGET IT! LET US GO AFTER THE GIRL, ALONE!
NEVER! WOULD YOU EXPECT ME TO DESERT HER WHEN SHE NEEDS ME? STRANGE TALK, COMING FROM YOU, CAP!
SORRY! I SHOULD HAVE KNOWN THE REAL GIANT-MAN WOULD DARE ANY-THING FOR THE WASP!
THEN, A SCANT FEW SECONDS LATER...
HOW DO YOU LIKE IT, MR. PYM?
YOU'RE A TALENTED DESIGNER, YOUNG LADY! BUT, I WOULDN'T CARE IF IT FIT LIKE A TENT RIGHT NOW--!
--ALL I WANT TO DO IS GO AFTER THE WASP!
THEN LET'S WASTE NO MORE TIME! BECOME GIANT-MAN BEFORE OUR EYES, AND WE'LL ACCEPT YOU BACK INTO THE RANKS!
HE'S A PHONY! HE'LL NEVER DO IT!
THAT REMAINS TO BE SEEN!
WE'LL HAVE TO STEP OUTSIDE--WHERE THERE'S MORE ROOM!
5

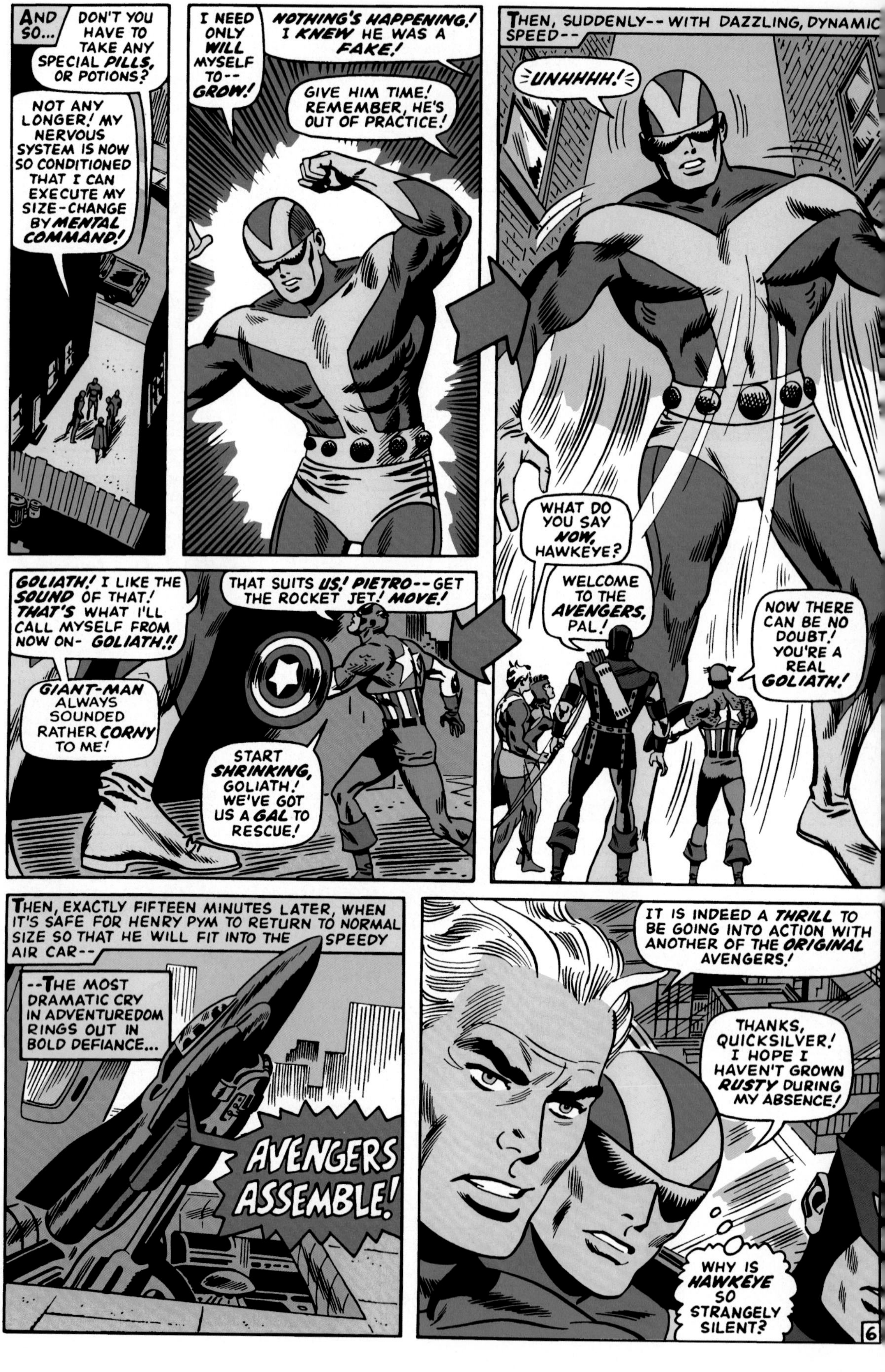
AND SO...
DON'T YOU HAVE TO TAKE ANY SPECIAL PILLS, OR POTIONS?
NOT ANY LONGER! MY NERVOUS SYSTEM IS NOW SO CONDITIONED THAT I CAN EXECUTE MY SIZE-CHANGE BY MENTAL COMMAND!
I NEED ONLY WILL MYSELF TO-- GROW!
NOTHING'S HAPPENING! I KNEW HE WAS A FAKE!
GIVE HIM TIME! REMEMBER, HE'S OUT OF PRACTICE!
THEN, SUDDENLY-- WITH DAZZLING, DYNAMIC SPEED--
UNHHHH!
WHAT DO YOU SAY NOW, HAWKEYE?
WELCOME TO THE AVENGERS, PAL!
NOW THERE CAN BE NO DOUBT! YOU'RE A REAL GOLIATH!
GOLIATH! I LIKE THE SOUND OF THAT! THAT'S WHAT I'LL CALL MYSELF FROM NOW ON- GOLIATH!!
GIANT-MAN ALWAYS SOUNDED RATHER CORNY TO ME!
THAT SUITS US! PIETRO--GET THE ROCKET JET! MOVE!
START SHRINKING, GOLIATH! WE'VE GOT US A GAL TO RESCUE!
THEN, EXACTLY FIFTEEN MINUTES LATER, WHEN IT'S SAFE FOR HENRY PYM TO RETURN TO NORMAL SIZE SO THAT HE WILL FIT INTO THE SPEEDY AIR CAR--
--THE MOST DRAMATIC CRY IN ADVENTUREDOM RINGS OUT IN BOLD DEFIANCE...
AVENGERS ASSEMBLE!
IT IS INDEED A THRILL TO BE GOING INTO ACTION WITH ANOTHER OF THE ORIGINAL AVENGERS!
THANKS, QUICKSILVER! I HOPE I HAVEN'T GROWN RUSTY DURING MY ABSENCE!
WHY IS HAWKEYE SO STRANGELY SILENT?
6

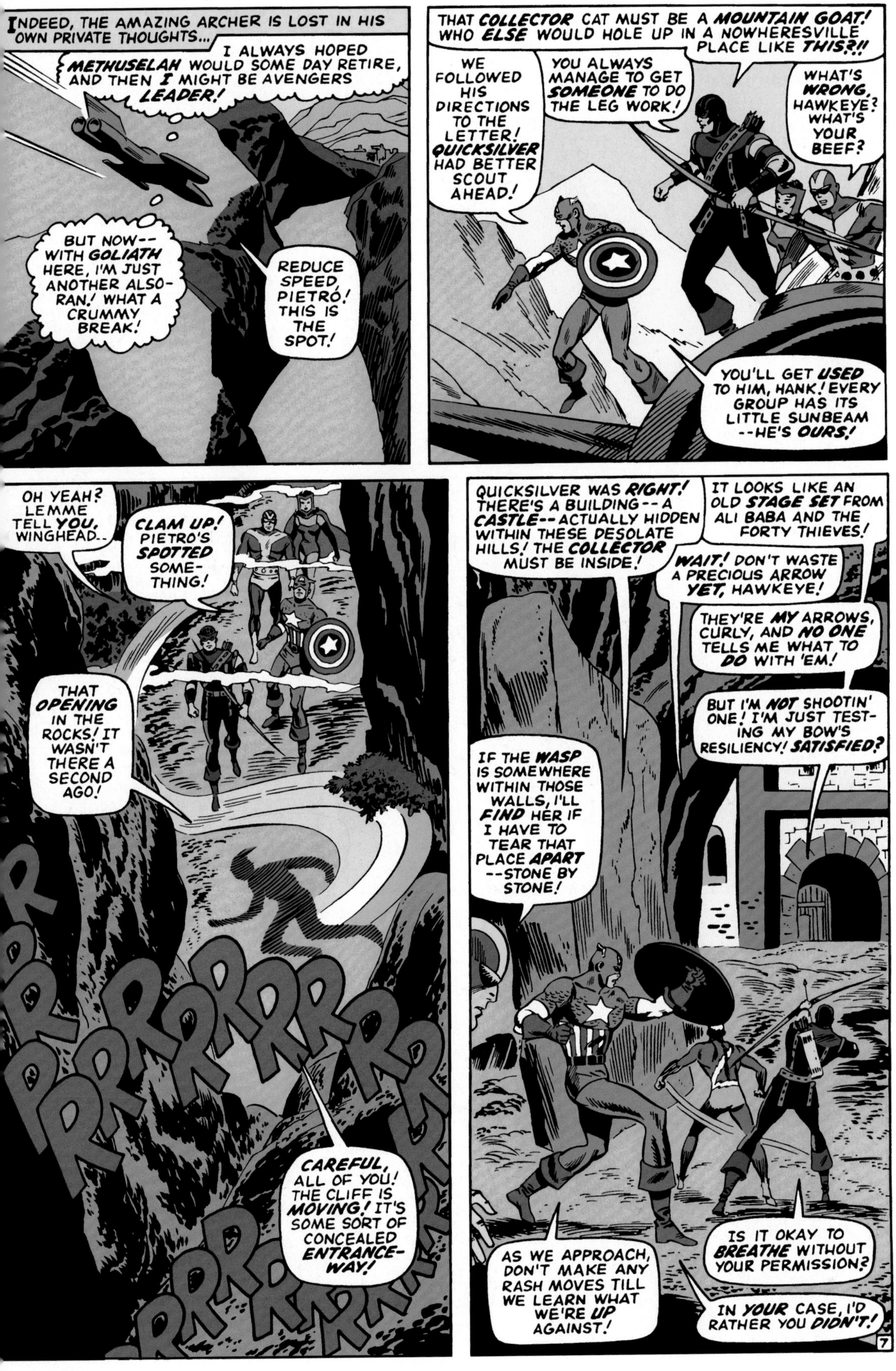
INDEED, THE AMAZING ARCHER IS LOST IN HIS OWN PRIVATE THOUGHTS...
I ALWAYS HOPED METHUSELAH WOULD SOME DAY RETIRE, AND THEN I MIGHT BE AVENGERS LEADER!
BUT NOW-- WITH GOLIATH HERE, I'M JUST ANOTHER ALSO-RAN! WHAT A CRUMMY BREAK!
REDUCE SPEED, PIETRO! THIS IS THE SPOT!
THAT COLLECTOR CAT MUST BE A MOUNTAIN GOAT! WHO ELSE WOULD HOLE UP IN A NOWHERESVILLE PLACE LIKE THIS?!!
WE FOLLOWED HIS DIRECTIONS TO THE LETTER! QUICKSILVER HAD BETTER SCOUT AHEAD!
YOU ALWAYS MANAGE TO GET SOMEONE TO DO THE LEG WORK!
WHAT'S WRONG, HAWKEYE? WHAT'S YOUR BEEF?
YOU'LL GET USED TO HIM, HANK! EVERY GROUP HAS ITS LITTLE SUNBEAM --HE'S OURS!
OH YEAH? LEMME TELL YOU, WINGHEAD..
CLAM UP! PIETRO'S SPOTTED SOME-THING!
THAT OPENING IN THE ROCKS! IT WASN'T THERE A SECOND AGO!
RRRRRRRRRRRRRRRRRR
CAREFUL, ALL OF YOU! THE CLIFF IS MOVING! IT'S SOME SORT OF CONCEALED ENTRANCE-WAY!
QUICKSILVER WAS RIGHT! THERE'S A BUILDING--A CASTLE--ACTUALLY HIDDEN WITHIN THESE DESOLATE HILLS! THE COLLECTOR MUST BE INSIDE!
IT LOOKS LIKE AN OLD STAGE SET FROM ALI BABA AND THE FORTY THIEVES!
WAIT! DON'T WASTE A PRECIOUS ARROW YET, HAWKEYE!
THEY'RE MY ARROWS, CURLY, AND NO ONE TELLS ME WHAT TO DO WITH 'EM!
BUT I'M NOT SHOOTIN' ONE! I'M JUST TEST-ING MY BOW'S RESILIENCY! SATISFIED?
IF THE WASP IS SOMEWHERE WITHIN THOSE WALLS, I'LL FIND HER IF I HAVE TO TEAR THAT PLACE APART --STONE BY STONE!
AS WE APPROACH, DON'T MAKE ANY RASH MOVES TILL WE LEARN WHAT WE'RE UP AGAINST!
IS IT OKAY TO BREATHE WITHOUT YOUR PERMISSION?
IN YOUR CASE, I'D RATHER YOU DIDN'T!
7

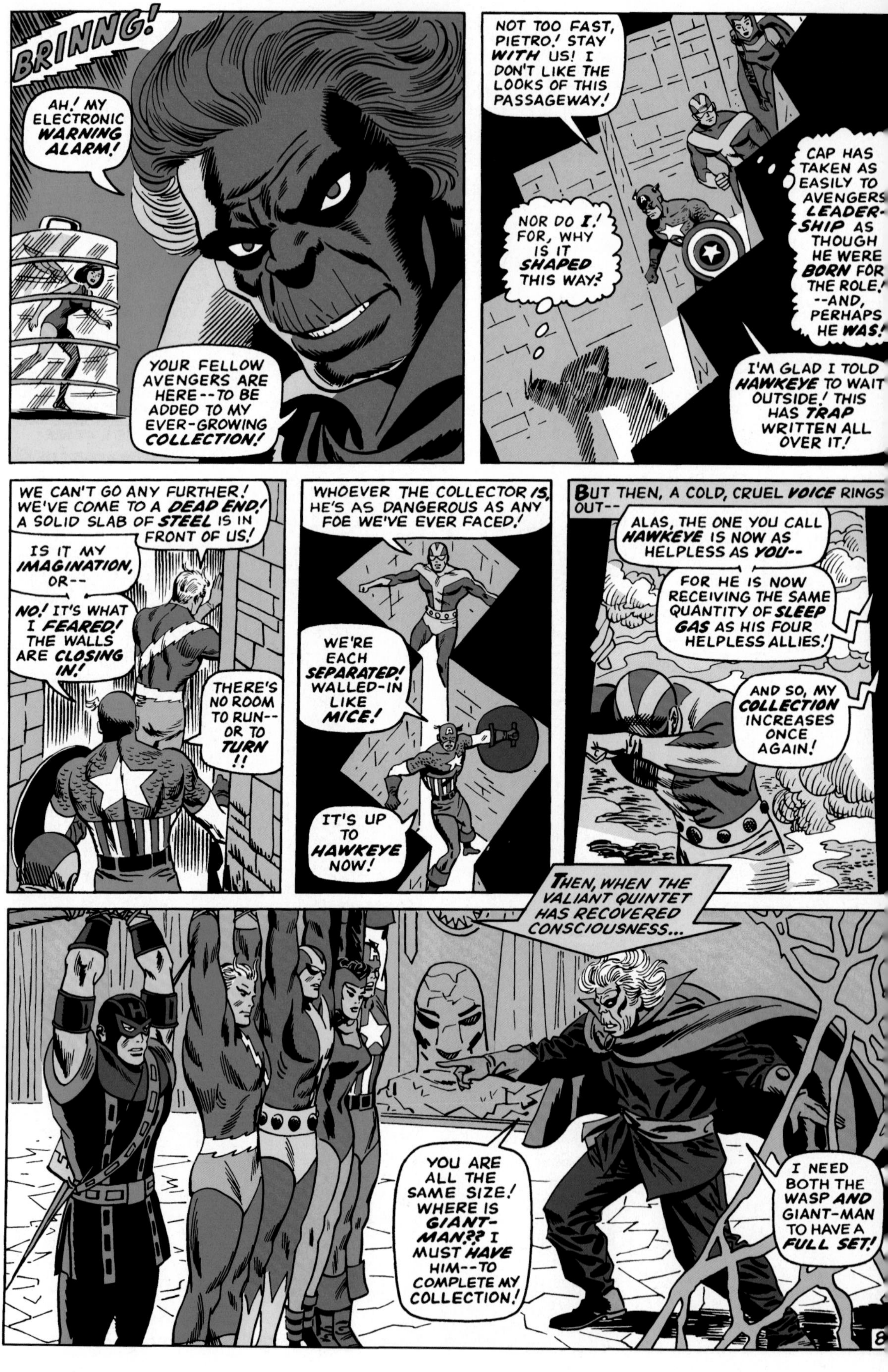
BRINNG!
AH! MY ELECTRONIC WARNING ALARM!
YOUR FELLOW AVENGERS ARE HERE--TO BE ADDED TO MY EVER-GROWING COLLECTION!
NOT TOO FAST, PIETRO! STAY WITH US! I DON'T LIKE THE LOOKS OF THIS PASSAGEWAY!
NOR DO I! FOR, WHY IS IT SHAPED THIS WAY?
CAP HAS TAKEN AS EASILY TO AVENGERS LEADER-SHIP AS THOUGH HE WERE BORN FOR THE ROLE! --AND, PERHAPS HE WAS!
I'M GLAD I TOLD HAWKEYE TO WAIT OUTSIDE! THIS HAS TRAP WRITTEN ALL OVER IT!
WE CAN'T GO ANY FURTHER! WE'VE COME TO A DEAD END! A SOLID SLAB OF STEEL IS IN FRONT OF US!
IS IT MY IMAGINATION, OR--
NO! IT'S WHAT I FEARED! THE WALLS ARE CLOSING IN!
THERE'S NO ROOM TO RUN--OR TO TURN!!
WHOEVER THE COLLECTOR IS, HE'S AS DANGEROUS AS ANY FOE WE'VE EVER FACED!
WE'RE EACH SEPARATED! WALLED-IN LIKE MICE!
IT'S UP TO HAWKEYE NOW!
BUT THEN, A COLD, CRUEL VOICE RINGS OUT--
ALAS, THE ONE YOU CALL HAWKEYE IS NOW AS HELPLESS AS YOU--
FOR HE IS NOW RECEIVING THE SAME QUANTITY OF SLEEP GAS AS HIS FOUR HELPLESS ALLIES!
AND SO, MY COLLECTION INCREASES ONCE AGAIN!
THEN, WHEN THE VALIANT QUINTET HAS RECOVERED CONSCIOUSNESS...
YOU ARE ALL THE SAME SIZE! WHERE IS GIANT-MAN?? I MUST HAVE HIM--TO COMPLETE MY COLLECTION!
I NEED BOTH THE WASP AND GIANT-MAN TO HAVE A FULL SET!
8

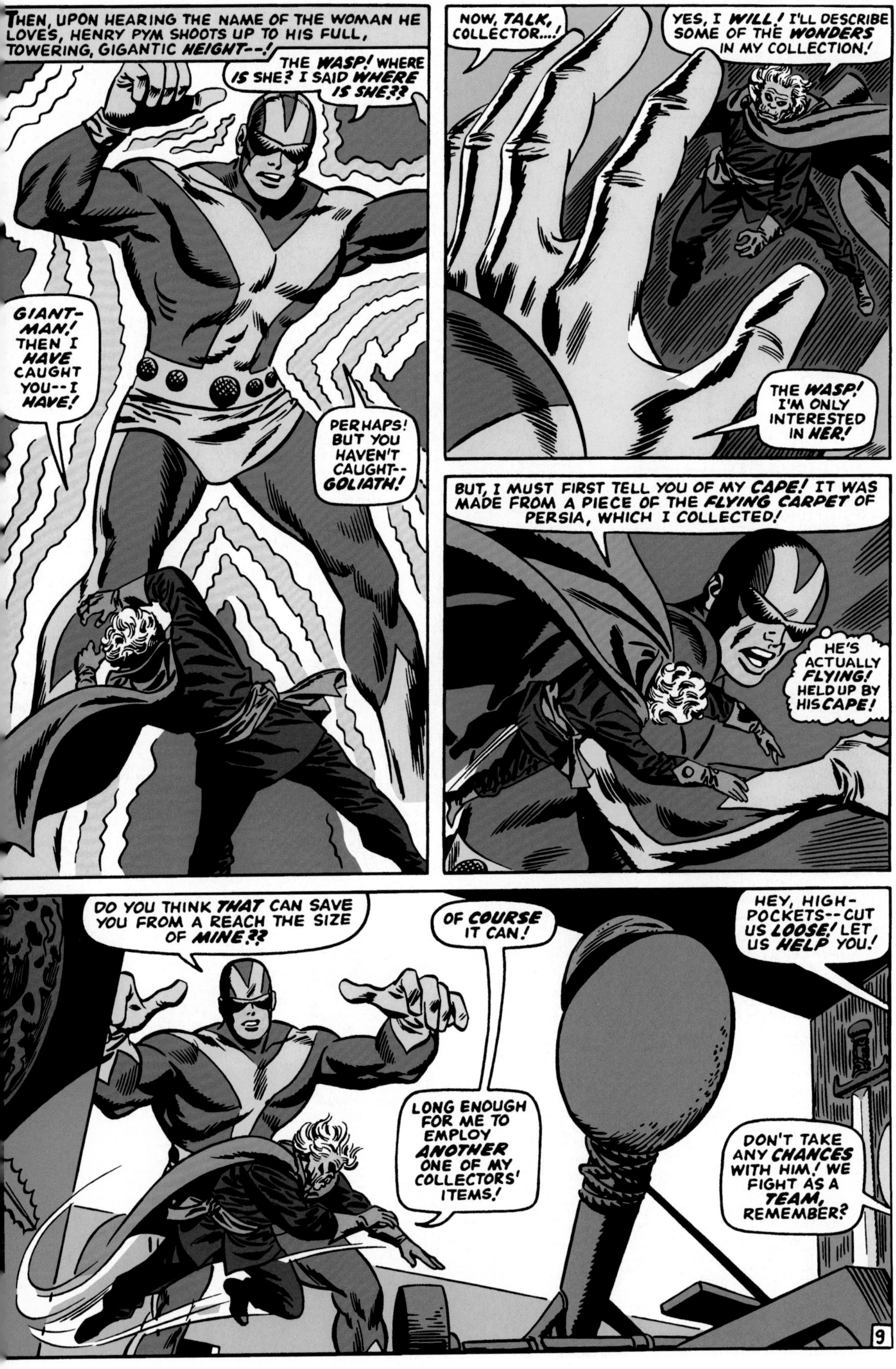

THEN, UPON HEARING THE NAME OF THE WOMAN HE LOVES, HENRY PYM SHOOTS UP TO HIS FULL, TOWERING, GIGANTIC HEIGHT--!
THE WASP! WHERE IS SHE? I SAID WHERE IS SHE??
GIANT-MAN! THEN I HAVE CAUGHT YOU--I HAVE!
PERHAPS! BUT YOU HAVEN'T CAUGHT--GOLIATH!
NOW, TALK, COLLECTOR....!
YES, I WILL! I'LL DESCRIBE SOME OF THE WONDERS IN MY COLLECTION!
THE WASP! I'M ONLY INTERESTED IN HER!
BUT, I MUST FIRST TELL YOU OF MY CAPE! IT WAS MADE FROM A PIECE OF THE FLYING CARPET OF PERSIA, WHICH I COLLECTED!
HE'S ACTUALLY FLYING! HELD UP BY HIS CAPE!
DO YOU THINK THAT CAN SAVE YOU FROM A REACH THE SIZE OF MINE??
OF COURSE IT CAN!
LONG ENOUGH FOR ME TO EMPLOY ANOTHER ONE OF MY COLLECTORS' ITEMS!
HEY, HIGH-POCKETS--CUT US LOOSE! LET US HELP YOU!
DON'T TAKE ANY CHANCES WITH HIM! WE FIGHT AS A TEAM, REMEMBER?
9

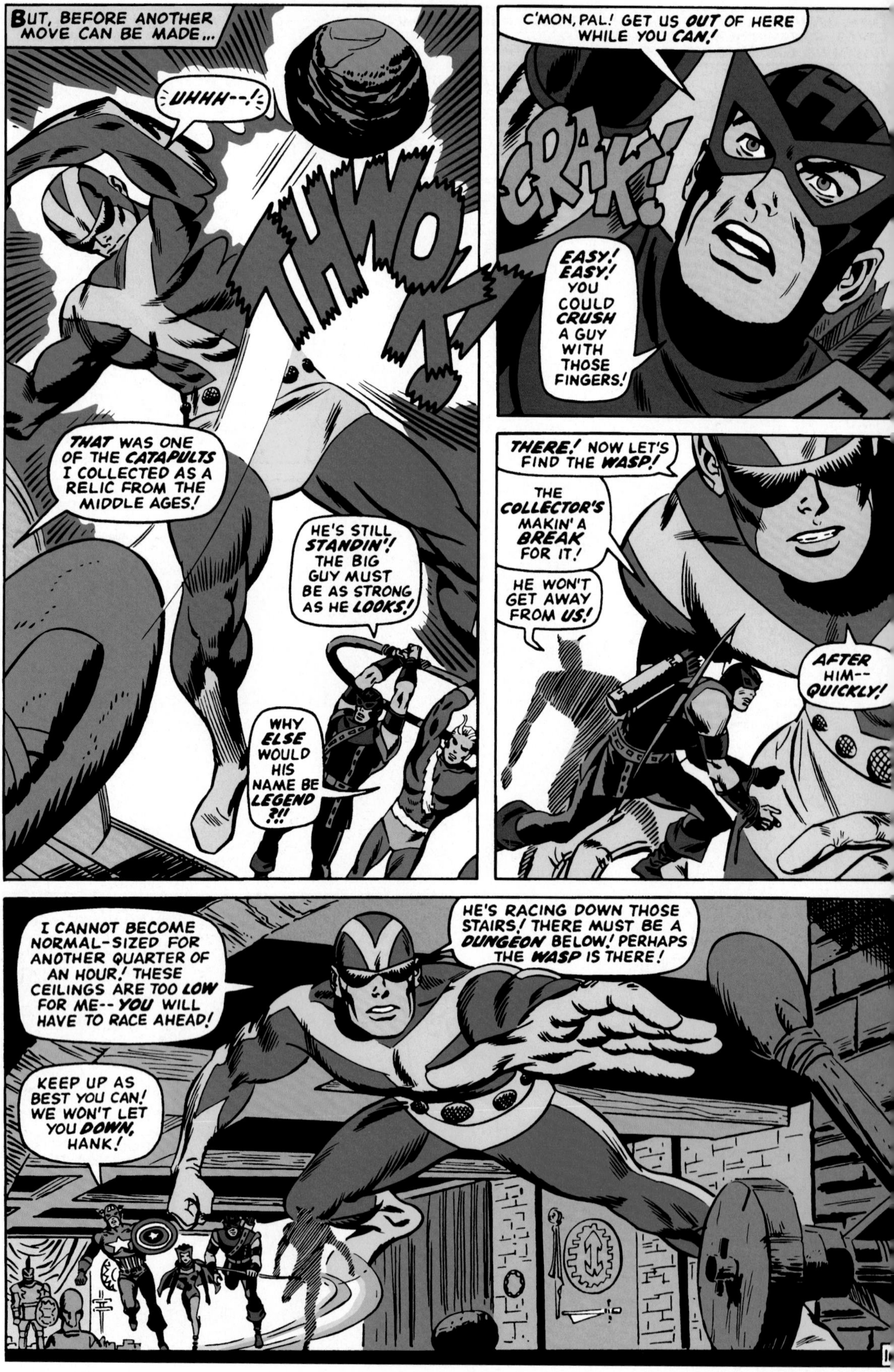
BUT, BEFORE ANOTHER MOVE CAN BE MADE...
UHHH--!
THWOK
THAT WAS ONE OF THE CATAPULTS I COLLECTED AS A RELIC FROM THE MIDDLE AGES!
HE'S STILL STANDIN'! THE BIG GUY MUST BE AS STRONG AS HE LOOKS!
WHY ELSE WOULD HIS NAME BE LEGEND?!!
C'MON, PAL! GET US OUT OF HERE WHILE YOU CAN!
CRAK!
EASY! EASY! YOU COULD CRUSH A GUY WITH THOSE FINGERS!
THERE! NOW LET'S FIND THE WASP!
THE COLLECTOR'S MAKIN' A BREAK FOR IT!
HE WON'T GET AWAY FROM US!
AFTER HIM-- QUICKLY!
I CANNOT BECOME NORMAL-SIZED FOR ANOTHER QUARTER OF AN HOUR! THESE CEILINGS ARE TOO LOW FOR ME-- YOU WILL HAVE TO RACE AHEAD!
HE'S RACING DOWN THOSE STAIRS! THERE MUST BE A DUNGEON BELOW! PERHAPS THE WASP IS THERE!
KEEP UP AS BEST YOU CAN! WE WON'T LET YOU DOWN, HANK!

SINCE YOU'RE THE LEADER, YOU SHALL BE MY FIRST CAPTIVE, CAPTAIN AMERICA!

WE'LL SEE WHO'S THE CAPTIVE-- AND WHO'S THE CAPTOR!

BLAST IT! I CAN'T USE MY BOW! YOU'RE IN THE LINE OF FIRE!

THIS CHARACTER HAS ALL SORTS OF TRICKY GIMMICKS HE CAN USE!

I WISH I WERE AS CONFIDENT AS I'M TRYING TO SOUND!

DON'T LOOK NOW, BUT WE'RE PLANNING TO PUT YOU UNDER WRAPS!

THWUMP!

KRRANNG!

*HISTORY WILL NEVER FORGET THAT GRIPPING TABLEAU FROM AVENGERS #27-- AND NEITHER WILL--SMILIN' STAN!

SO THAT'S WHO HE IS! HE'S THE CREEP WHO ATTACKED ME BACK AT HQ BEFORE I TOOK OFF FOR ATTUMA!*

TAKE COVER, BOTH OF YOU! HE'S CAPABLE OF ANYTHING! I RECOGNIZE HIM-- HE'S THE BEETLE!

THIS IS MY CHANCE! PERHAPS, IF I CAPTURE THE AVENGERS FOR HIM, THE COLLECTOR WILL GIVE ME THE ANTIDOTE FOR THE OBEDIENCE POTION HE HAS FED TO ME-- AND I'LL BE FREE AGAIN!

LOOK OUT! THERE'S SOMEONE ABOVE US! HE--HE'S ABOUT TO POUNCE--!

CALL IT A SIXTH SENSE-- CALL IT A WOMAN'S INTUITION-- BUT, AT THAT INSTANT, THE QUICK-WITTED SCARLET WITCH CRIES OUT IN ALARM...

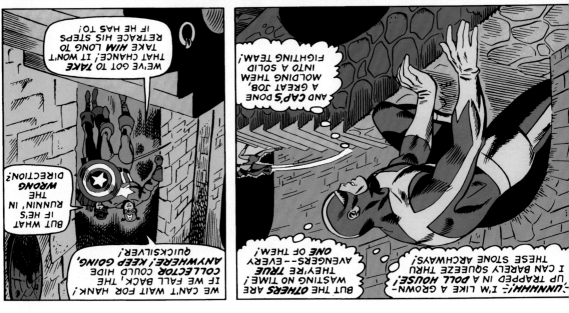

WE CAN'T WAIT FOR HANK! IF WE FALL BACK, THE COLLECTOR COULD HIDE ANYWHERE! KEEP GOING, QUICKSILVER!

BUT WHAT IF HE'S RUNNIN' IN THE WRONG DIRECTION?

WE'VE GOT TO TAKE THAT CHANCE! IT WON'T TAKE HIM LONG TO RETRACE HIS STEPS IF HE HAS TO!

AND CAP'S DONE A GREAT JOB, MOLDING THEM INTO A SOLID FIGHTING TEAM!

BUT THE OTHERS ARE WASTING NO TIME! THEY'RE TRUE AVENGERS-- EVERY ONE OF THEM!

UNNNHH! I'M LIKE A GROWN-UP TRAPPED IN A DOLL HOUSE! I CAN BARELY SQUEEZE THRU THESE STONE ARCHWAYS!

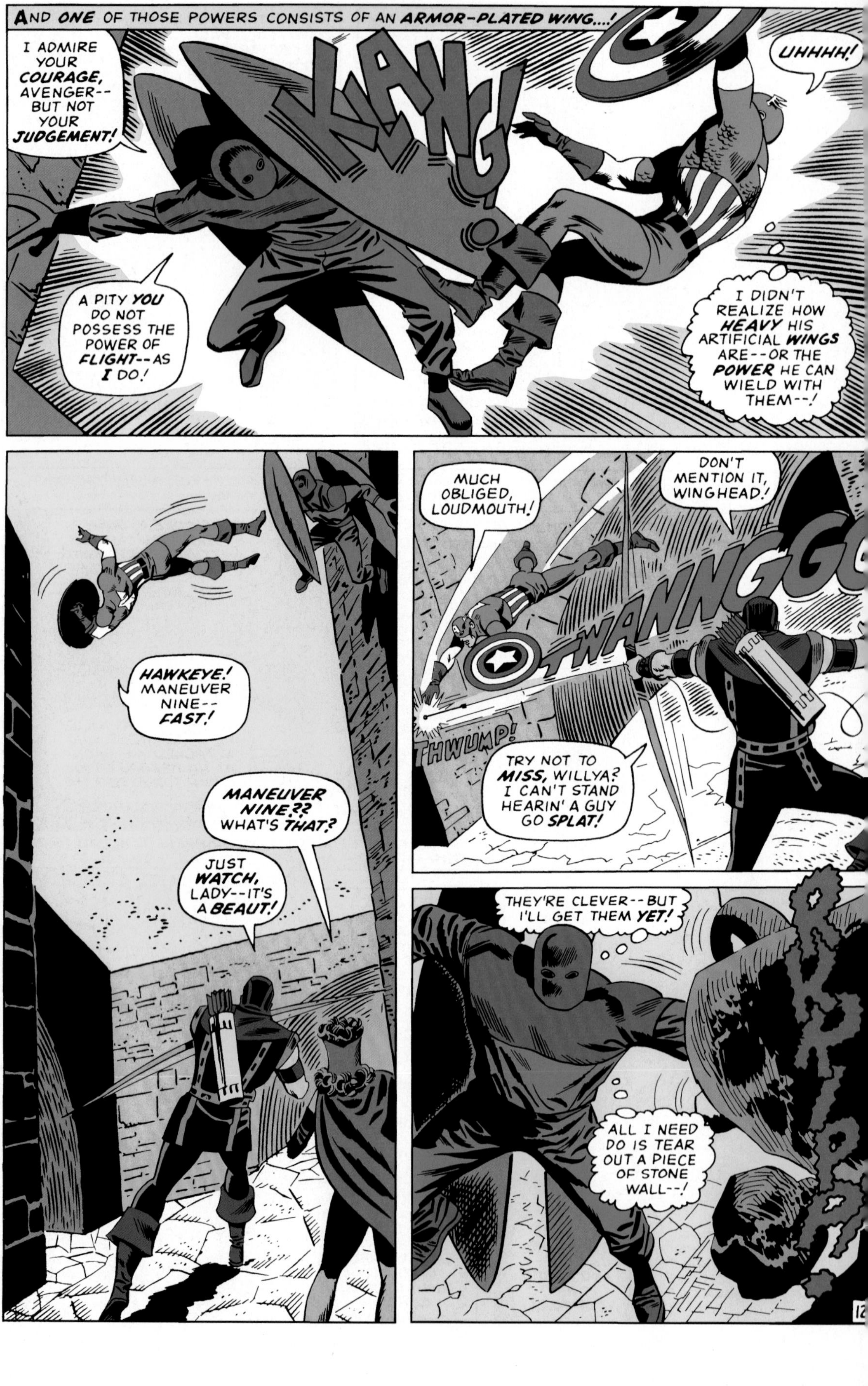
AND ONE OF THOSE POWERS CONSISTS OF AN ARMOR-PLATED WING...!
I ADMIRE YOUR COURAGE, AVENGER-- BUT NOT YOUR JUDGEMENT!
KLANG!
UHHHH!
A PITY YOU DO NOT POSSESS THE POWER OF FLIGHT--AS I DO!
I DIDN'T REALIZE HOW HEAVY HIS ARTIFICIAL WINGS ARE--OR THE POWER HE CAN WIELD WITH THEM--!
HAWKEYE! MANEUVER NINE-- FAST!
MANEUVER NINE?? WHAT'S THAT?
JUST WATCH, LADY--IT'S A BEAUT!
MUCH OBLIGED, LOUDMOUTH!
DON'T MENTION IT, WINGHEAD!
THWANNGG
THWUMP!
TRY NOT TO MISS, WILLYA? I CAN'T STAND HEARIN' A GUY GO SPLAT!
THEY'RE CLEVER--BUT I'LL GET THEM YET!
ALL I NEED DO IS TEAR OUT A PIECE OF STONE WALL--!
12

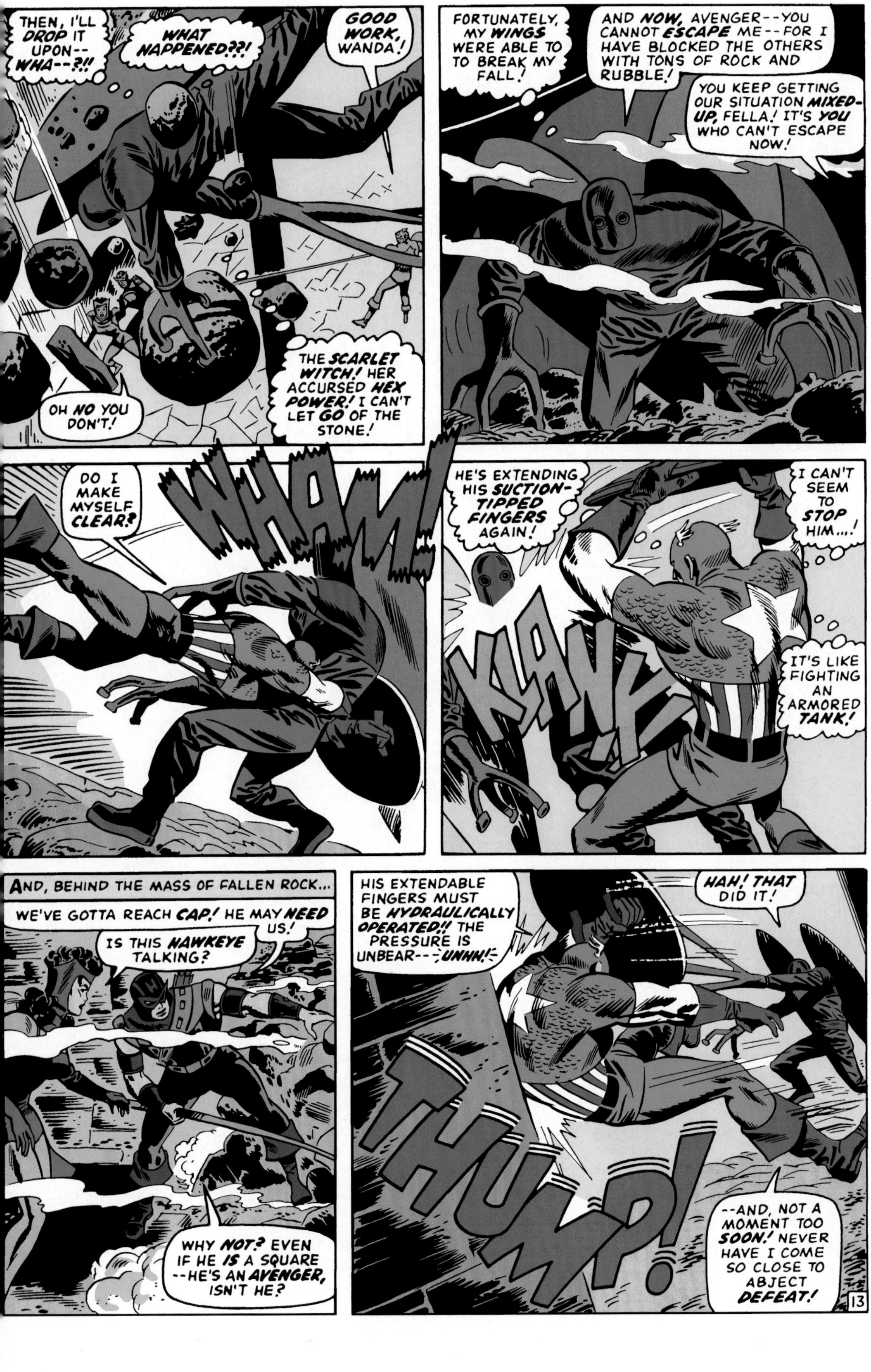
THEN, I'LL DROP IT UPON-- WHA--?!!
WHAT HAPPENED??!
GOOD WORK, WANDA!
THE SCARLET WITCH! HER ACCURSED HEX POWER! I CAN'T LET GO OF THE STONE!
OH NO YOU DON'T!
FORTUNATELY, MY WINGS WERE ABLE TO TO BREAK MY FALL!
AND NOW, AVENGER--YOU CANNOT ESCAPE ME--FOR I HAVE BLOCKED THE OTHERS WITH TONS OF ROCK AND RUBBLE!
YOU KEEP GETTING OUR SITUATION MIXED-UP, FELLA! IT'S YOU WHO CAN'T ESCAPE NOW!
DO I MAKE MYSELF CLEAR?
WHAM!
HE'S EXTENDING HIS SUCTION-TIPPED FINGERS AGAIN!
I CAN'T SEEM TO STOP HIM....!
KLANK
IT'S LIKE FIGHTING AN ARMORED TANK!
AND, BEHIND THE MASS OF FALLEN ROCK...
WE'VE GOTTA REACH CAP! HE MAY NEED US!
IS THIS HAWKEYE TALKING?
WHY NOT? EVEN IF HE IS A SQUARE --HE'S AN AVENGER, ISN'T HE?
HIS EXTENDABLE FINGERS MUST BE HYDRAULICALLY OPERATED!! THE PRESSURE IS UNBEAR-- UNHH!
HAH! THAT DID IT!
THUMP!
--AND, NOT A MOMENT TOO SOON! NEVER HAVE I COME SO CLOSE TO ABJECT DEFEAT!
13

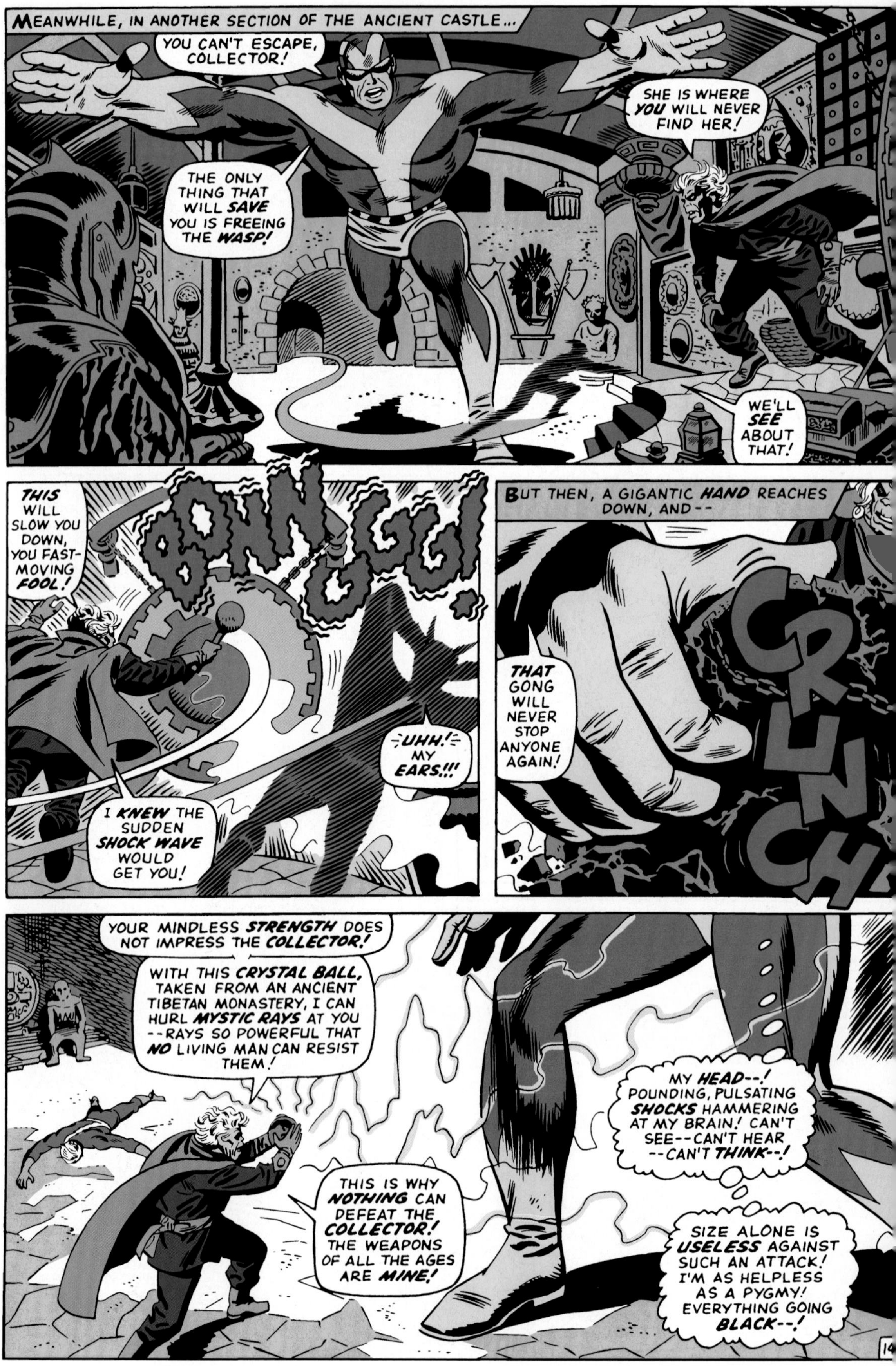
MEANWHILE, IN ANOTHER SECTION OF THE ANCIENT CASTLE...
YOU CAN'T ESCAPE, COLLECTOR!
THE ONLY THING THAT WILL SAVE YOU IS FREEING THE WASP!
SHE IS WHERE YOU WILL NEVER FIND HER!
WE'LL SEE ABOUT THAT!
THIS WILL SLOW YOU DOWN, YOU FAST-MOVING FOOL!
BONNGGG!
UHH! MY EARS!!!
I KNEW THE SUDDEN SHOCK WAVE WOULD GET YOU!
BUT THEN, A GIGANTIC HAND REACHES DOWN, AND--
THAT GONG WILL NEVER STOP ANYONE AGAIN!
CRUNCH
YOUR MINDLESS STRENGTH DOES NOT IMPRESS THE COLLECTOR!
WITH THIS CRYSTAL BALL, TAKEN FROM AN ANCIENT TIBETAN MONASTERY, I CAN HURL MYSTIC RAYS AT YOU --RAYS SO POWERFUL THAT NO LIVING MAN CAN RESIST THEM!
THIS IS WHY NOTHING CAN DEFEAT THE COLLECTOR! THE WEAPONS OF ALL THE AGES ARE MINE!
MY HEAD--! POUNDING, PULSATING SHOCKS HAMMERING AT MY BRAIN! CAN'T SEE--CAN'T HEAR --CAN'T THINK--!
SIZE ALONE IS USELESS AGAINST SUCH AN ATTACK! I'M AS HELPLESS AS A PYGMY! EVERYTHING GOING BLACK--!

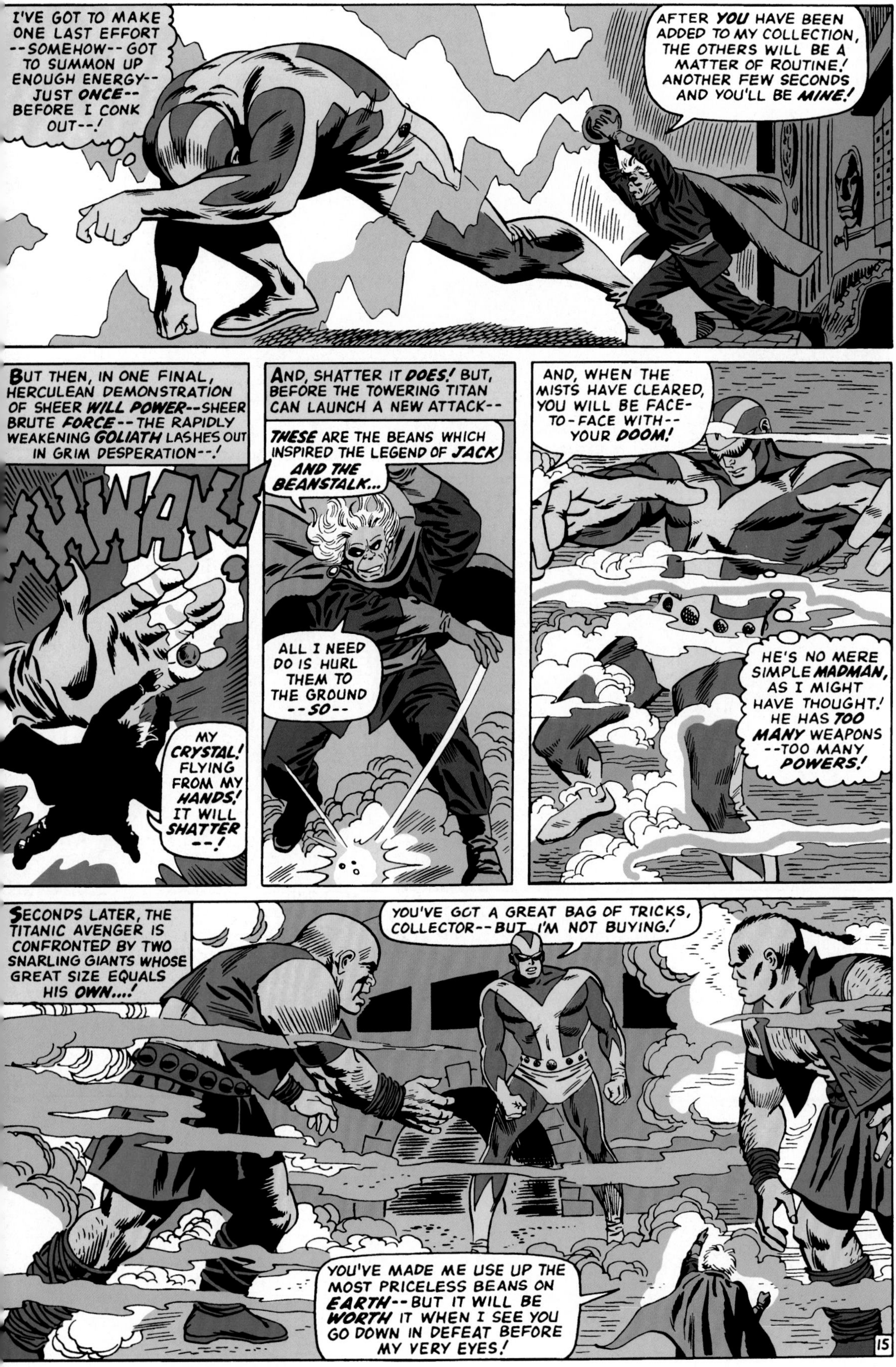
I'VE GOT TO MAKE ONE LAST EFFORT --SOMEHOW-- GOT TO SUMMON UP ENOUGH ENERGY-- JUST ONCE-- BEFORE I CONK OUT--!
AFTER YOU HAVE BEEN ADDED TO MY COLLECTION, THE OTHERS WILL BE A MATTER OF ROUTINE! ANOTHER FEW SECONDS AND YOU'LL BE MINE!
BUT THEN, IN ONE FINAL, HERCULEAN DEMONSTRATION OF SHEER WILL POWER--SHEER BRUTE FORCE--THE RAPIDLY WEAKENING GOLIATH LASHES OUT IN GRIM DESPERATION--!
THWAK!
MY CRYSTAL! FLYING FROM MY HANDS! IT WILL SHATTER --!
AND, SHATTER IT DOES! BUT, BEFORE THE TOWERING TITAN CAN LAUNCH A NEW ATTACK--
THESE ARE THE BEANS WHICH INSPIRED THE LEGEND OF JACK AND THE BEANSTALK...
ALL I NEED DO IS HURL THEM TO THE GROUND --SO--
AND, WHEN THE MISTS HAVE CLEARED, YOU WILL BE FACE-TO-FACE WITH-- YOUR DOOM!
HE'S NO MERE SIMPLE MADMAN, AS I MIGHT HAVE THOUGHT! HE HAS TOO MANY WEAPONS --TOO MANY POWERS!
SECONDS LATER, THE TITANIC AVENGER IS CONFRONTED BY TWO SNARLING GIANTS WHOSE GREAT SIZE EQUALS HIS OWN...!
YOU'VE GOT A GREAT BAG OF TRICKS, COLLECTOR--BUT I'M NOT BUYING!
YOU'VE MADE ME USE UP THE MOST PRICELESS BEANS ON EARTH--BUT IT WILL BE WORTH IT WHEN I SEE YOU GO DOWN IN DEFEAT BEFORE MY VERY EYES!
15

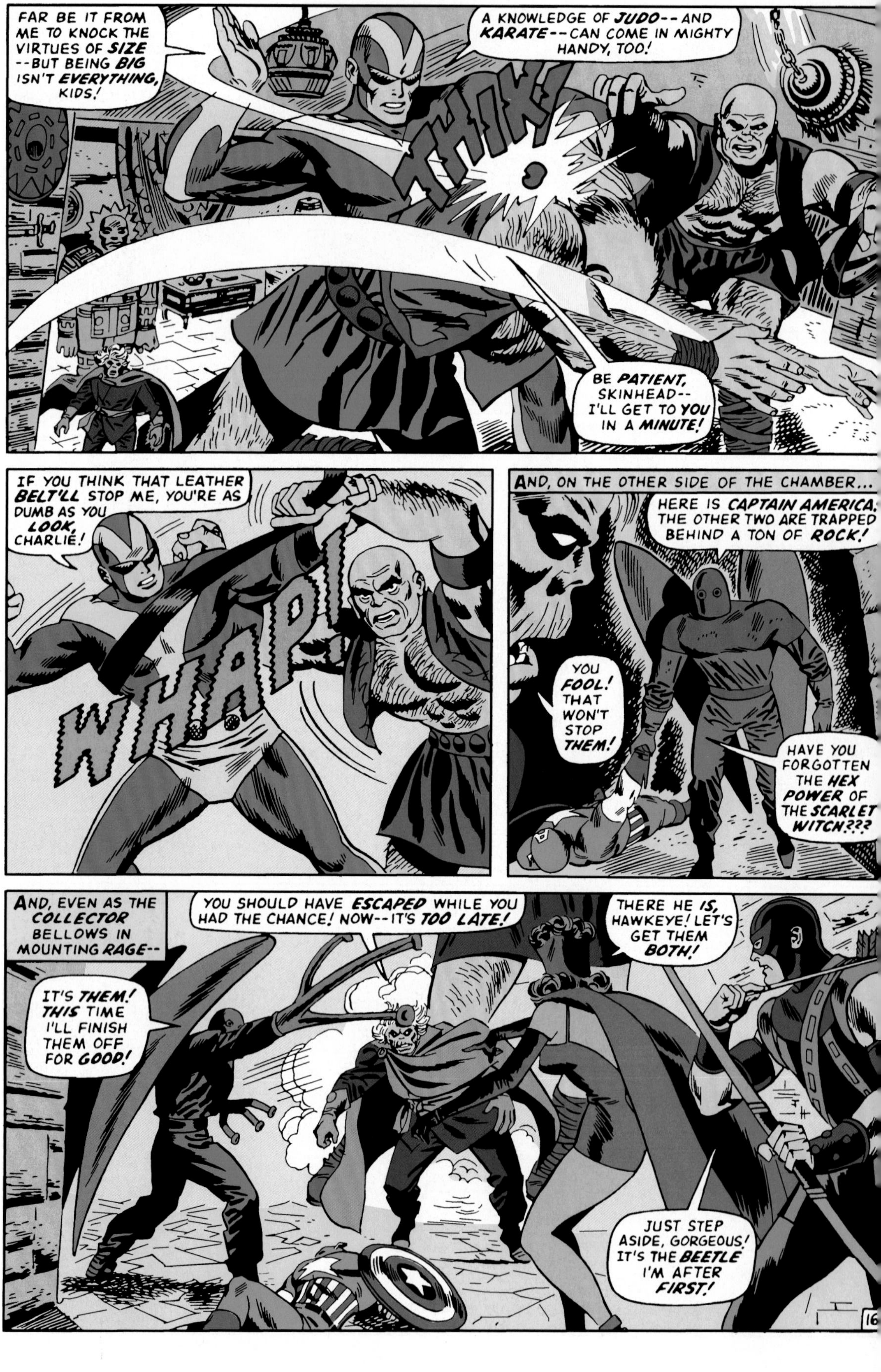
FAR BE IT FROM ME TO KNOCK THE VIRTUES OF SIZE --BUT BEING BIG ISN'T EVERYTHING, KIDS!
A KNOWLEDGE OF JUDO--AND KARATE--CAN COME IN MIGHTY HANDY, TOO!
THUK!
BE PATIENT, SKINHEAD-- I'LL GET TO YOU IN A MINUTE!
IF YOU THINK THAT LEATHER BELT'LL STOP ME, YOU'RE AS DUMB AS YOU LOOK, CHARLIE!
WHAP!
AND, ON THE OTHER SIDE OF THE CHAMBER...
HERE IS CAPTAIN AMERICA! THE OTHER TWO ARE TRAPPED BEHIND A TON OF ROCK!
YOU FOOL! THAT WON'T STOP THEM!
HAVE YOU FORGOTTEN THE HEX POWER OF THE SCARLET WITCH???
AND, EVEN AS THE COLLECTOR BELLOWS IN MOUNTING RAGE--
YOU SHOULD HAVE ESCAPED WHILE YOU HAD THE CHANCE! NOW--IT'S TOO LATE!
THERE HE IS, HAWKEYE! LET'S GET THEM BOTH!
IT'S THEM! THIS TIME I'LL FINISH THEM OFF FOR GOOD!
JUST STEP ASIDE, GORGEOUS! IT'S THE BEETLE I'M AFTER FIRST!
16

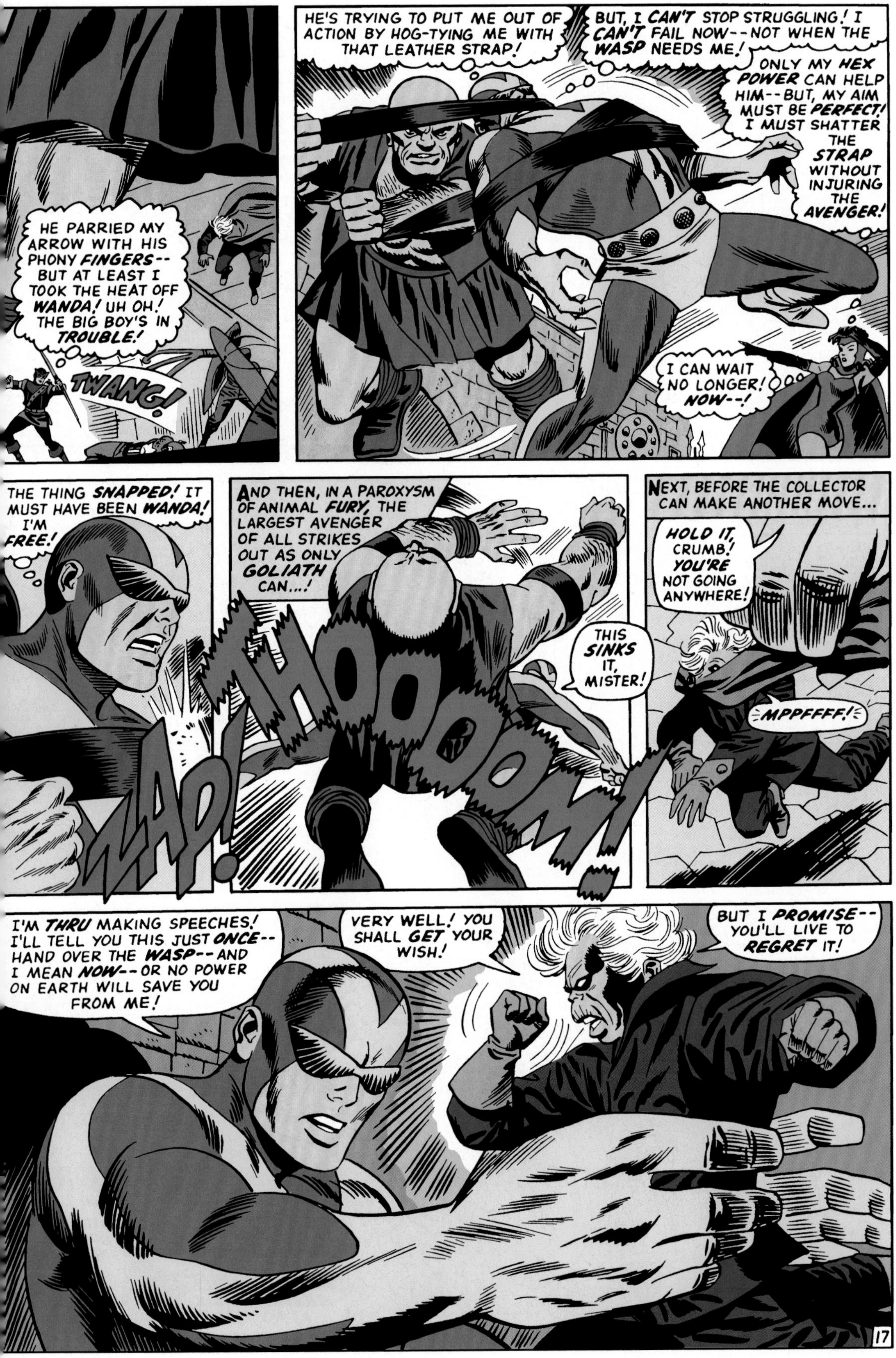

HE PARRIED MY ARROW WITH HIS PHONY FINGERS-- BUT AT LEAST I TOOK THE HEAT OFF WANDA! UH OH! THE BIG BOY'S IN TROUBLE!
TWANG!
HE'S TRYING TO PUT ME OUT OF ACTION BY HOG-TYING ME WITH THAT LEATHER STRAP!
BUT, I CAN'T STOP STRUGGLING! I CAN'T FAIL NOW--NOT WHEN THE WASP NEEDS ME!
ONLY MY HEX POWER CAN HELP HIM--BUT, MY AIM MUST BE PERFECT! I MUST SHATTER THE STRAP WITHOUT INJURING THE AVENGER!
I CAN WAIT NO LONGER! NOW--!
THE THING SNAPPED! IT MUST HAVE BEEN WANDA! I'M FREE!
ZAP!
AND THEN, IN A PAROXYSM OF ANIMAL FURY, THE LARGEST AVENGER OF ALL STRIKES OUT AS ONLY GOLIATH CAN...!
THOOOOM!
THIS SINKS IT, MISTER!
NEXT, BEFORE THE COLLECTOR CAN MAKE ANOTHER MOVE...
HOLD IT, CRUMB! YOU'RE NOT GOING ANYWHERE!
MPPFFFF!
I'M THRU MAKING SPEECHES! I'LL TELL YOU THIS JUST ONCE-- HAND OVER THE WASP--AND I MEAN NOW--OR NO POWER ON EARTH WILL SAVE YOU FROM ME!
VERY WELL! YOU SHALL GET YOUR WISH!
BUT I PROMISE-- YOU'LL LIVE TO REGRET IT!

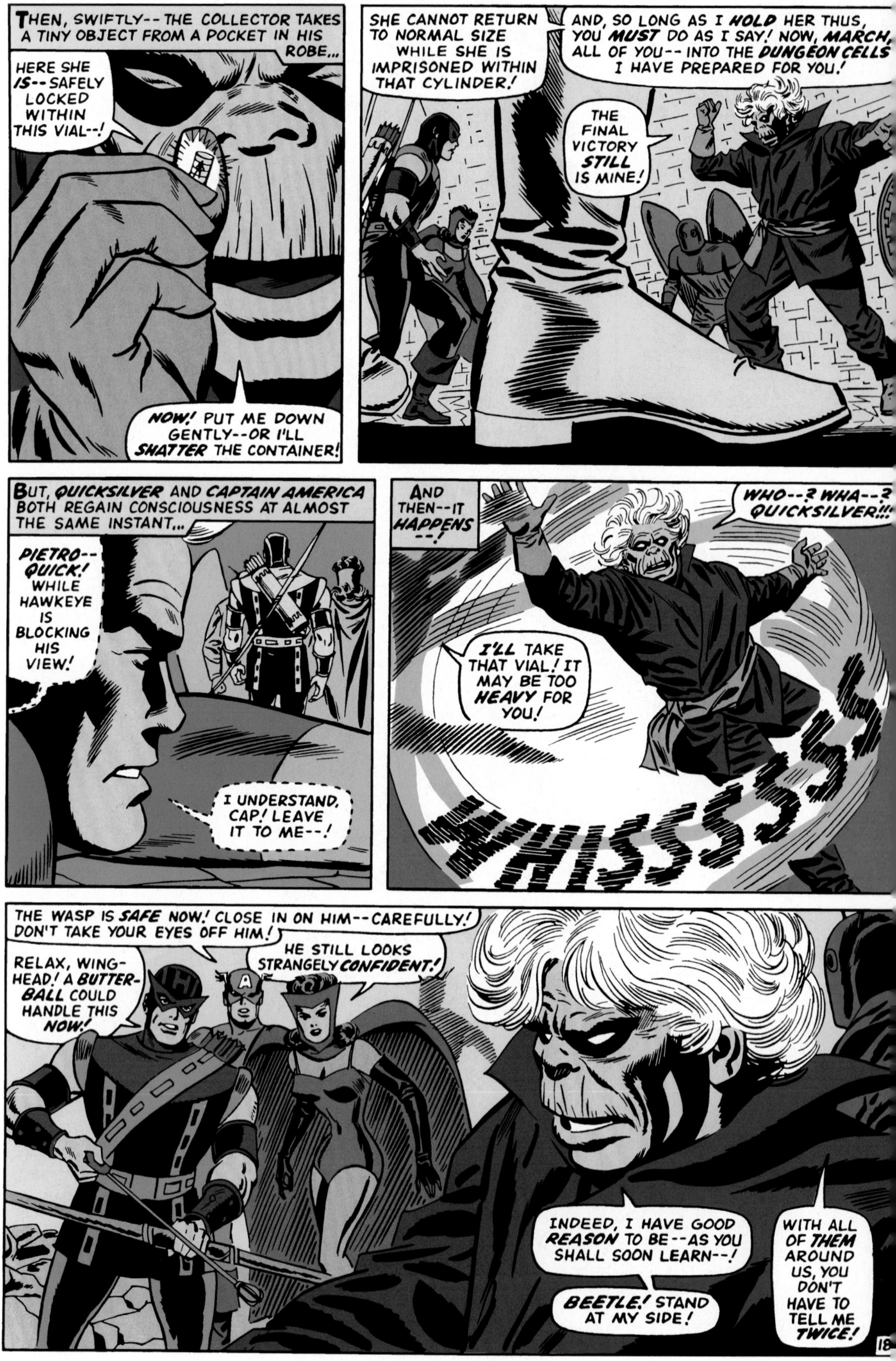
THEN, SWIFTLY-- THE COLLECTOR TAKES A TINY OBJECT FROM A POCKET IN HIS ROBE...
HERE SHE IS-- SAFELY LOCKED WITHIN THIS VIAL--!
NOW! PUT ME DOWN GENTLY--OR I'LL SHATTER THE CONTAINER!
SHE CANNOT RETURN TO NORMAL SIZE WHILE SHE IS IMPRISONED WITHIN THAT CYLINDER!
AND, SO LONG AS I HOLD HER THUS, YOU MUST DO AS I SAY! NOW, MARCH, ALL OF YOU-- INTO THE DUNGEON CELLS I HAVE PREPARED FOR YOU!
THE FINAL VICTORY STILL IS MINE!
BUT, QUICKSILVER AND CAPTAIN AMERICA BOTH REGAIN CONSCIOUSNESS AT ALMOST THE SAME INSTANT...
PIETRO-- QUICK! WHILE HAWKEYE IS BLOCKING HIS VIEW!
I UNDERSTAND, CAP! LEAVE IT TO ME--!
AND THEN--IT HAPPENS--!
WHO--? WHA--? QUICKSILVER!!!
I'LL TAKE THAT VIAL! IT MAY BE TOO HEAVY FOR YOU!
WHISSSSS
THE WASP IS SAFE NOW! CLOSE IN ON HIM--CAREFULLY! DON'T TAKE YOUR EYES OFF HIM!
HE STILL LOOKS STRANGELY CONFIDENT!
RELAX, WING-HEAD! A BUTTER-BALL COULD HANDLE THIS NOW!
INDEED, I HAVE GOOD REASON TO BE--AS YOU SHALL SOON LEARN--!
BEETLE! STAND AT MY SIDE!
WITH ALL OF THEM AROUND US, YOU DON'T HAVE TO TELL ME TWICE!

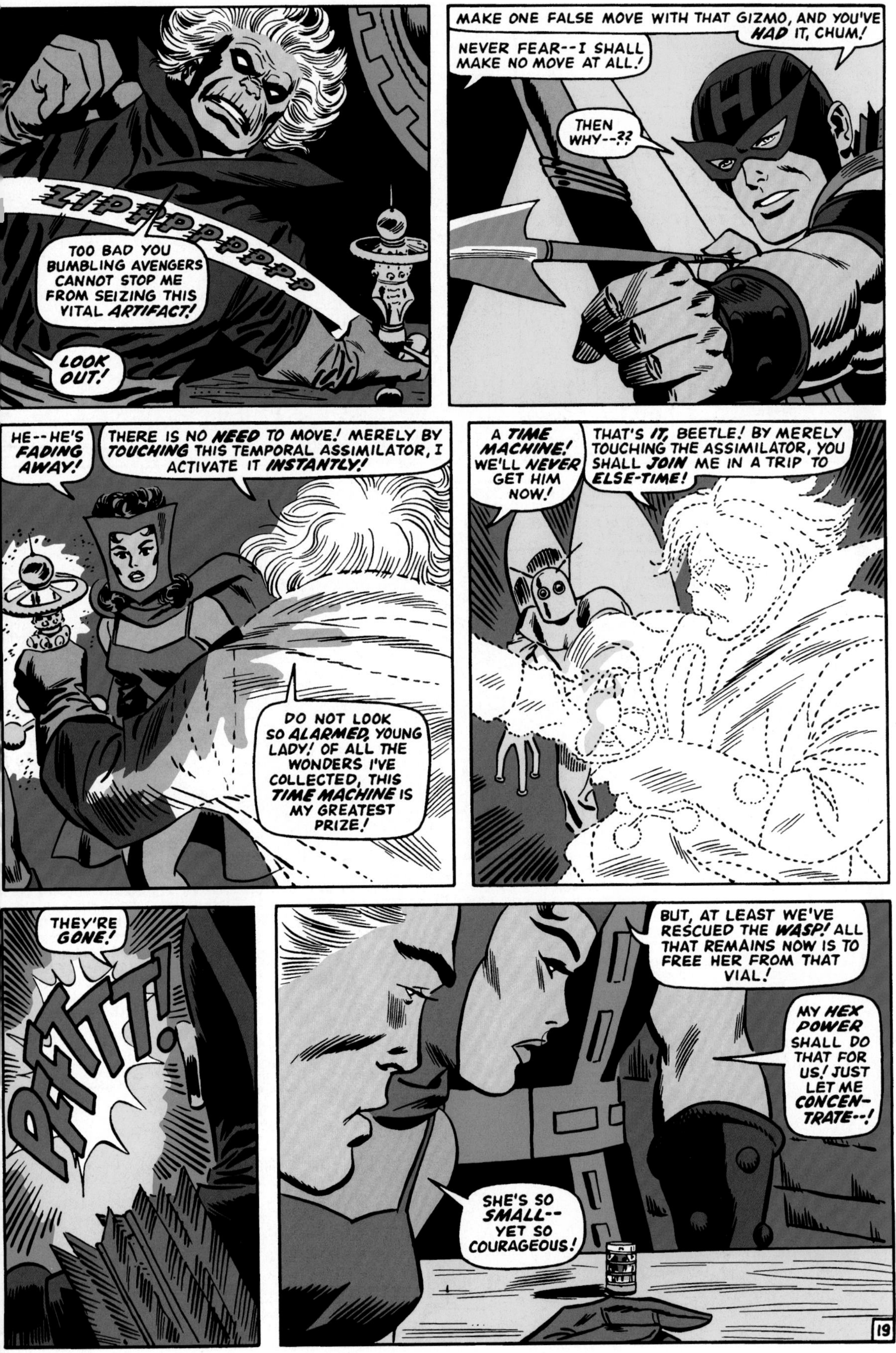
ZIPPPPPPPPP
TOO BAD YOU BUMBLING AVENGERS CANNOT STOP ME FROM SEIZING THIS VITAL ARTIFACT!
LOOK OUT!
MAKE ONE FALSE MOVE WITH THAT GIZMO, AND YOU'VE HAD IT, CHUM!
NEVER FEAR--I SHALL MAKE NO MOVE AT ALL!
THEN WHY--??
HE--HE'S FADING AWAY!
THERE IS NO NEED TO MOVE! MERELY BY TOUCHING THIS TEMPORAL ASSIMILATOR, I ACTIVATE IT INSTANTLY!
DO NOT LOOK SO ALARMED, YOUNG LADY! OF ALL THE WONDERS I'VE COLLECTED, THIS TIME MACHINE IS MY GREATEST PRIZE!
A TIME MACHINE! WE'LL NEVER GET HIM NOW!
THAT'S IT, BEETLE! BY MERELY TOUCHING THE ASSIMILATOR, YOU SHALL JOIN ME IN A TRIP TO ELSE-TIME!
THEY'RE GONE!
PFFTTT!
BUT, AT LEAST WE'VE RESCUED THE WASP! ALL THAT REMAINS NOW IS TO FREE HER FROM THAT VIAL!
MY HEX POWER SHALL DO THAT FOR US! JUST LET ME CONCEN-TRATE--!
SHE'S SO SMALL--YET SO COURAGEOUS!

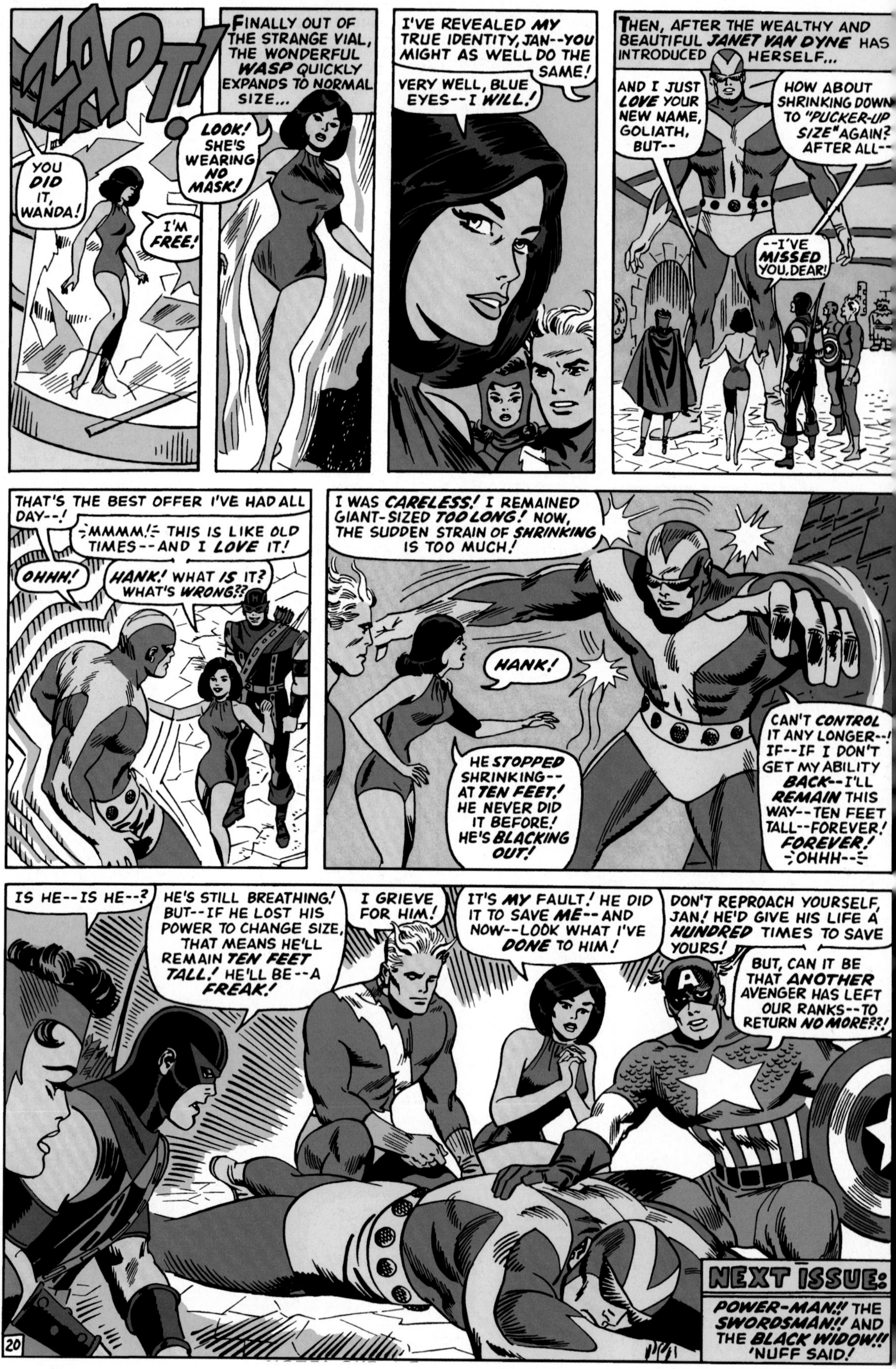
ZAPT!
YOU DID IT, WANDA!
I'M FREE!
FINALLY OUT OF THE STRANGE VIAL, THE WONDERFUL WASP QUICKLY EXPANDS TO NORMAL SIZE...
LOOK! SHE'S WEARING NO MASK!
I'VE REVEALED MY TRUE IDENTITY, JAN--YOU MIGHT AS WELL DO THE SAME!
VERY WELL, BLUE EYES--I WILL!
THEN, AFTER THE WEALTHY AND BEAUTIFUL JANET VAN DYNE HAS INTRODUCED HERSELF...
AND I JUST LOVE YOUR NEW NAME, GOLIATH, BUT--
HOW ABOUT SHRINKING DOWN TO "PUCKER-UP SIZE" AGAIN? AFTER ALL--
--I'VE MISSED YOU, DEAR!
THAT'S THE BEST OFFER I'VE HAD ALL DAY--!
MMMM! THIS IS LIKE OLD TIMES--AND I LOVE IT!
OHHH!
HANK! WHAT IS IT? WHAT'S WRONG??
I WAS CARELESS! I REMAINED GIANT-SIZED TOO LONG! NOW, THE SUDDEN STRAIN OF SHRINKING IS TOO MUCH!
HANK!
HE STOPPED SHRINKING--AT TEN FEET! HE NEVER DID IT BEFORE! HE'S BLACKING OUT!
CAN'T CONTROL IT ANY LONGER--! IF--IF I DON'T GET MY ABILITY BACK--I'LL REMAIN THIS WAY--TEN FEET TALL--FOREVER! FOREVER! OHHH--
IS HE--IS HE--?
HE'S STILL BREATHING! BUT--IF HE LOST HIS POWER TO CHANGE SIZE, THAT MEANS HE'LL REMAIN TEN FEET TALL! HE'LL BE--A FREAK!
I GRIEVE FOR HIM!
IT'S MY FAULT! HE DID IT TO SAVE ME--AND NOW--LOOK WHAT I'VE DONE TO HIM!
DON'T REPROACH YOURSELF, JAN! HE'D GIVE HIS LIFE A HUNDRED TIMES TO SAVE YOURS!
BUT, CAN IT BE THAT ANOTHER AVENGER HAS LEFT OUR RANKS--TO RETURN NO MORE??!
NEXT ISSUE:
POWER-MAN!! THE SWORDSMAN!! AND THE BLACK WIDOW!! 'NUFF SAID!
20

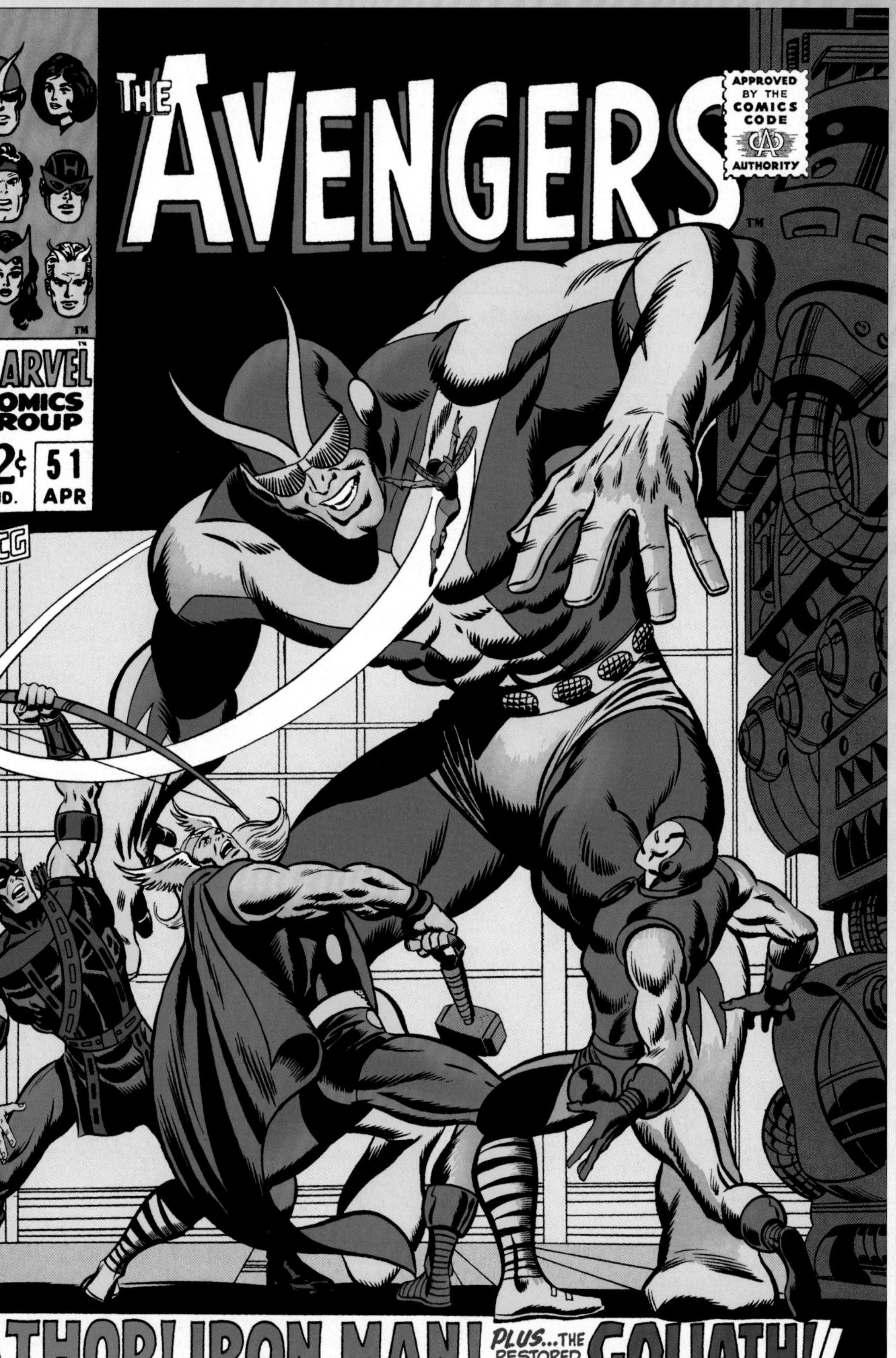
THE AVENGERS
APPROVED BY THE COMICS CODE AUTHORITY
MARVEL COMICS GROUP
12¢ IND.
51 APR
MCG
THOR! IRON MAN! PLUS... THE RESTORED POWER OF... GOLIATH!

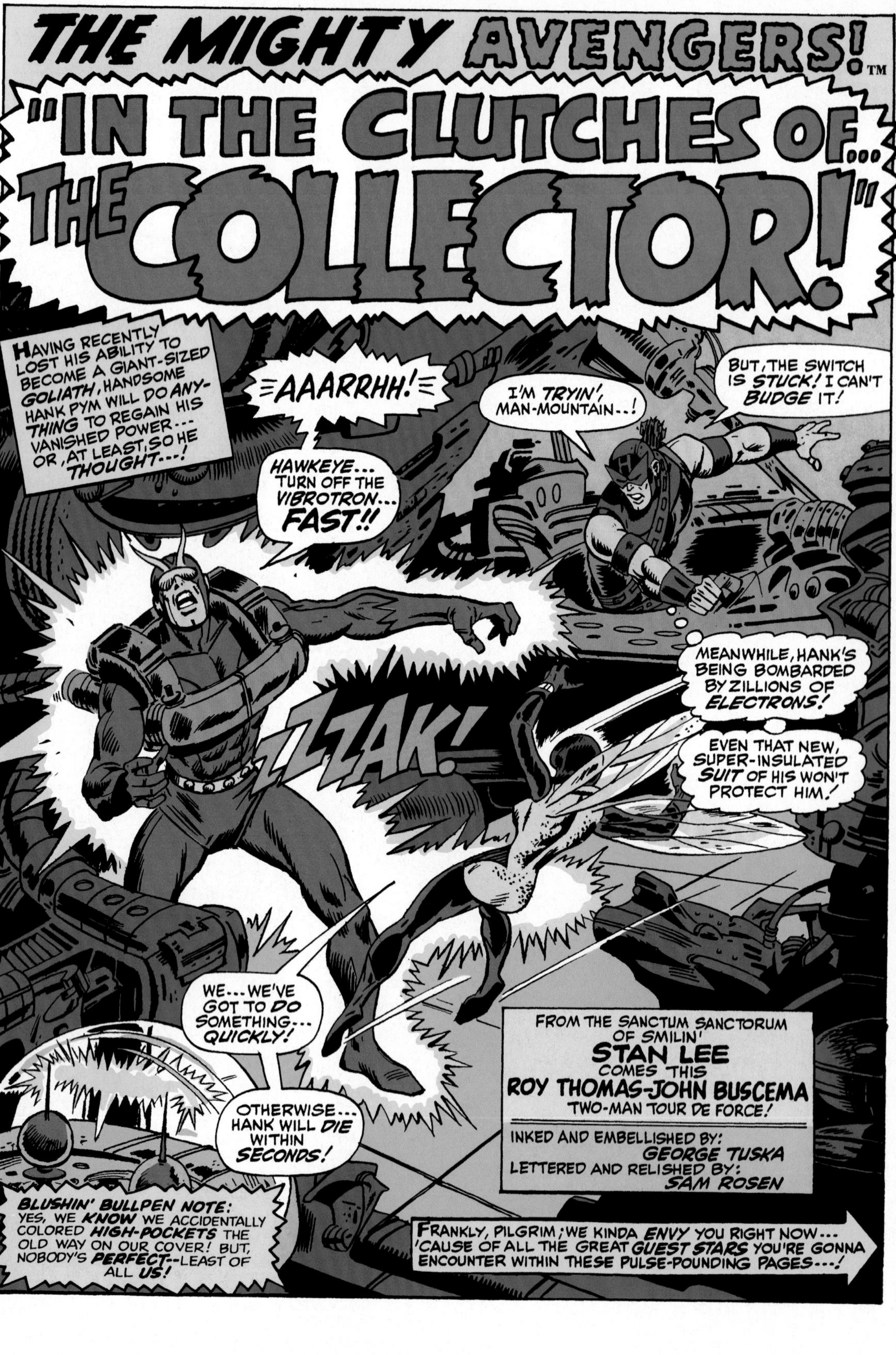
THE MIGHTY AVENGERS!™
"IN THE CLUTCHES OF... THE COLLECTOR!"
HAVING RECENTLY LOST HIS ABILITY TO BECOME A GIANT-SIZED GOLIATH, HANDSOME HANK PYM WILL DO ANYTHING TO REGAIN HIS VANISHED POWER... OR, AT LEAST, SO HE THOUGHT...!
AAARRHH!
HAWKEYE... TURN OFF THE VIBROTRON... FAST!!
I'M TRYIN', MAN-MOUNTAIN..!
BUT, THE SWITCH IS STUCK! I CAN'T BUDGE IT!
MEANWHILE, HANK'S BEING BOMBARDED BY ZILLIONS OF ELECTRONS!
EVEN THAT NEW, SUPER-INSULATED SUIT OF HIS WON'T PROTECT HIM!
ZZAK!
WE... WE'VE GOT TO DO SOMETHING... QUICKLY!
OTHERWISE... HANK WILL DIE WITHIN SECONDS!
FROM THE SANCTUM SANCTORUM OF SMILIN' STAN LEE COMES THIS ROY THOMAS-JOHN BUSCEMA TWO-MAN TOUR DE FORCE!
INKED AND EMBELLISHED BY: GEORGE TUSKA
LETTERED AND RELISHED BY: SAM ROSEN
BLUSHIN' BULLPEN NOTE: YES, WE KNOW WE ACCIDENTALLY COLORED HIGH-POCKETS THE OLD WAY ON OUR COVER! BUT, NOBODY'S PERFECT--LEAST OF ALL US!
FRANKLY, PILGRIM; WE KINDA ENVY YOU RIGHT NOW... 'CAUSE OF ALL THE GREAT GUEST STARS YOU'RE GONNA ENCOUNTER WITHIN THESE PULSE-POUNDING PAGES...!

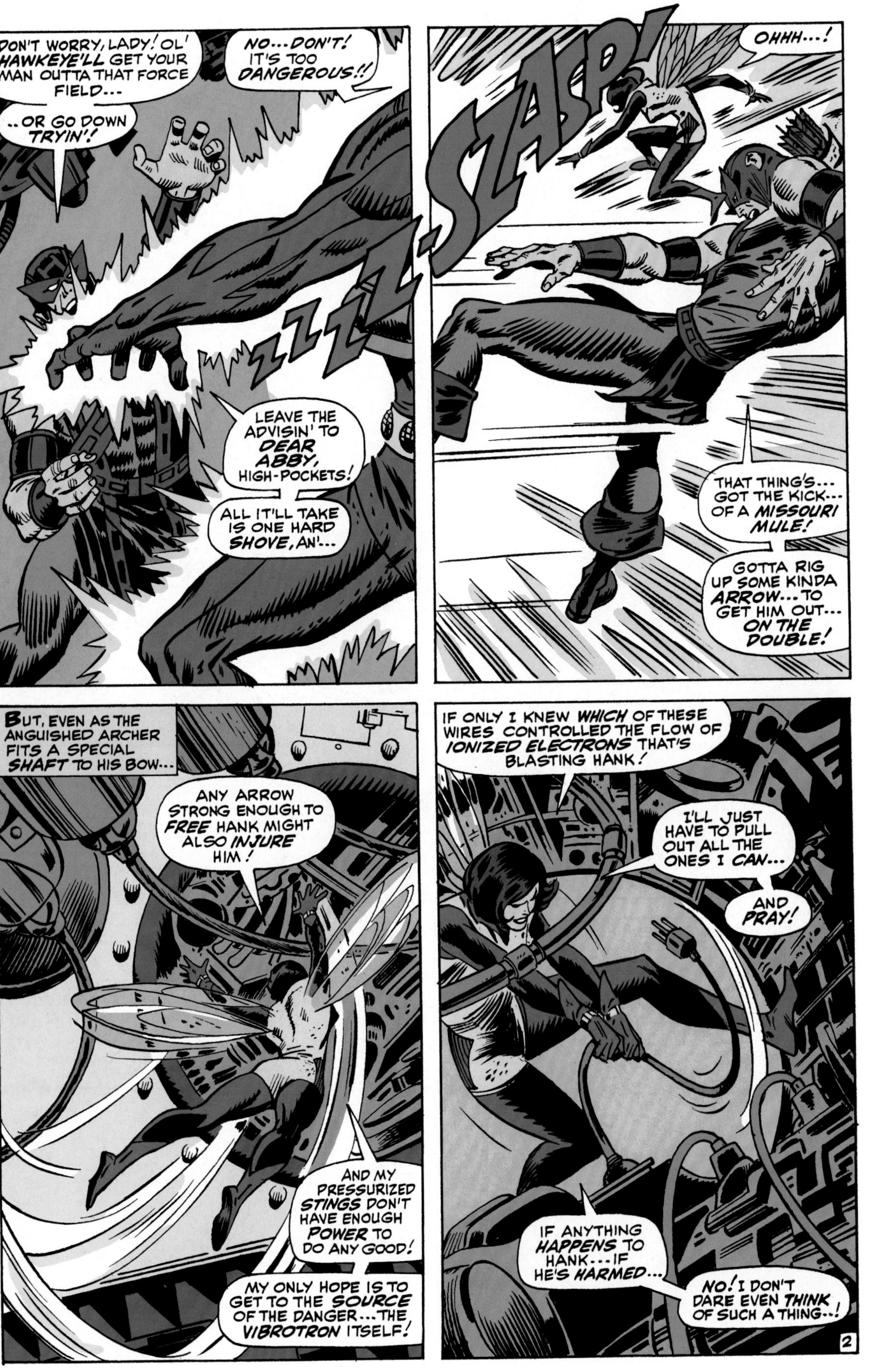
DON'T WORRY, LADY! OL' HAWKEYE'LL GET YOUR MAN OUTTA THAT FORCE FIELD...
..OR GO DOWN TRYIN'!
NO...DON'T! IT'S TOO DANGEROUS!!
ZZZZ-SZASP!
OHHH...!
LEAVE THE ADVISIN' TO DEAR ABBY, HIGH-POCKETS!
ALL IT'LL TAKE IS ONE HARD SHOVE, AN'...
THAT THING'S... GOT THE KICK... OF A MISSOURI MULE!
GOTTA RIG UP SOME KINDA ARROW...TO GET HIM OUT... ON THE DOUBLE!
BUT, EVEN AS THE ANGUISHED ARCHER FITS A SPECIAL SHAFT TO HIS BOW...
ANY ARROW STRONG ENOUGH TO FREE HANK MIGHT ALSO INJURE HIM!
AND MY PRESSURIZED STINGS DON'T HAVE ENOUGH POWER TO DO ANY GOOD!
MY ONLY HOPE IS TO GET TO THE SOURCE OF THE DANGER...THE VIBROTRON ITSELF!
IF ONLY I KNEW WHICH OF THESE WIRES CONTROLLED THE FLOW OF IONIZED ELECTRONS THAT'S BLASTING HANK!
I'LL JUST HAVE TO PULL OUT ALL THE ONES I CAN...
AND PRAY!
IF ANYTHING HAPPENS TO HANK...IF HE'S HARMED...
NO! I DON'T DARE EVEN THINK OF SUCH A THING..!
2

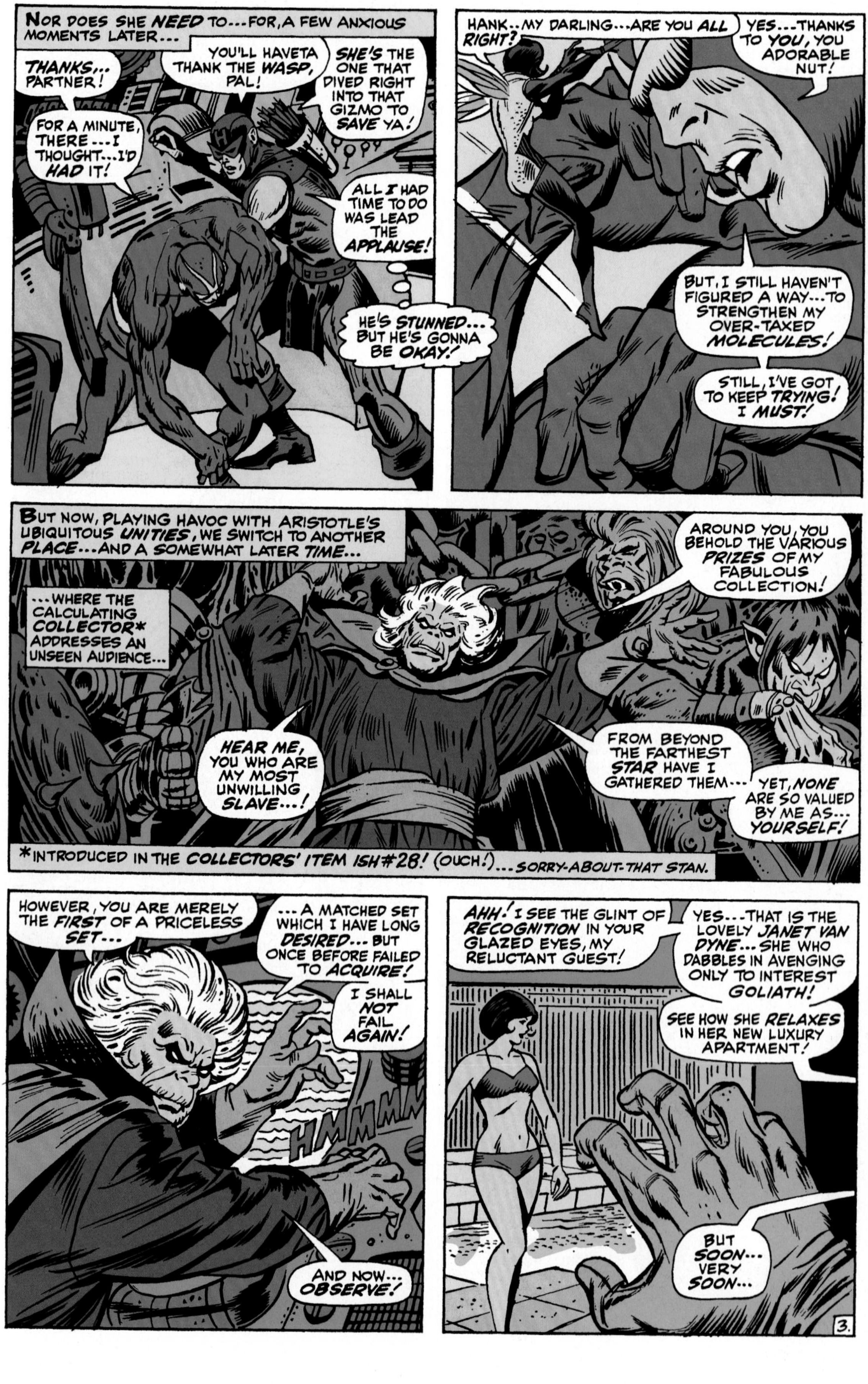
NOR DOES SHE NEED TO... FOR, A FEW ANXIOUS MOMENTS LATER...
THANKS,... PARTNER!
FOR A MINUTE, THERE... I THOUGHT... I'D HAD IT!
YOU'LL HAVETA THANK THE WASP, PAL!
SHE'S THE ONE THAT DIVED RIGHT INTO THAT GIZMO TO SAVE YA!
ALL I HAD TIME TO DO WAS LEAD THE APPLAUSE!
HE'S STUNNED... BUT HE'S GONNA BE OKAY!
HANK... MY DARLING... ARE YOU ALL RIGHT?
YES... THANKS TO YOU, YOU ADORABLE NUT!
BUT, I STILL HAVEN'T FIGURED A WAY... TO STRENGTHEN MY OVER-TAXED MOLECULES!
STILL, I'VE GOT TO KEEP TRYING! I MUST!
BUT NOW, PLAYING HAVOC WITH ARISTOTLE'S UBIQUITOUS UNITIES, WE SWITCH TO ANOTHER PLACE... AND A SOMEWHAT LATER TIME...
...WHERE THE CALCULATING COLLECTOR* ADDRESSES AN UNSEEN AUDIENCE...
AROUND YOU, YOU BEHOLD THE VARIOUS PRIZES OF MY FABULOUS COLLECTION!
HEAR ME, YOU WHO ARE MY MOST UNWILLING SLAVE...!
FROM BEYOND THE FARTHEST STAR HAVE I GATHERED THEM...
YET, NONE ARE SO VALUED BY ME AS... YOURSELF!
*INTRODUCED IN THE COLLECTORS' ITEM ISH #28! (OUCH!)... SORRY-ABOUT-THAT STAN.
HOWEVER, YOU ARE MERELY THE FIRST OF A PRICELESS SET...
...A MATCHED SET WHICH I HAVE LONG DESIRED... BUT ONCE BEFORE FAILED TO ACQUIRE!
I SHALL NOT FAIL AGAIN!
HMMMM
AND NOW... OBSERVE!
AHH! I SEE THE GLINT OF RECOGNITION IN YOUR GLAZED EYES, MY RELUCTANT GUEST!
YES... THAT IS THE LOVELY JANET VAN DYNE... SHE WHO DABBLES IN AVENGING ONLY TO INTEREST GOLIATH!
SEE HOW SHE RELAXES IN HER NEW LUXURY APARTMENT!
BUT SOON... VERY SOON...
3.

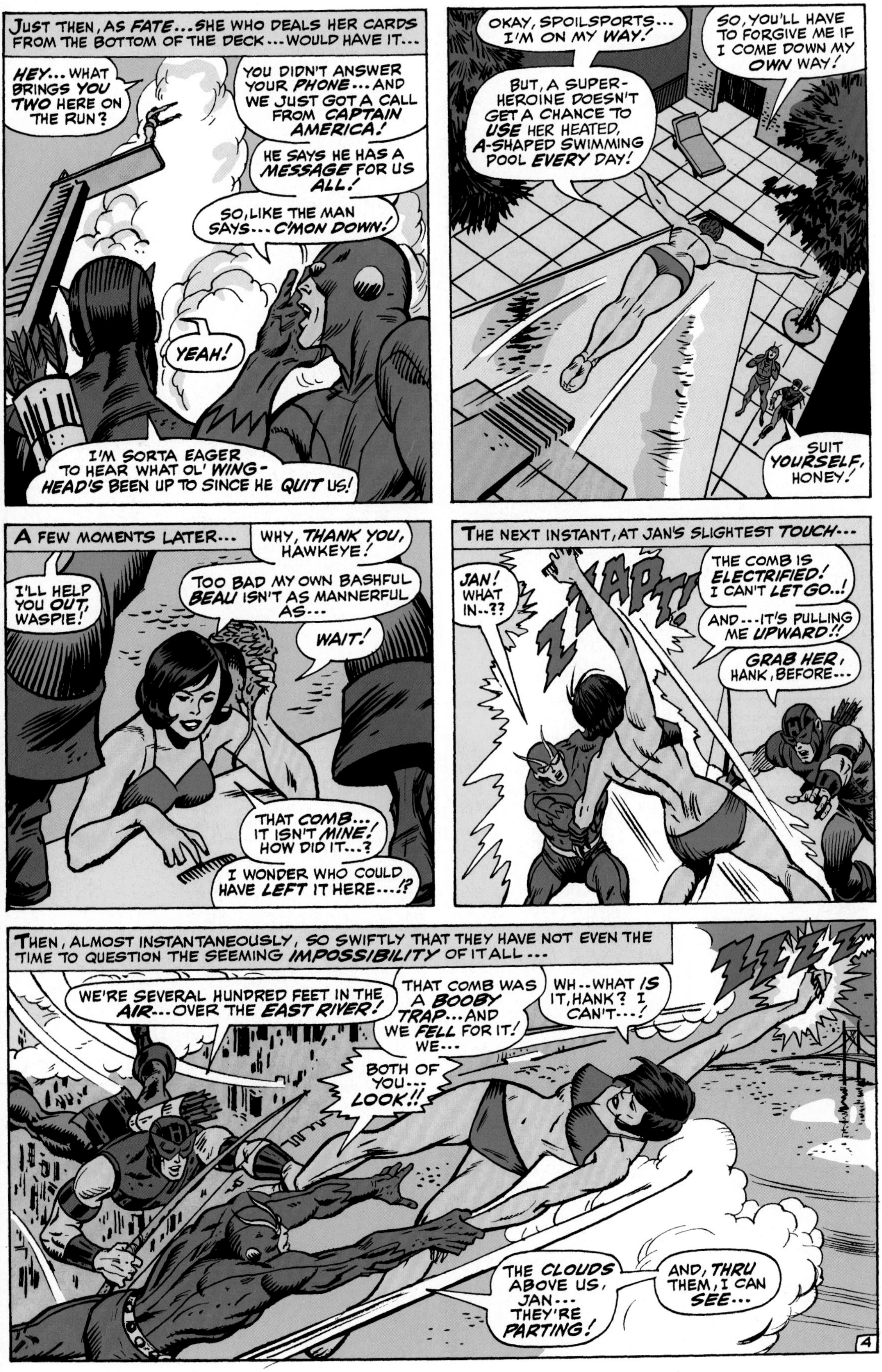
JUST THEN, AS FATE... SHE WHO DEALS HER CARDS FROM THE BOTTOM OF THE DECK... WOULD HAVE IT...
HEY... WHAT BRINGS YOU TWO HERE ON THE RUN?
YOU DIDN'T ANSWER YOUR PHONE... AND WE JUST GOT A CALL FROM CAPTAIN AMERICA!
HE SAYS HE HAS A MESSAGE FOR US ALL!
SO, LIKE THE MAN SAYS... C'MON DOWN!
YEAH!
I'M SORTA EAGER TO HEAR WHAT OL' WING-HEAD'S BEEN UP TO SINCE HE QUIT US!
OKAY, SPOILSPORTS... I'M ON MY WAY!
BUT, A SUPER-HEROINE DOESN'T GET A CHANCE TO USE HER HEATED, A-SHAPED SWIMMING POOL EVERY DAY!
SO, YOU'LL HAVE TO FORGIVE ME IF I COME DOWN MY OWN WAY!
SUIT YOURSELF, HONEY!
A FEW MOMENTS LATER...
WHY, THANK YOU, HAWKEYE!
I'LL HELP YOU OUT, WASPIE!
TOO BAD MY OWN BASHFUL BEAU ISN'T AS MANNERFUL AS...
WAIT!
THAT COMB... IT ISN'T MINE! HOW DID IT...?
I WONDER WHO COULD HAVE LEFT IT HERE...!?
THE NEXT INSTANT, AT JAN'S SLIGHTEST TOUCH...
JAN! WHAT IN..??
ZZAPT!
THE COMB IS ELECTRIFIED! I CAN'T LET GO..!
AND... IT'S PULLING ME UPWARD!!
GRAB HER, HANK, BEFORE...
THEN, ALMOST INSTANTANEOUSLY, SO SWIFTLY THAT THEY HAVE NOT EVEN THE TIME TO QUESTION THE SEEMING IMPOSSIBILITY OF IT ALL...
ZZZZ
WE'RE SEVERAL HUNDRED FEET IN THE AIR... OVER THE EAST RIVER!
THAT COMB WAS A BOOBY TRAP... AND WE FELL FOR IT! WE...
WH.. WHAT IS IT, HANK? I CAN'T...!
BOTH OF YOU... LOOK!!
THE CLOUDS ABOVE US, JAN... THEY'RE PARTING!
AND, THRU THEM, I CAN SEE...
4

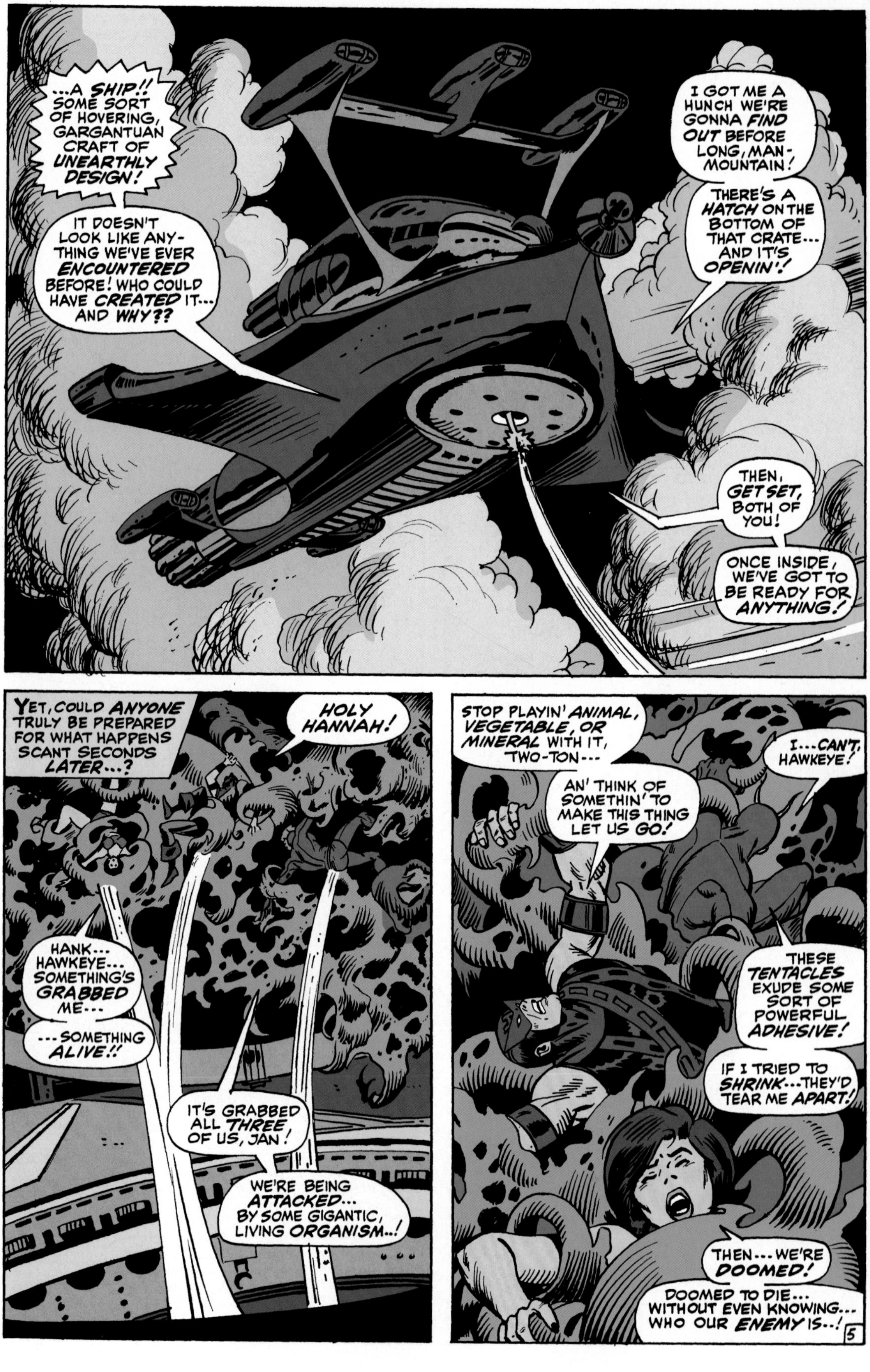
...A SHIP!! SOME SORT OF HOVERING, GARGANTUAN CRAFT OF UNEARTHLY DESIGN!
IT DOESN'T LOOK LIKE ANYTHING WE'VE EVER ENCOUNTERED BEFORE! WHO COULD HAVE CREATED IT... AND WHY??
I GOT ME A HUNCH WE'RE GONNA FIND OUT BEFORE LONG, MAN-MOUNTAIN!
THERE'S A HATCH ON THE BOTTOM OF THAT CRATE... AND IT'S OPENIN'!
THEN, GET SET, BOTH OF YOU!
ONCE INSIDE, WE'VE GOT TO BE READY FOR ANYTHING!
YET, COULD ANYONE TRULY BE PREPARED FOR WHAT HAPPENS SCANT SECONDS LATER...?
HOLY HANNAH!
HANK... HAWKEYE... SOMETHING'S GRABBED ME...
...SOMETHING ALIVE!!
IT'S GRABBED ALL THREE OF US, JAN!
WE'RE BEING ATTACKED... BY SOME GIGANTIC, LIVING ORGANISM..!
STOP PLAYIN' ANIMAL, VEGETABLE, OR MINERAL WITH IT, TWO-TON---
AN' THINK OF SOMETHIN' TO MAKE THIS THING LET US GO!
I...CAN'T, HAWKEYE!
THESE TENTACLES EXUDE SOME SORT OF POWERFUL ADHESIVE!
IF I TRIED TO SHRINK...THEY'D TEAR ME APART!
THEN... WE'RE DOOMED!
DOOMED TO DIE... WITHOUT EVEN KNOWING... WHO OUR ENEMY IS..!
5

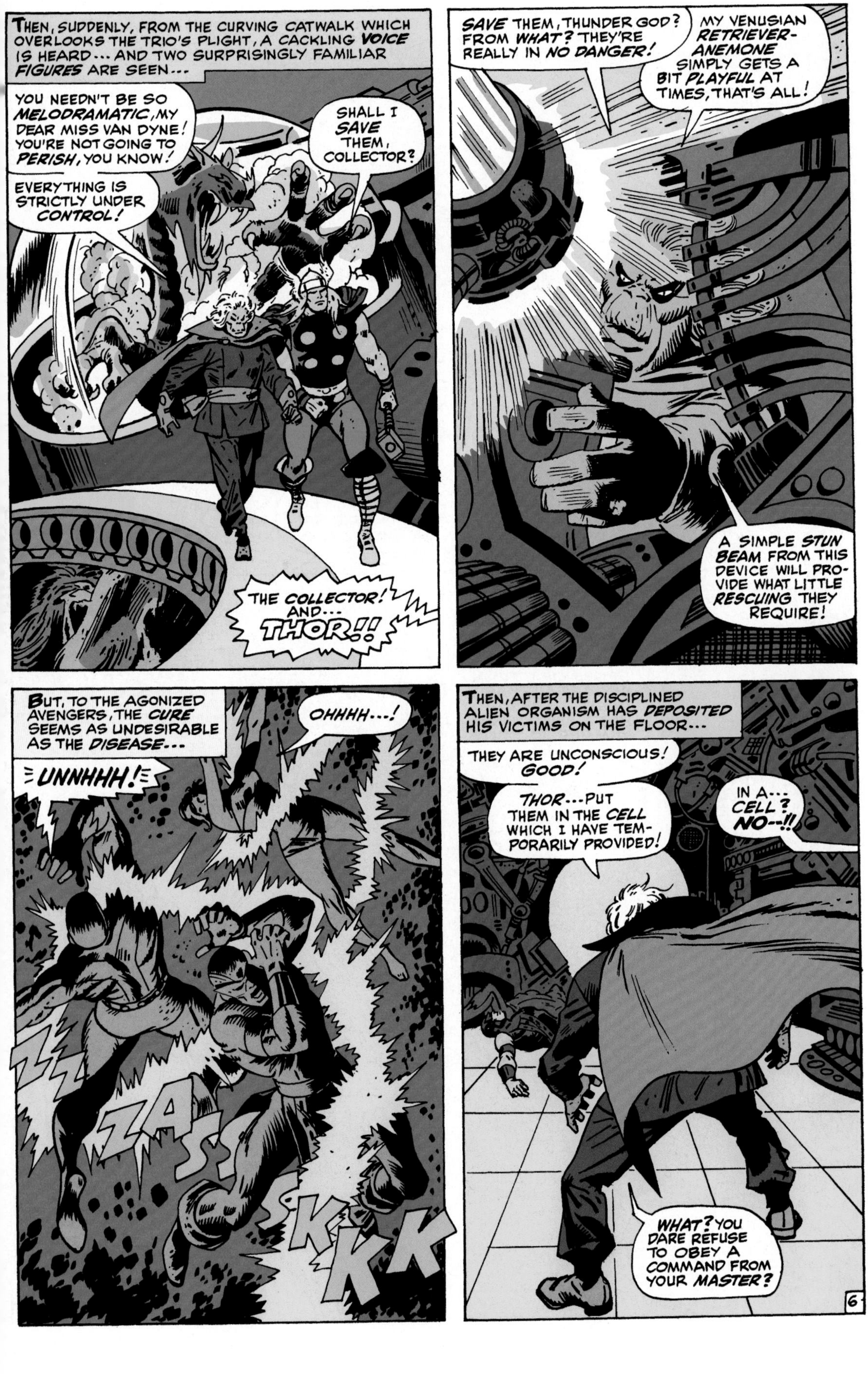
THEN, SUDDENLY, FROM THE CURVING CATWALK WHICH OVERLOOKS THE TRIO'S PLIGHT, A CACKLING VOICE IS HEARD... AND TWO SURPRISINGLY FAMILIAR FIGURES ARE SEEN...
YOU NEEDN'T BE SO MELODRAMATIC, MY DEAR MISS VAN DYNE! YOU'RE NOT GOING TO PERISH, YOU KNOW!
EVERYTHING IS STRICTLY UNDER CONTROL!
SHALL I SAVE THEM, COLLECTOR?
THE COLLECTOR! AND... THOR!!
SAVE THEM, THUNDER GOD? FROM WHAT? THEY'RE REALLY IN NO DANGER!
MY VENUSIAN RETRIEVER-ANEMONE SIMPLY GETS A BIT PLAYFUL AT TIMES, THAT'S ALL!
A SIMPLE STUN BEAM FROM THIS DEVICE WILL PROVIDE WHAT LITTLE RESCUING THEY REQUIRE!
BUT, TO THE AGONIZED AVENGERS, THE CURE SEEMS AS UNDESIRABLE AS THE DISEASE...
OHHHH...!
UNNHHH!
ZASSKKK
THEN, AFTER THE DISCIPLINED ALIEN ORGANISM HAS DEPOSITED HIS VICTIMS ON THE FLOOR...
THEY ARE UNCONSCIOUS! GOOD!
THOR...PUT THEM IN THE CELL WHICH I HAVE TEMPORARILY PROVIDED!
IN A... CELL? NO--!!
WHAT? YOU DARE REFUSE TO OBEY A COMMAND FROM YOUR MASTER?
6

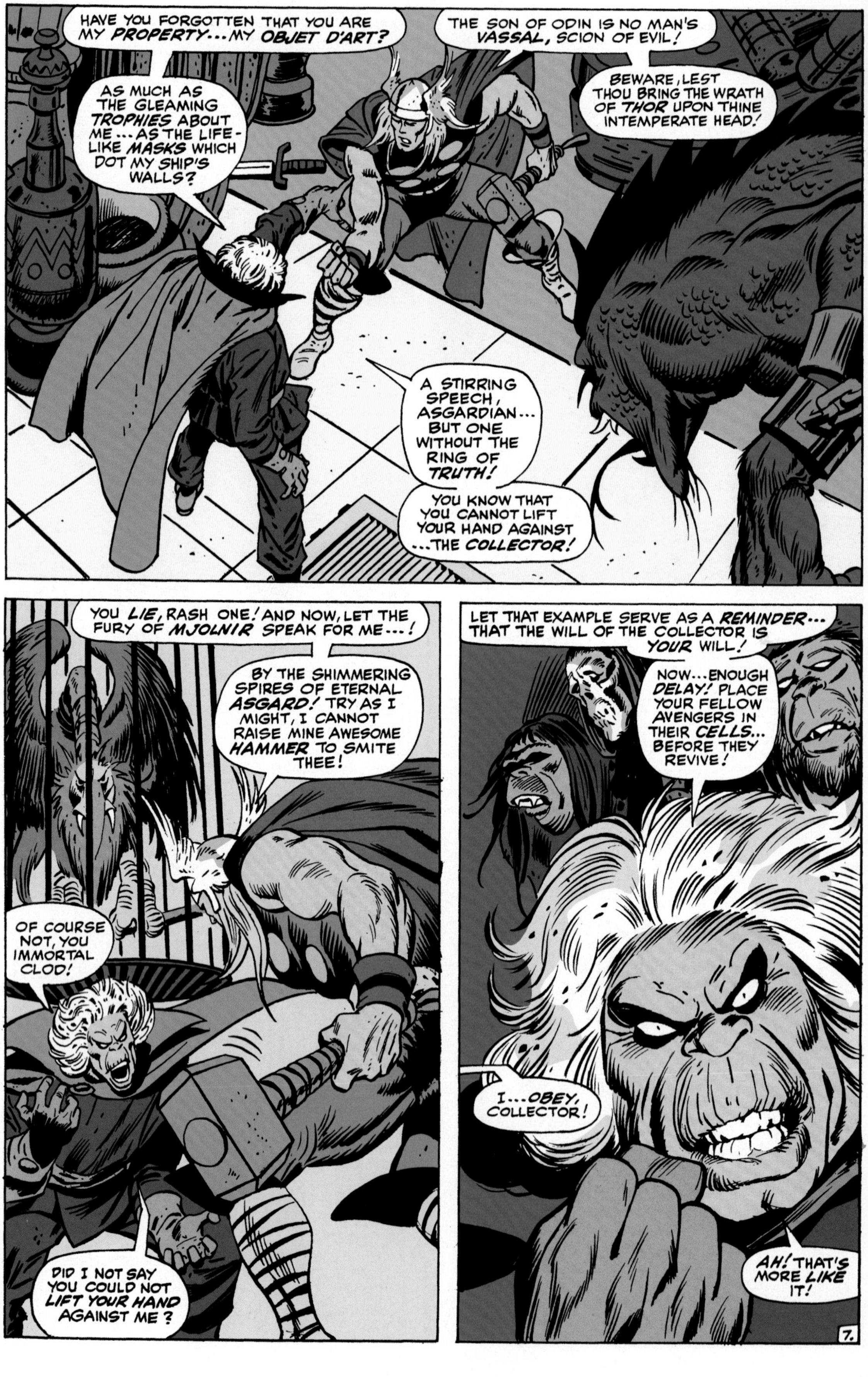
HAVE YOU FORGOTTEN THAT YOU ARE MY PROPERTY... MY OBJET D'ART?
AS MUCH AS THE GLEAMING TROPHIES ABOUT ME... AS THE LIFE-LIKE MASKS WHICH DOT MY SHIP'S WALLS?
THE SON OF ODIN IS NO MAN'S VASSAL, SCION OF EVIL!
BEWARE, LEST THOU BRING THE WRATH OF THOR UPON THINE INTEMPERATE HEAD!
A STIRRING SPEECH, ASGARDIAN... BUT ONE WITHOUT THE RING OF TRUTH!
YOU KNOW THAT YOU CANNOT LIFT YOUR HAND AGAINST ...THE COLLECTOR!
YOU LIE, RASH ONE! AND NOW, LET THE FURY OF MJOLNIR SPEAK FOR ME...!
BY THE SHIMMERING SPIRES OF ETERNAL ASGARD! TRY AS I MIGHT, I CANNOT RAISE MINE AWESOME HAMMER TO SMITE THEE!
OF COURSE NOT, YOU IMMORTAL CLOD!
DID I NOT SAY YOU COULD NOT LIFT YOUR HAND AGAINST ME?
LET THAT EXAMPLE SERVE AS A REMINDER... THAT THE WILL OF THE COLLECTOR IS YOUR WILL!
NOW... ENOUGH DELAY! PLACE YOUR FELLOW AVENGERS IN THEIR CELLS... BEFORE THEY REVIVE!
I...OBEY, COLLECTOR!
AH! THAT'S MORE LIKE IT!
7.

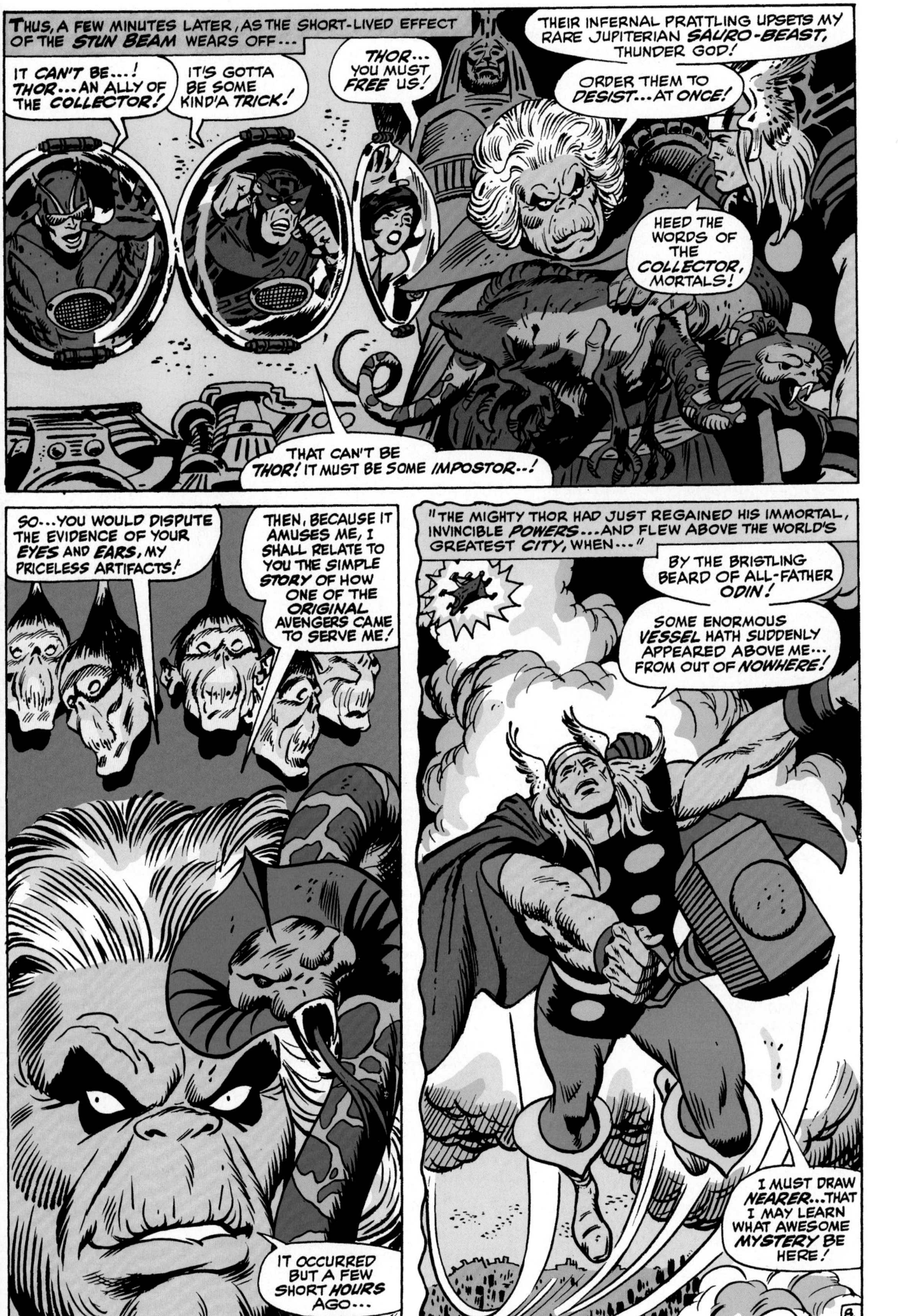
THUS, A FEW MINUTES LATER, AS THE SHORT-LIVED EFFECT OF THE STUN BEAM WEARS OFF...
IT CAN'T BE...! THOR...AN ALLY OF THE COLLECTOR!
IT'S GOTTA BE SOME KIND'A TRICK!
THOR... YOU MUST FREE US!
THEIR INFERNAL PRATTLING UPSETS MY RARE JUPITERIAN SAURO-BEAST, THUNDER GOD!
ORDER THEM TO DESIST...AT ONCE!
HEED THE WORDS OF THE COLLECTOR, MORTALS!
THAT CAN'T BE THOR! IT MUST BE SOME IMPOSTOR..!
SO...YOU WOULD DISPUTE THE EVIDENCE OF YOUR EYES AND EARS, MY PRICELESS ARTIFACTS!
THEN, BECAUSE IT AMUSES ME, I SHALL RELATE TO YOU THE SIMPLE STORY OF HOW ONE OF THE ORIGINAL AVENGERS CAME TO SERVE ME!
IT OCCURRED BUT A FEW SHORT HOURS AGO...
"THE MIGHTY THOR HAD JUST REGAINED HIS IMMORTAL, INVINCIBLE POWERS...AND FLEW ABOVE THE WORLD'S GREATEST CITY, WHEN..."
BY THE BRISTLING BEARD OF ALL-FATHER ODIN!
SOME ENORMOUS VESSEL HATH SUDDENLY APPEARED ABOVE ME... FROM OUT OF NOWHERE!
I MUST DRAW NEARER...THAT I MAY LEARN WHAT AWESOME MYSTERY BE HERE!
8.

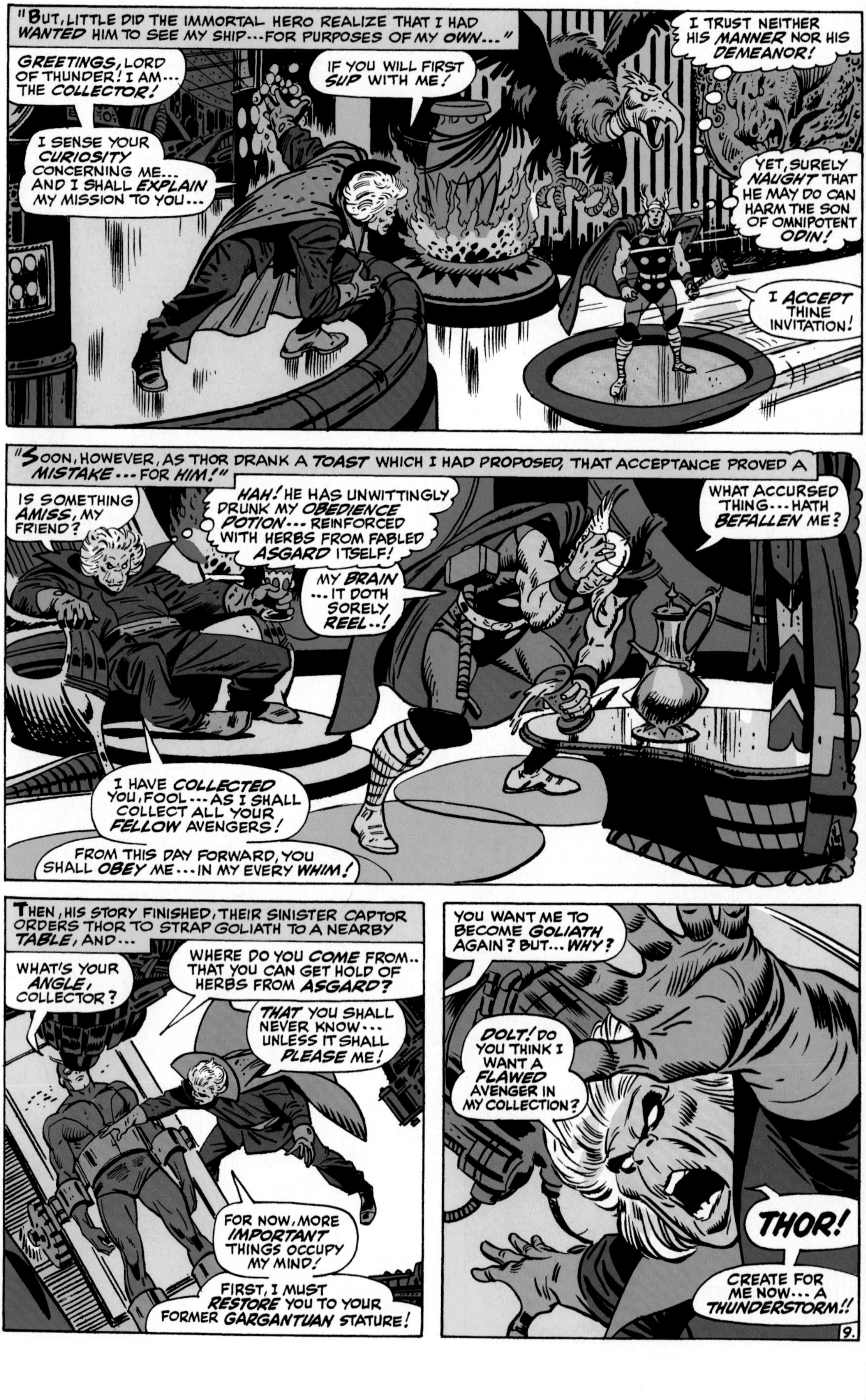
"BUT, LITTLE DID THE IMMORTAL HERO REALIZE THAT I HAD WANTED HIM TO SEE MY SHIP---FOR PURPOSES OF MY OWN..."
GREETINGS, LORD OF THUNDER! I AM--- THE COLLECTOR!
I SENSE YOUR CURIOSITY CONCERNING ME... AND I SHALL EXPLAIN MY MISSION TO YOU...
IF YOU WILL FIRST SUP WITH ME!
I TRUST NEITHER HIS MANNER NOR HIS DEMEANOR!
YET, SURELY NAUGHT THAT HE MAY DO CAN HARM THE SON OF OMNIPOTENT ODIN!
I ACCEPT THINE INVITATION!
"SOON, HOWEVER, AS THOR DRANK A TOAST WHICH I HAD PROPOSED, THAT ACCEPTANCE PROVED A MISTAKE --- FOR HIM!"
IS SOMETHING AMISS, MY FRIEND?
HAH! HE HAS UNWITTINGLY DRUNK MY OBEDIENCE POTION--- REINFORCED WITH HERBS FROM FABLED ASGARD ITSELF!
MY BRAIN ...IT DOTH SORELY REEL..!
WHAT ACCURSED THING---HATH BEFALLEN ME?
I HAVE COLLECTED YOU, FOOL---AS I SHALL COLLECT ALL YOUR FELLOW AVENGERS!
FROM THIS DAY FORWARD, YOU SHALL OBEY ME---IN MY EVERY WHIM!
THEN, HIS STORY FINISHED, THEIR SINISTER CAPTOR ORDERS THOR TO STRAP GOLIATH TO A NEARBY TABLE, AND...
WHAT'S YOUR ANGLE, COLLECTOR?
WHERE DO YOU COME FROM.. THAT YOU CAN GET HOLD OF HERBS FROM ASGARD?
THAT YOU SHALL NEVER KNOW--- UNLESS IT SHALL PLEASE ME!
FOR NOW, MORE IMPORTANT THINGS OCCUPY MY MIND!
FIRST, I MUST RESTORE YOU TO YOUR FORMER GARGANTUAN STATURE!
YOU WANT ME TO BECOME GOLIATH AGAIN? BUT... WHY?
DOLT! DO YOU THINK I WANT A FLAWED AVENGER IN MY COLLECTION?
THOR!
CREATE FOR ME NOW... A THUNDERSTORM!!
9.

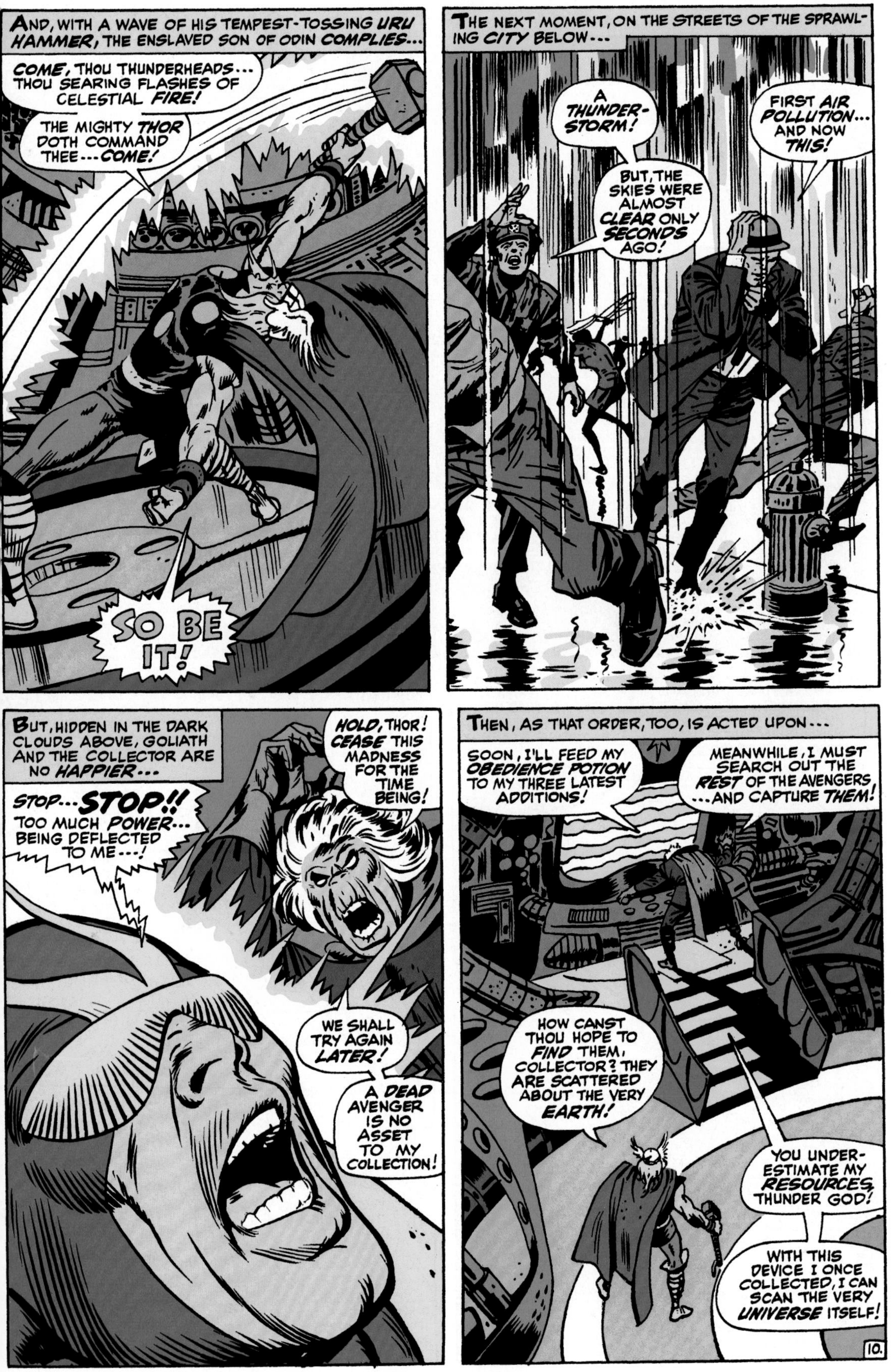
AND, WITH A WAVE OF HIS TEMPEST-TOSSING URU HAMMER, THE ENSLAVED SON OF ODIN COMPLIES...
COME, THOU THUNDERHEADS... THOU SEARING FLASHES OF CELESTIAL FIRE!
THE MIGHTY THOR DOTH COMMAND THEE... COME!
SO BE IT!
THE NEXT MOMENT, ON THE STREETS OF THE SPRAWLING CITY BELOW...
A THUNDER-STORM!
BUT, THE SKIES WERE ALMOST CLEAR ONLY SECONDS AGO!
FIRST AIR POLLUTION... AND NOW THIS!
BUT, HIDDEN IN THE DARK CLOUDS ABOVE, GOLIATH AND THE COLLECTOR ARE NO HAPPIER...
STOP... STOP!! TOO MUCH POWER... BEING DEFLECTED TO ME...!
HOLD, THOR! CEASE THIS MADNESS FOR THE TIME BEING!
WE SHALL TRY AGAIN LATER!
A DEAD AVENGER IS NO ASSET TO MY COLLECTION!
THEN, AS THAT ORDER, TOO, IS ACTED UPON...
SOON, I'LL FEED MY OBEDIENCE POTION TO MY THREE LATEST ADDITIONS!
MEANWHILE, I MUST SEARCH OUT THE REST OF THE AVENGERS ...AND CAPTURE THEM!
HOW CANST THOU HOPE TO FIND THEM, COLLECTOR? THEY ARE SCATTERED ABOUT THE VERY EARTH!
YOU UNDER-ESTIMATE MY RESOURCES, THUNDER GOD!
WITH THIS DEVICE I ONCE COLLECTED, I CAN SCAN THE VERY UNIVERSE ITSELF!
10.

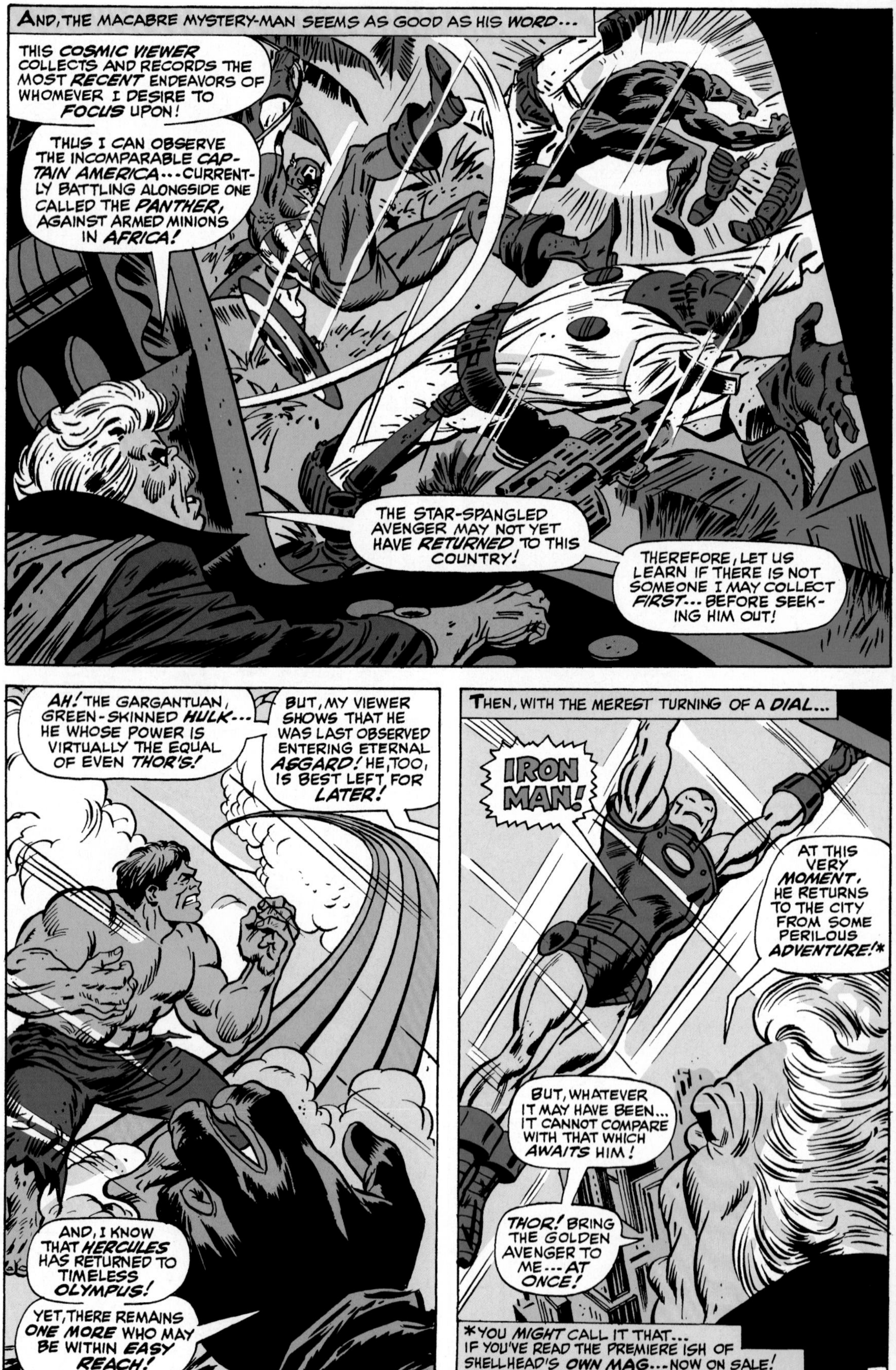
AND, THE MACABRE MYSTERY-MAN SEEMS AS GOOD AS HIS WORD...
THIS COSMIC VIEWER COLLECTS AND RECORDS THE MOST RECENT ENDEAVORS OF WHOMEVER I DESIRE TO FOCUS UPON!
THUS I CAN OBSERVE THE INCOMPARABLE CAPTAIN AMERICA... CURRENTLY BATTLING ALONGSIDE ONE CALLED THE PANTHER, AGAINST ARMED MINIONS IN AFRICA!
THE STAR-SPANGLED AVENGER MAY NOT YET HAVE RETURNED TO THIS COUNTRY!
THEREFORE, LET US LEARN IF THERE IS NOT SOMEONE I MAY COLLECT FIRST... BEFORE SEEKING HIM OUT!
AH! THE GARGANTUAN, GREEN-SKINNED HULK... HE WHOSE POWER IS VIRTUALLY THE EQUAL OF EVEN THOR'S!
BUT, MY VIEWER SHOWS THAT HE WAS LAST OBSERVED ENTERING ETERNAL ASGARD! HE, TOO, IS BEST LEFT FOR LATER!
AND, I KNOW THAT HERCULES HAS RETURNED TO TIMELESS OLYMPUS!
YET, THERE REMAINS ONE MORE WHO MAY BE WITHIN EASY REACH!
THEN, WITH THE MEREST TURNING OF A DIAL...
IRON MAN!
AT THIS VERY MOMENT, HE RETURNS TO THE CITY FROM SOME PERILOUS ADVENTURE!*
BUT, WHATEVER IT MAY HAVE BEEN... IT CANNOT COMPARE WITH THAT WHICH AWAITS HIM!
THOR! BRING THE GOLDEN AVENGER TO ME... AT ONCE!
*YOU MIGHT CALL IT THAT... IF YOU'VE READ THE PREMIERE ISH OF SHELLHEAD'S OWN MAG... NOW ON SALE! --SALESMAN STAN.
11.

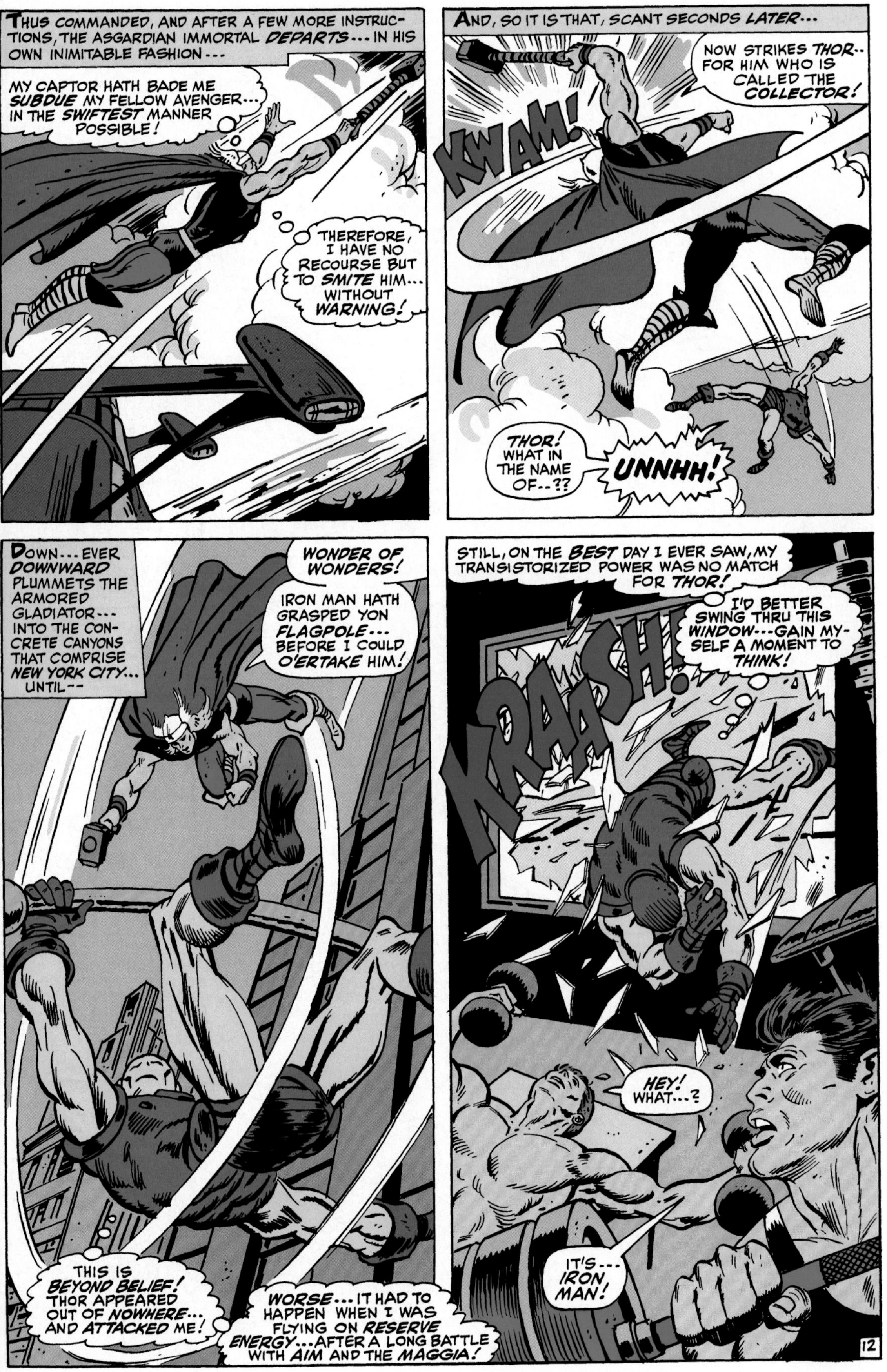
THUS COMMANDED, AND AFTER A FEW MORE INSTRUCTIONS, THE ASGARDIAN IMMORTAL DEPARTS... IN HIS OWN INIMITABLE FASHION...
MY CAPTOR HATH BADE ME SUBDUE MY FELLOW AVENGER... IN THE SWIFTEST MANNER POSSIBLE!
THEREFORE, I HAVE NO RECOURSE BUT TO SMITE HIM... WITHOUT WARNING!
AND, SO IT IS THAT, SCANT SECONDS LATER...
NOW STRIKES THOR.. FOR HIM WHO IS CALLED THE COLLECTOR!
KWAM!
THOR! WHAT IN THE NAME OF--??
UNNHH!
DOWN... EVER DOWNWARD PLUMMETS THE ARMORED GLADIATOR... INTO THE CONCRETE CANYONS THAT COMPRISE NEW YORK CITY... UNTIL--
WONDER OF WONDERS!
IRON MAN HATH GRASPED YON FLAGPOLE... BEFORE I COULD O'ERTAKE HIM!
THIS IS BEYOND BELIEF! THOR APPEARED OUT OF NOWHERE... AND ATTACKED ME!
WORSE... IT HAD TO HAPPEN WHEN I WAS FLYING ON RESERVE ENERGY... AFTER A LONG BATTLE WITH AIM AND THE MAGGIA!
STILL, ON THE BEST DAY I EVER SAW, MY TRANSISTORIZED POWER WAS NO MATCH FOR THOR!
I'D BETTER SWING THRU THIS WINDOW... GAIN MYSELF A MOMENT TO THINK!
KRAASH!
HEY! WHAT...?
IT'S... IRON MAN!
12

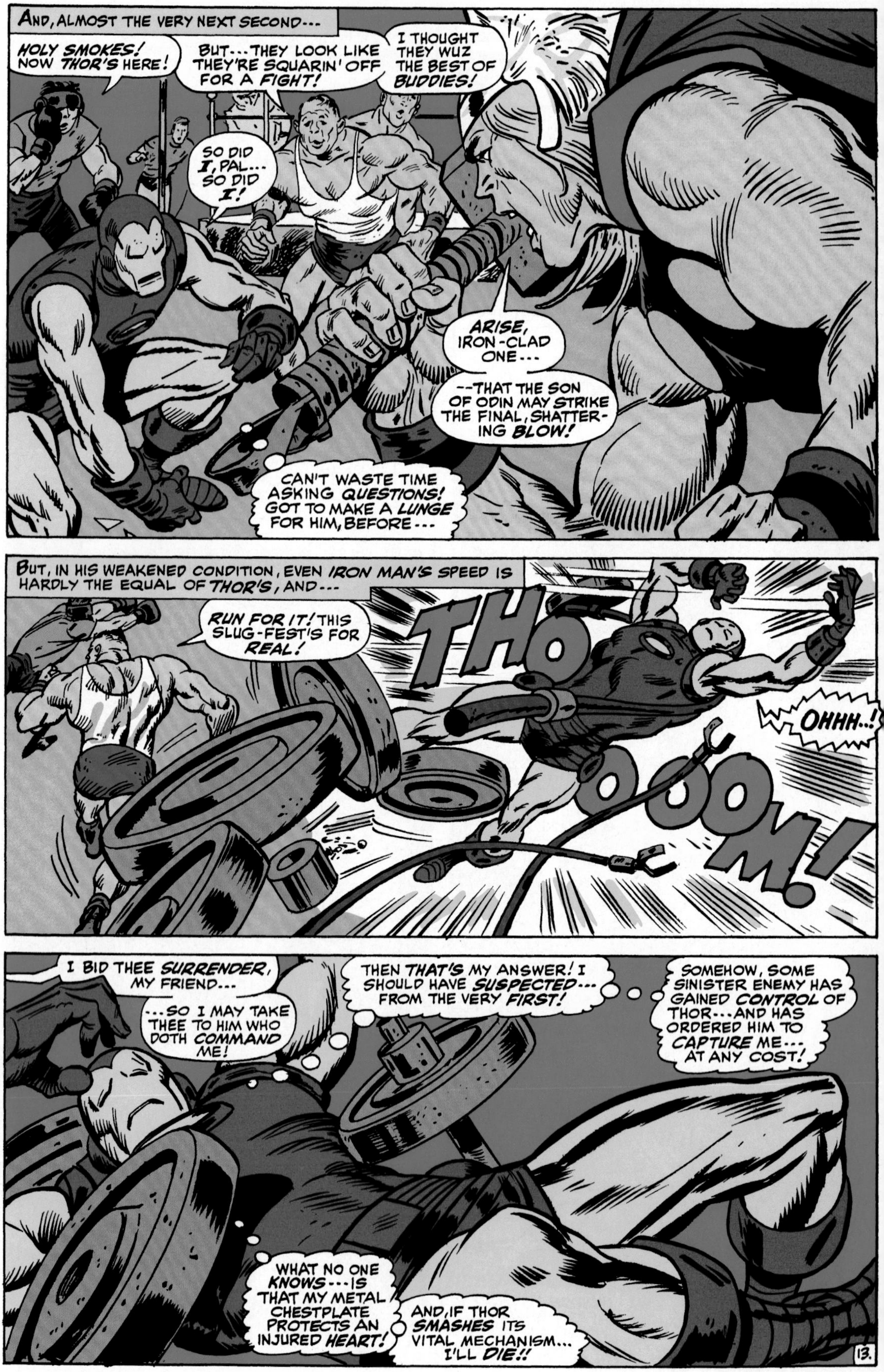
AND, ALMOST THE VERY NEXT SECOND---
HOLY SMOKES! NOW THOR'S HERE!
BUT--- THEY LOOK LIKE THEY'RE SQUARIN' OFF FOR A FIGHT!
I THOUGHT THEY WUZ THE BEST OF BUDDIES!
SO DID I, PAL... SO DID I!
ARISE, IRON-CLAD ONE---
--THAT THE SON OF ODIN MAY STRIKE THE FINAL, SHATTERING BLOW!
CAN'T WASTE TIME ASKING QUESTIONS! GOT TO MAKE A LUNGE FOR HIM, BEFORE---
BUT, IN HIS WEAKENED CONDITION, EVEN IRON MAN'S SPEED IS HARDLY THE EQUAL OF THOR'S, AND---
RUN FOR IT! THIS SLUG-FEST'S FOR REAL!
THOOOOM!
OHHH..!
I BID THEE SURRENDER, MY FRIEND---
---SO I MAY TAKE THEE TO HIM WHO DOTH COMMAND ME!
THEN THAT'S MY ANSWER! I SHOULD HAVE SUSPECTED--- FROM THE VERY FIRST!
SOMEHOW, SOME SINISTER ENEMY HAS GAINED CONTROL OF THOR---AND HAS ORDERED HIM TO CAPTURE ME--- AT ANY COST!
WHAT NO ONE KNOWS---IS THAT MY METAL CHESTPLATE PROTECTS AN INJURED HEART!
AND, IF THOR SMASHES ITS VITAL MECHANISM... I'LL DIE!!
13.

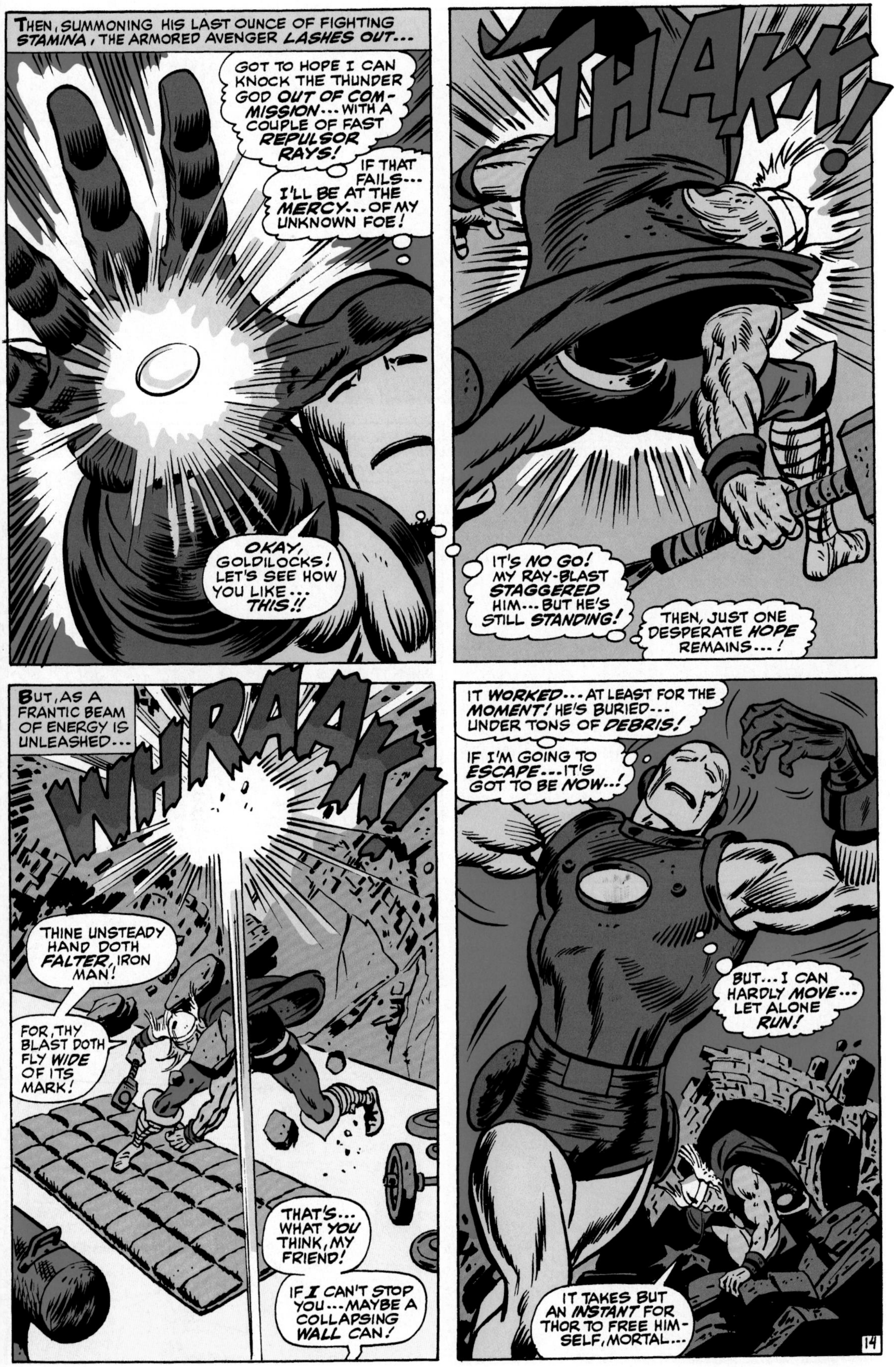
THEN, SUMMONING HIS LAST OUNCE OF FIGHTING STAMINA, THE ARMORED AVENGER LASHES OUT...
GOT TO HOPE I CAN KNOCK THE THUNDER GOD OUT OF COM-MISSION... WITH A COUPLE OF FAST REPULSOR RAYS!
IF THAT FAILS... I'LL BE AT THE MERCY... OF MY UNKNOWN FOE!
OKAY, GOLDILOCKS! LET'S SEE HOW YOU LIKE... THIS!!
THAKK!
IT'S NO GO! MY RAY-BLAST STAGGERED HIM... BUT HE'S STILL STANDING!
THEN, JUST ONE DESPERATE HOPE REMAINS...!
BUT, AS A FRANTIC BEAM OF ENERGY IS UNLEASHED...
WHRAAK!
THINE UNSTEADY HAND DOTH FALTER, IRON MAN!
FOR, THY BLAST DOTH FLY WIDE OF ITS MARK!
THAT'S... WHAT YOU THINK, MY FRIEND!
IF I CAN'T STOP YOU... MAYBE A COLLAPSING WALL CAN!
IT WORKED... AT LEAST FOR THE MOMENT! HE'S BURIED... UNDER TONS OF DEBRIS!
IF I'M GOING TO ESCAPE... IT'S GOT TO BE NOW...!
BUT... I CAN HARDLY MOVE... LET ALONE RUN!
IT TAKES BUT AN INSTANT FOR THOR TO FREE HIM-SELF, MORTAL...
14

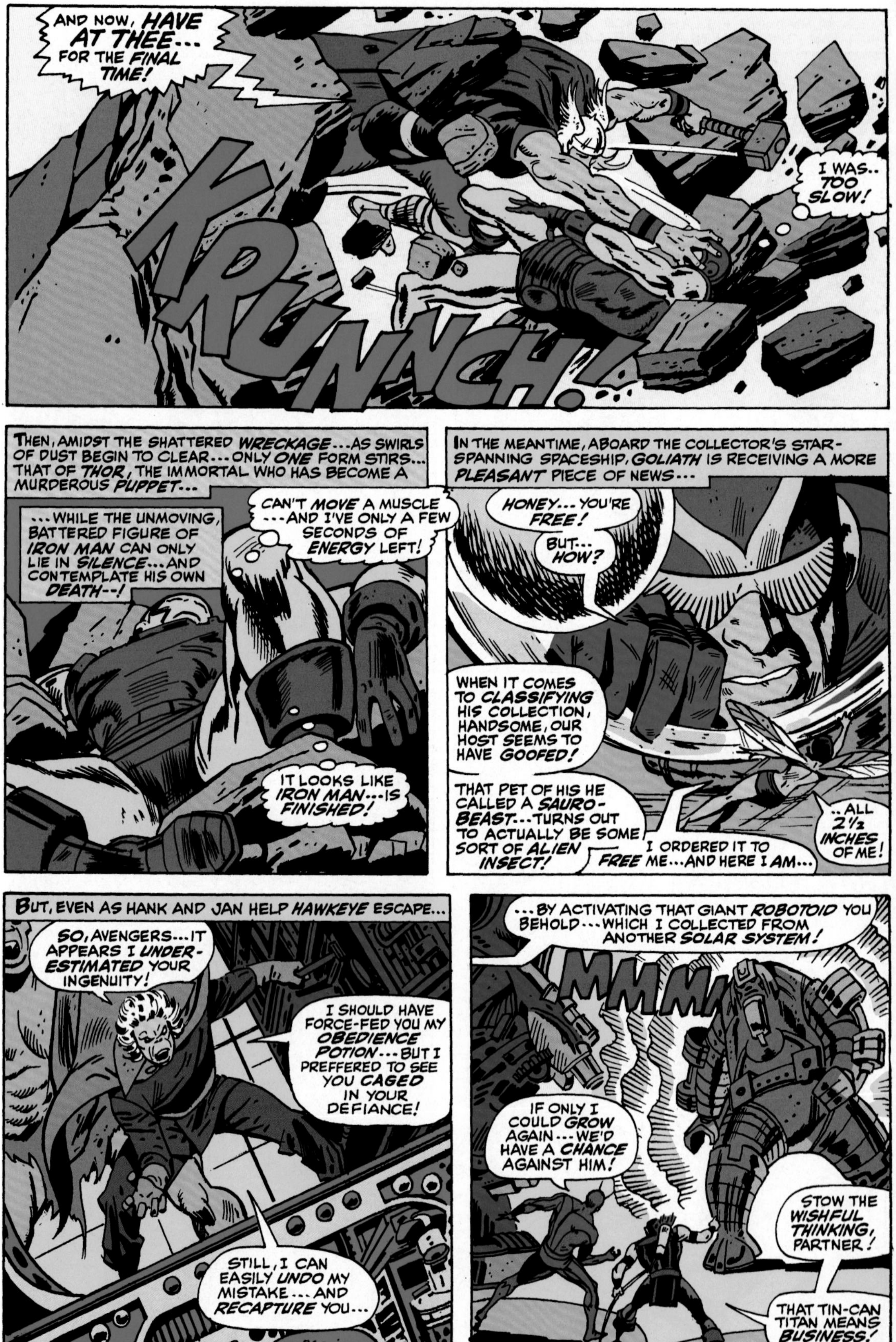
AND NOW, HAVE AT THEE... FOR THE FINAL TIME!
KRUNNCH!
I WAS.. TOO SLOW!
THEN, AMIDST THE SHATTERED WRECKAGE...AS SWIRLS OF DUST BEGIN TO CLEAR...ONLY ONE FORM STIRS... THAT OF THOR, THE IMMORTAL WHO HAS BECOME A MURDEROUS PUPPET...
...WHILE THE UNMOVING, BATTERED FIGURE OF IRON MAN CAN ONLY LIE IN SILENCE...AND CONTEMPLATE HIS OWN DEATH--!
CAN'T MOVE A MUSCLE ---AND I'VE ONLY A FEW SECONDS OF ENERGY LEFT!
IT LOOKS LIKE IRON MAN...IS FINISHED!
IN THE MEANTIME, ABOARD THE COLLECTOR'S STAR-SPANNING SPACESHIP, GOLIATH IS RECEIVING A MORE PLEASANT PIECE OF NEWS...
HONEY... YOU'RE FREE!
BUT... HOW?
WHEN IT COMES TO CLASSIFYING HIS COLLECTION, HANDSOME, OUR HOST SEEMS TO HAVE GOOFED!
THAT PET OF HIS HE CALLED A SAURO-BEAST...TURNS OUT TO ACTUALLY BE SOME SORT OF ALIEN INSECT!
I ORDERED IT TO FREE ME...AND HERE I AM...
..ALL 2½ INCHES OF ME!
BUT, EVEN AS HANK AND JAN HELP HAWKEYE ESCAPE...
SO, AVENGERS...IT APPEARS I UNDER-ESTIMATED YOUR INGENUITY!
I SHOULD HAVE FORCE-FED YOU MY OBEDIENCE POTION...BUT I PREFFERED TO SEE YOU CAGED IN YOUR DEFIANCE!
STILL, I CAN EASILY UNDO MY MISTAKE...AND RECAPTURE YOU...
...BY ACTIVATING THAT GIANT ROBOTOID YOU BEHOLD...WHICH I COLLECTED FROM ANOTHER SOLAR SYSTEM!
MMMM
IF ONLY I COULD GROW AGAIN...WE'D HAVE A CHANCE AGAINST HIM!
STOW THE WISHFUL THINKING, PARTNER!
THAT TIN-CAN TITAN MEANS BUSINESS!

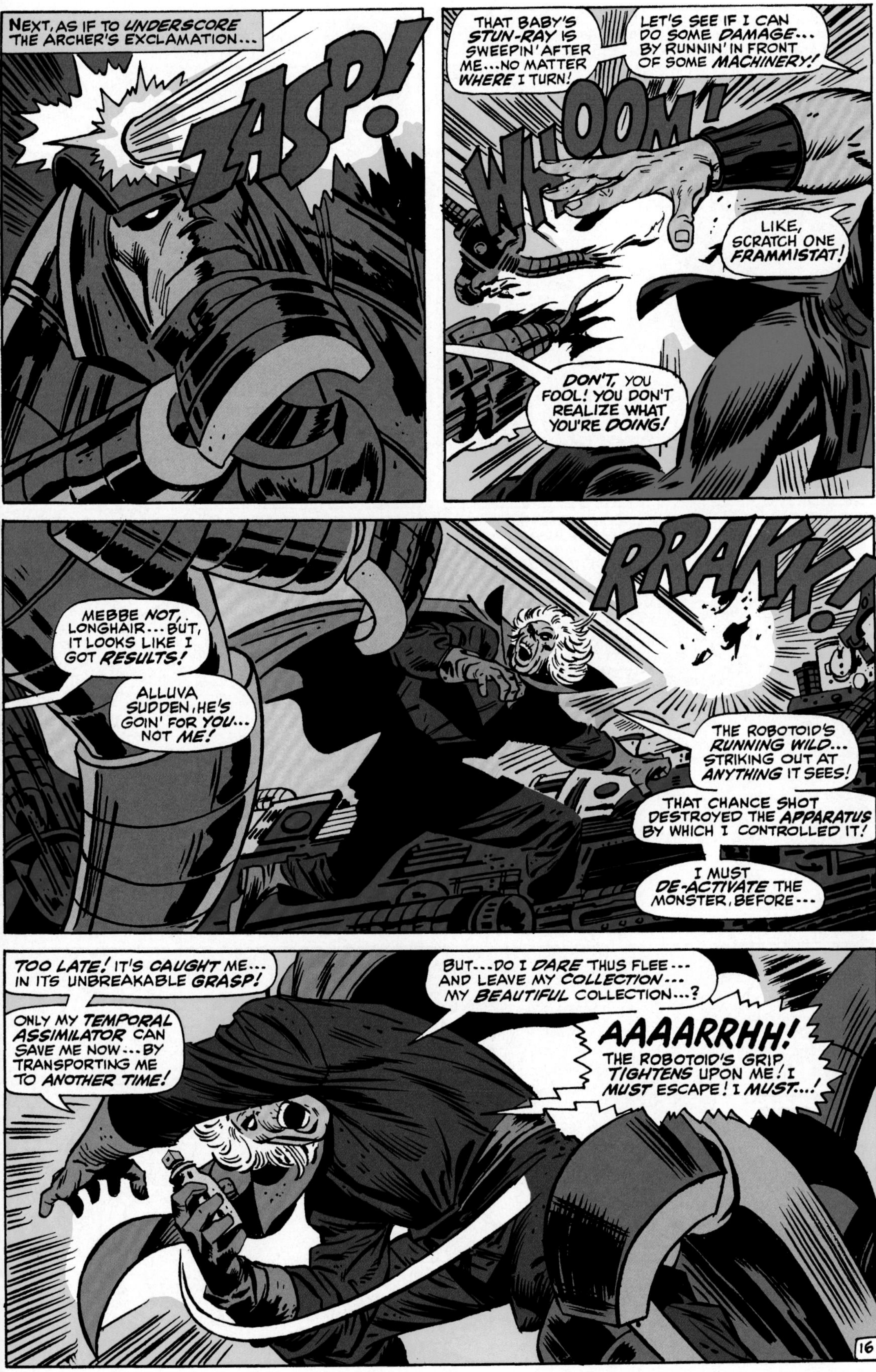
NEXT, AS IF TO UNDERSCORE THE ARCHER'S EXCLAMATION...
ZASP!
THAT BABY'S STUN-RAY IS SWEEPIN' AFTER ME...NO MATTER WHERE I TURN!
LET'S SEE IF I CAN DO SOME DAMAGE... BY RUNNIN' IN FRONT OF SOME MACHINERY!
WHOOM!
LIKE, SCRATCH ONE FRAMMISTAT!
DON'T, YOU FOOL! YOU DON'T REALIZE WHAT YOU'RE DOING!
RRAKK!
MEBBE NOT, LONGHAIR... BUT, IT LOOKS LIKE I GOT RESULTS!
ALLUVA SUDDEN, HE'S GOIN' FOR YOU... NOT ME!
THE ROBOTOID'S RUNNING WILD... STRIKING OUT AT ANYTHING IT SEES!
THAT CHANCE SHOT DESTROYED THE APPARATUS BY WHICH I CONTROLLED IT!
I MUST DE-ACTIVATE THE MONSTER, BEFORE---
TOO LATE! IT'S CAUGHT ME... IN ITS UNBREAKABLE GRASP!
ONLY MY TEMPORAL ASSIMILATOR CAN SAVE ME NOW... BY TRANSPORTING ME TO ANOTHER TIME!
BUT---DO I DARE THUS FLEE--- AND LEAVE MY COLLECTION--- MY BEAUTIFUL COLLECTION...?
AAAARRHH! THE ROBOTOID'S GRIP TIGHTENS UPON ME! I MUST ESCAPE! I MUST...!
16

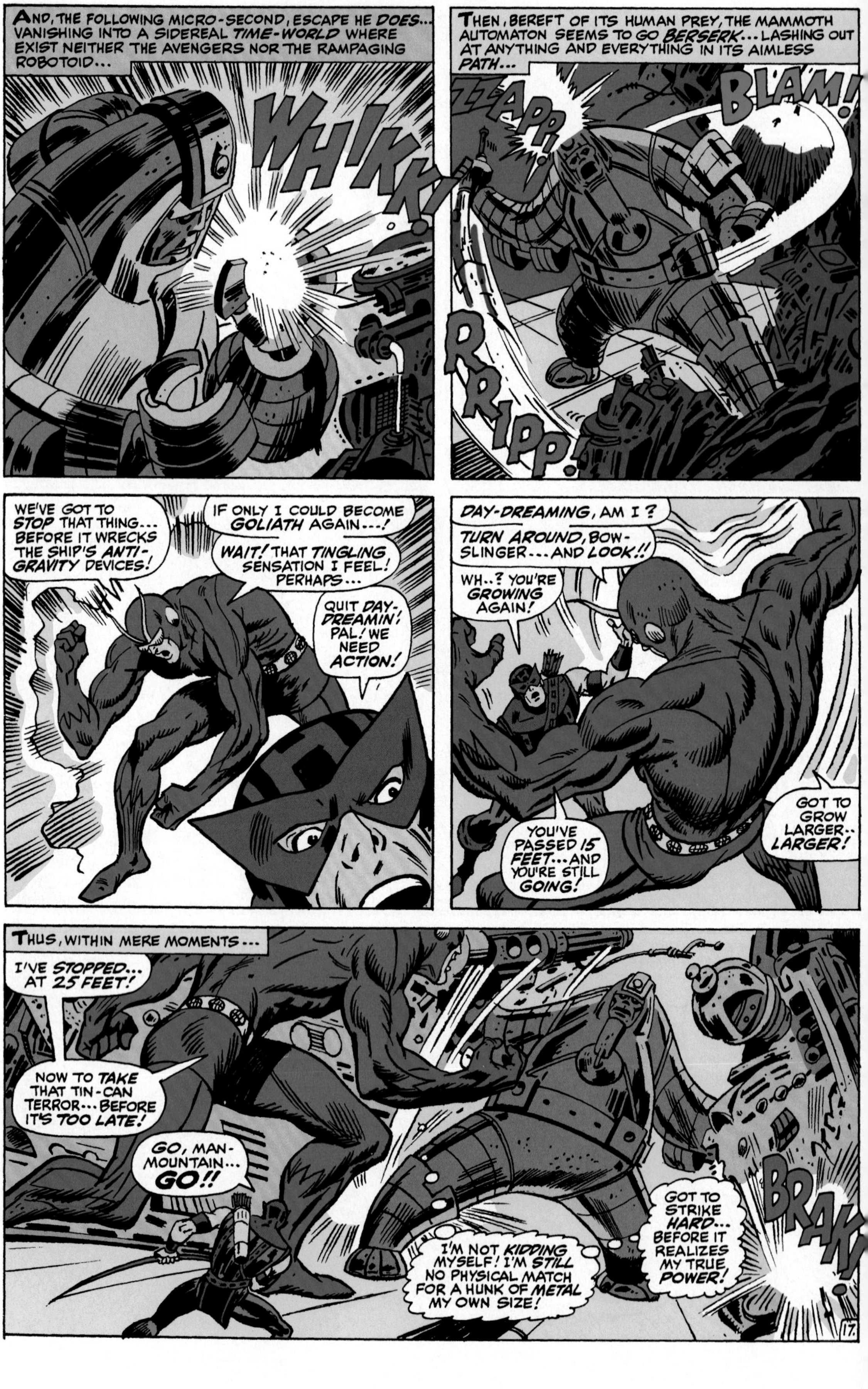
AND, THE FOLLOWING MICRO-SECOND, ESCAPE HE DOES... VANISHING INTO A SIDEREAL TIME-WORLD WHERE EXIST NEITHER THE AVENGERS NOR THE RAMPAGING ROBOTOID...
WHIKK!
THEN, BEREFT OF ITS HUMAN PREY, THE MAMMOTH AUTOMATON SEEMS TO GO BERSERK... LASHING OUT AT ANYTHING AND EVERYTHING IN ITS AIMLESS PATH...
ZZZAPP!
BLAM!
RRIPP!
WE'VE GOT TO STOP THAT THING... BEFORE IT WRECKS THE SHIP'S ANTI-GRAVITY DEVICES!
IF ONLY I COULD BECOME GOLIATH AGAIN---!
WAIT! THAT TINGLING SENSATION I FEEL! PERHAPS...
QUIT DAY-DREAMIN', PAL! WE NEED ACTION!
DAY-DREAMING, AM I?
TURN AROUND, BOW-SLINGER---AND LOOK!!
WH..? YOU'RE GROWING AGAIN!
YOU'VE PASSED 15 FEET...AND YOU'RE STILL GOING!
GOT TO GROW LARGER.. LARGER!
THUS, WITHIN MERE MOMENTS...
I'VE STOPPED... AT 25 FEET!
NOW TO TAKE THAT TIN-CAN TERROR... BEFORE IT'S TOO LATE!
GO, MAN-MOUNTAIN... GO!!
I'M NOT KIDDING MYSELF! I'M STILL NO PHYSICAL MATCH FOR A HUNK OF METAL MY OWN SIZE!
GOT TO STRIKE HARD... BEFORE IT REALIZES MY TRUE POWER!
BRAKK!
17

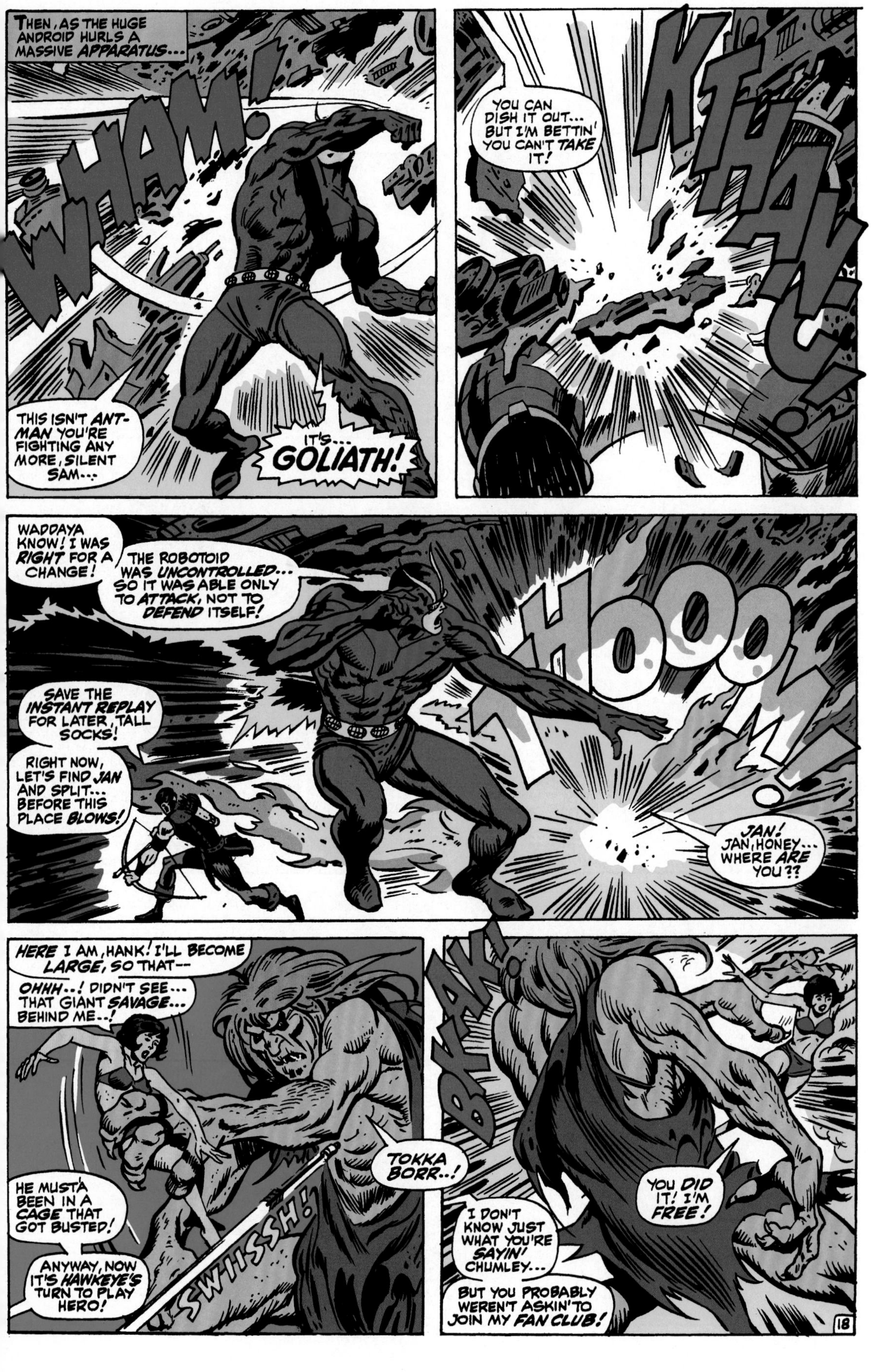
THEN, AS THE HUGE ANDROID HURLS A MASSIVE *APPARATUS*...
WHAM!
THIS ISN'T *ANT-MAN* YOU'RE FIGHTING ANY MORE, SILENT SAM...
IT'S... GOLIATH!
YOU CAN DISH IT OUT... BUT I'M BETTIN' YOU CAN'T *TAKE* IT!
KTHAKK!
WADDAYA KNOW! I WAS *RIGHT* FOR A CHANGE!
THE ROBOTOID WAS *UNCONTROLLED*... SO IT WAS ABLE ONLY TO *ATTACK*, NOT TO *DEFEND* ITSELF!
SAVE THE *INSTANT REPLAY* FOR LATER, TALL SOCKS!
RIGHT NOW, LET'S FIND *JAN* AND SPLIT... BEFORE THIS PLACE *BLOWS*!
WHOOOM!
JAN! JAN, HONEY... WHERE *ARE* YOU??
HERE I AM, HANK! I'LL BECOME *LARGE*, SO THAT--
OHHH..! DIDN'T SEE... THAT GIANT *SAVAGE*... BEHIND ME..!
TOKKA BORR..!
HE MUSTA BEEN IN A *CAGE* THAT GOT BUSTED!
ANYWAY, NOW IT'S *HAWKEYE'S* TURN TO PLAY HERO!
SWHISSSH!
BAKK!
YOU *DID* IT! I'M *FREE*!
I DON'T KNOW JUST WHAT YOU'RE *SAYIN'* CHUMLEY...
BUT YOU PROBABLY WEREN'T ASKIN' TO JOIN MY *FAN CLUB*!
18

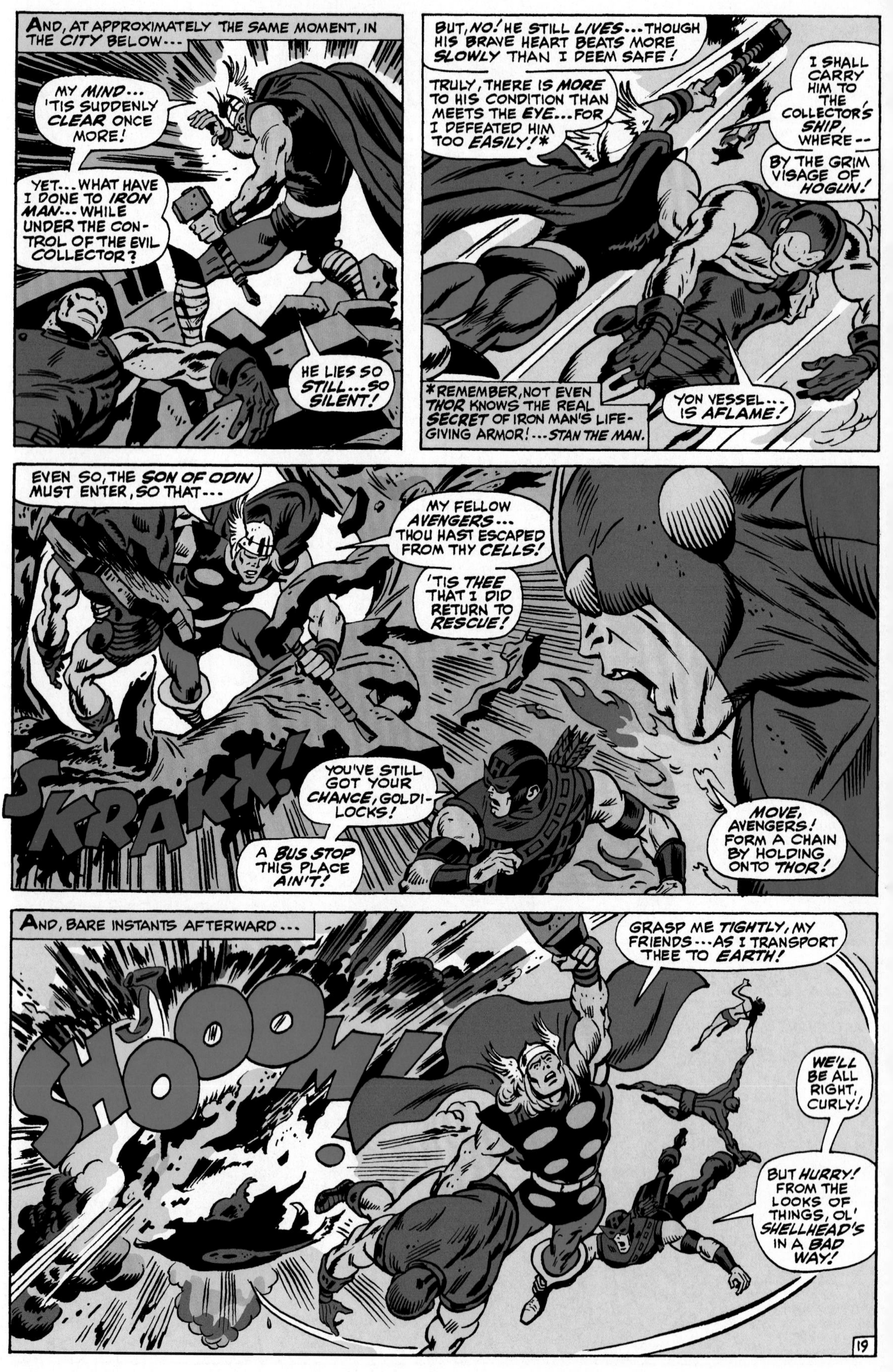

AND, AT APPROXIMATELY THE SAME MOMENT, IN THE CITY BELOW...
MY MIND... 'TIS SUDDENLY CLEAR ONCE MORE!
YET... WHAT HAVE I DONE TO IRON MAN... WHILE UNDER THE CONTROL OF THE EVIL COLLECTOR?
HE LIES SO STILL... SO SILENT!
BUT, NO! HE STILL LIVES... THOUGH HIS BRAVE HEART BEATS MORE SLOWLY THAN I DEEM SAFE!
TRULY, THERE IS MORE TO HIS CONDITION THAN MEETS THE EYE... FOR I DEFEATED HIM TOO EASILY!*
I SHALL CARRY HIM TO THE COLLECTOR'S SHIP, WHERE --
BY THE GRIM VISAGE OF HOGUN!
*REMEMBER, NOT EVEN THOR KNOWS THE REAL SECRET OF IRON MAN'S LIFE-GIVING ARMOR! ...STAN THE MAN.
YON VESSEL... IS AFLAME!
EVEN SO, THE SON OF ODIN MUST ENTER, SO THAT...
MY FELLOW AVENGERS... THOU HAST ESCAPED FROM THY CELLS!
'TIS THEE THAT I DID RETURN TO RESCUE!
SKRAKK!
YOU'VE STILL GOT YOUR CHANCE, GOLDILOCKS!
A BUS STOP THIS PLACE AIN'T!
MOVE, AVENGERS! FORM A CHAIN BY HOLDING ONTO THOR!
AND, BARE INSTANTS AFTERWARD...
GRASP ME TIGHTLY, MY FRIENDS... AS I TRANSPORT THEE TO EARTH!
SHOOM!
WE'LL BE ALL RIGHT, CURLY!
BUT HURRY! FROM THE LOOKS OF THINGS, OL' SHELLHEAD'S IN A BAD WAY!

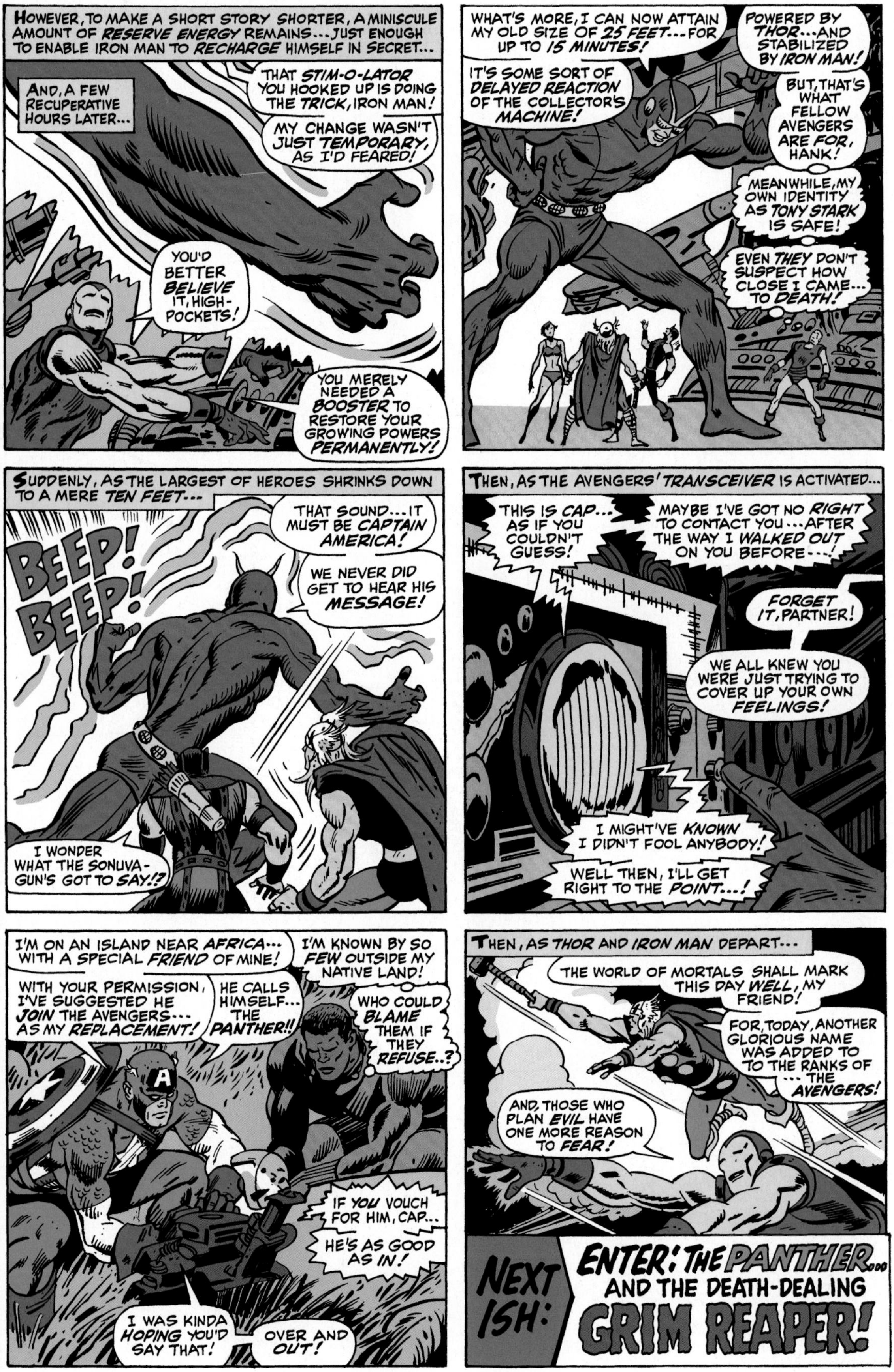
HOWEVER, TO MAKE A SHORT STORY SHORTER, A MINISCULE AMOUNT OF RESERVE ENERGY REMAINS... JUST ENOUGH TO ENABLE IRON MAN TO RECHARGE HIMSELF IN SECRET...
AND, A FEW RECUPERATIVE HOURS LATER...
THAT STIM-O-LATOR YOU HOOKED UP IS DOING THE TRICK, IRON MAN!
MY CHANGE WASN'T JUST TEMPORARY, AS I'D FEARED!
YOU'D BETTER BELIEVE IT, HIGH-POCKETS!
YOU MERELY NEEDED A BOOSTER TO RESTORE YOUR GROWING POWERS PERMANENTLY!
WHAT'S MORE, I CAN NOW ATTAIN MY OLD SIZE OF 25 FEET... FOR UP TO 15 MINUTES!
IT'S SOME SORT OF DELAYED REACTION OF THE COLLECTOR'S MACHINE!
POWERED BY THOR... AND STABILIZED BY IRON MAN!
BUT, THAT'S WHAT FELLOW AVENGERS ARE FOR, HANK!
MEANWHILE, MY OWN IDENTITY AS TONY STARK IS SAFE!
EVEN THEY DON'T SUSPECT HOW CLOSE I CAME... TO DEATH!
SUDDENLY, AS THE LARGEST OF HEROES SHRINKS DOWN TO A MERE TEN FEET...
THAT SOUND... IT MUST BE CAPTAIN AMERICA!
BEEP! BEEP!
WE NEVER DID GET TO HEAR HIS MESSAGE!
I WONDER WHAT THE SONUVA-GUN'S GOT TO SAY!?
THEN, AS THE AVENGERS' TRANSCEIVER IS ACTIVATED...
THIS IS CAP... AS IF YOU COULDN'T GUESS!
MAYBE I'VE GOT NO RIGHT TO CONTACT YOU... AFTER THE WAY I WALKED OUT ON YOU BEFORE...!
FORGET IT, PARTNER!
WE ALL KNEW YOU WERE JUST TRYING TO COVER UP YOUR OWN FEELINGS!
I MIGHT'VE KNOWN I DIDN'T FOOL ANYBODY!
WELL THEN, I'LL GET RIGHT TO THE POINT...!
I'M ON AN ISLAND NEAR AFRICA... WITH A SPECIAL FRIEND OF MINE!
I'M KNOWN BY SO FEW OUTSIDE MY NATIVE LAND!
WITH YOUR PERMISSION, I'VE SUGGESTED HE JOIN THE AVENGERS... AS MY REPLACEMENT!
HE CALLS HIMSELF... THE PANTHER!!
WHO COULD BLAME THEM IF THEY REFUSE..?
IF YOU VOUCH FOR HIM, CAP...
HE'S AS GOOD AS IN!
I WAS KINDA HOPING YOU'D SAY THAT!
OVER AND OUT!
THEN, AS THOR AND IRON MAN DEPART...
THE WORLD OF MORTALS SHALL MARK THIS DAY WELL, MY FRIEND!
FOR, TODAY, ANOTHER GLORIOUS NAME WAS ADDED TO THE RANKS OF ... THE AVENGERS!
AND, THOSE WHO PLAN EVIL HAVE ONE MORE REASON TO FEAR!
NEXT ISH:
ENTER: THE PANTHER... AND THE DEATH-DEALING GRIM REAPER!

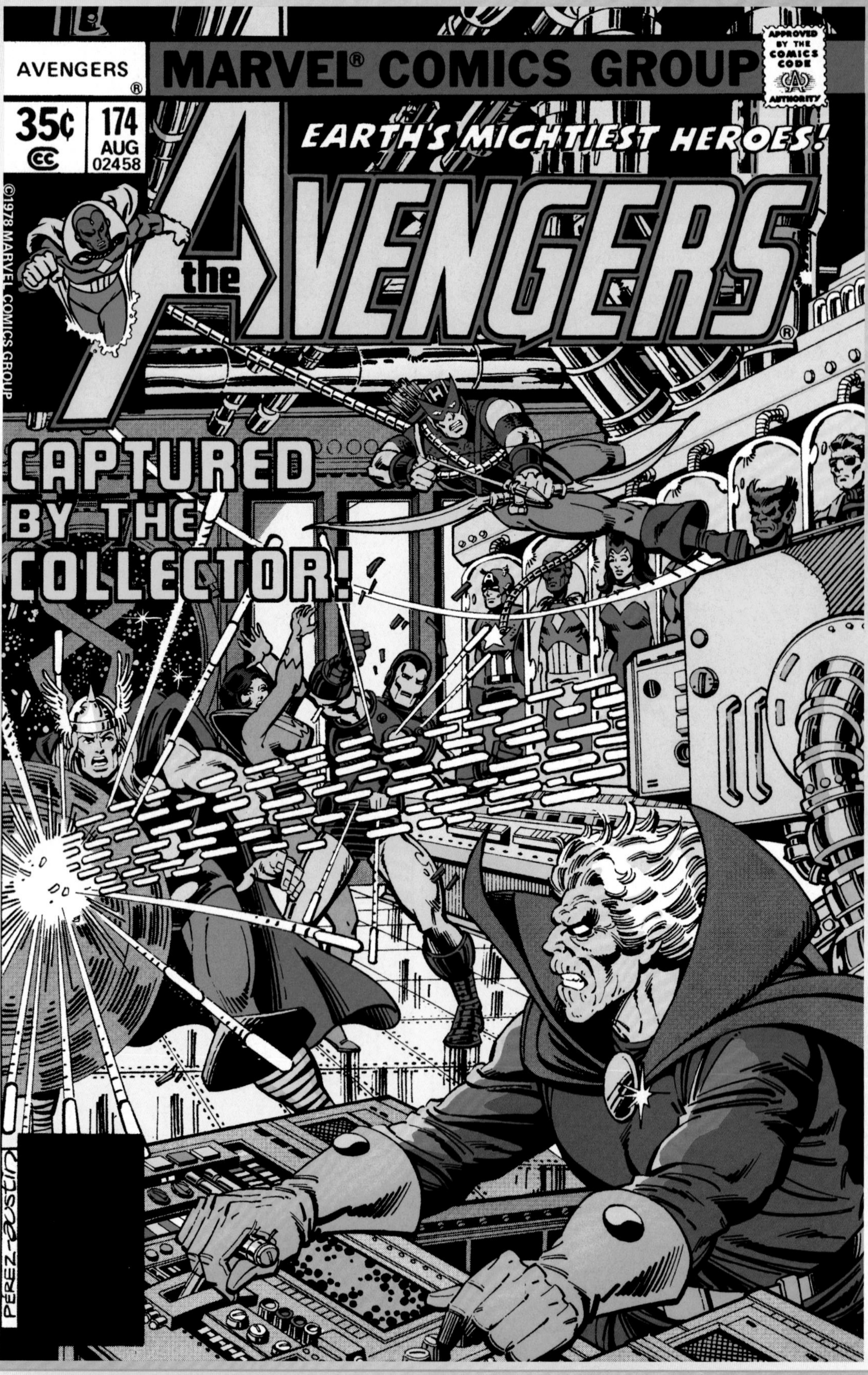
AVENGERS
MARVEL® COMICS GROUP
APPROVED BY THE COMICS CODE AUTHORITY
35¢
174
AUG
02458
EARTH'S MIGHTIEST HEROES!
the AVENGERS®
©1978 MARVEL COMICS GROUP
CAPTURED BY THE COLLECTOR!
PEREZ-AUSTIN

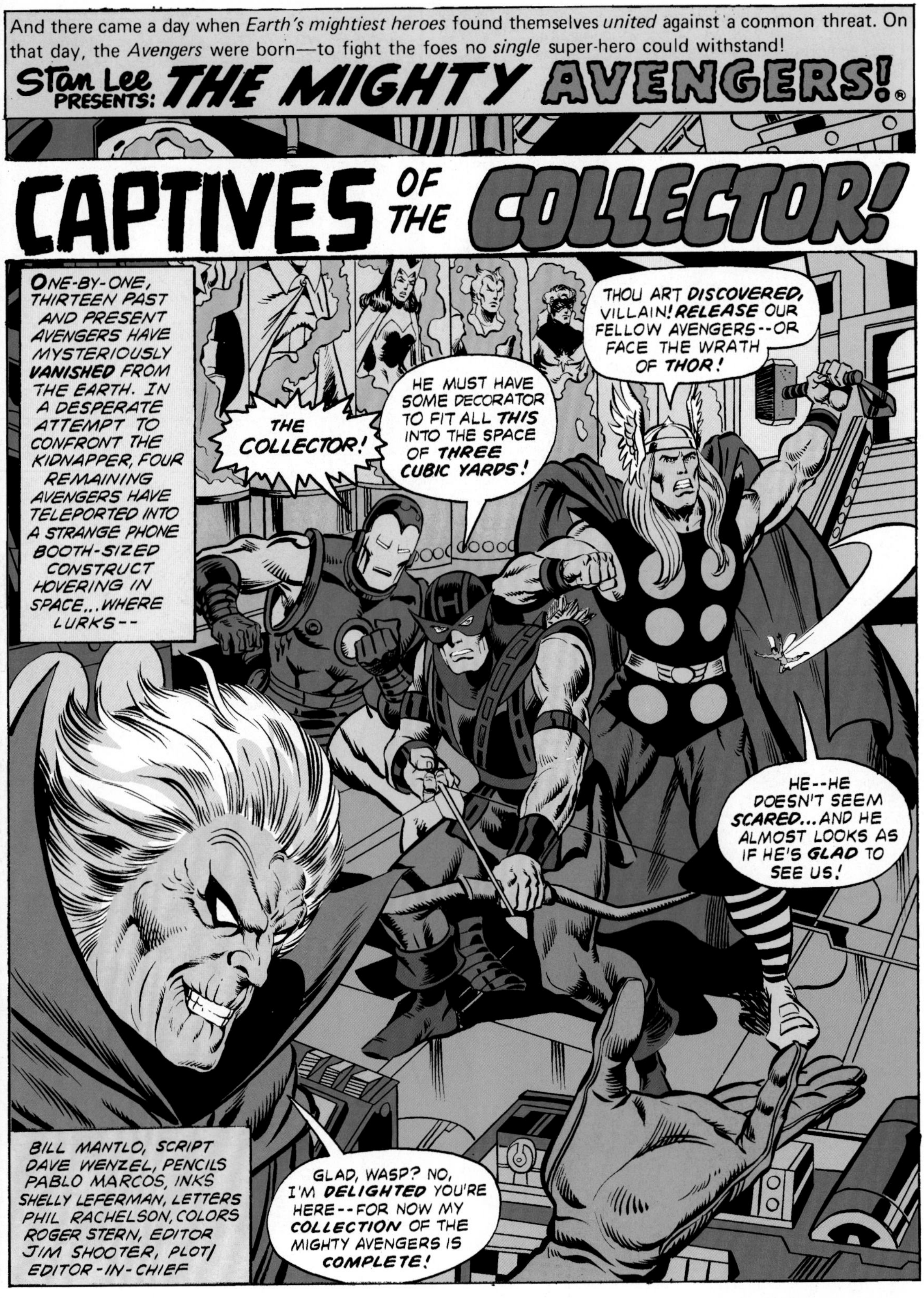

And there came a day when *Earth's mightiest heroes* found themselves *united* against a common threat. On that day, the *Avengers* were born—to fight the foes no *single* super-hero could withstand!
Stan Lee PRESENTS: THE MIGHTY AVENGERS!
CAPTIVES OF THE COLLECTOR!
ONE-BY-ONE, THIRTEEN PAST AND PRESENT AVENGERS HAVE MYSTERIOUSLY VANISHED FROM THE EARTH. IN A DESPERATE ATTEMPT TO CONFRONT THE KIDNAPPER, FOUR REMAINING AVENGERS HAVE TELEPORTED INTO A STRANGE PHONE BOOTH-SIZED CONSTRUCT HOVERING IN SPACE...WHERE LURKS--
THE COLLECTOR!
HE MUST HAVE SOME DECORATOR TO FIT ALL THIS INTO THE SPACE OF THREE CUBIC YARDS!
THOU ART DISCOVERED, VILLAIN! RELEASE OUR FELLOW AVENGERS--OR FACE THE WRATH OF THOR!
HE--HE DOESN'T SEEM SCARED...AND HE ALMOST LOOKS AS IF HE'S GLAD TO SEE US!
GLAD, WASP? NO, I'M DELIGHTED YOU'RE HERE--FOR NOW MY COLLECTION OF THE MIGHTY AVENGERS IS COMPLETE!
BILL MANTLO, SCRIPT
DAVE WENZEL, PENCILS
PABLO MARCOS, INKS
SHELLY LEFERMAN, LETTERS
PHIL RACHELSON, COLORS
ROGER STERN, EDITOR
JIM SHOOTER, PLOT/ EDITOR-IN-CHIEF

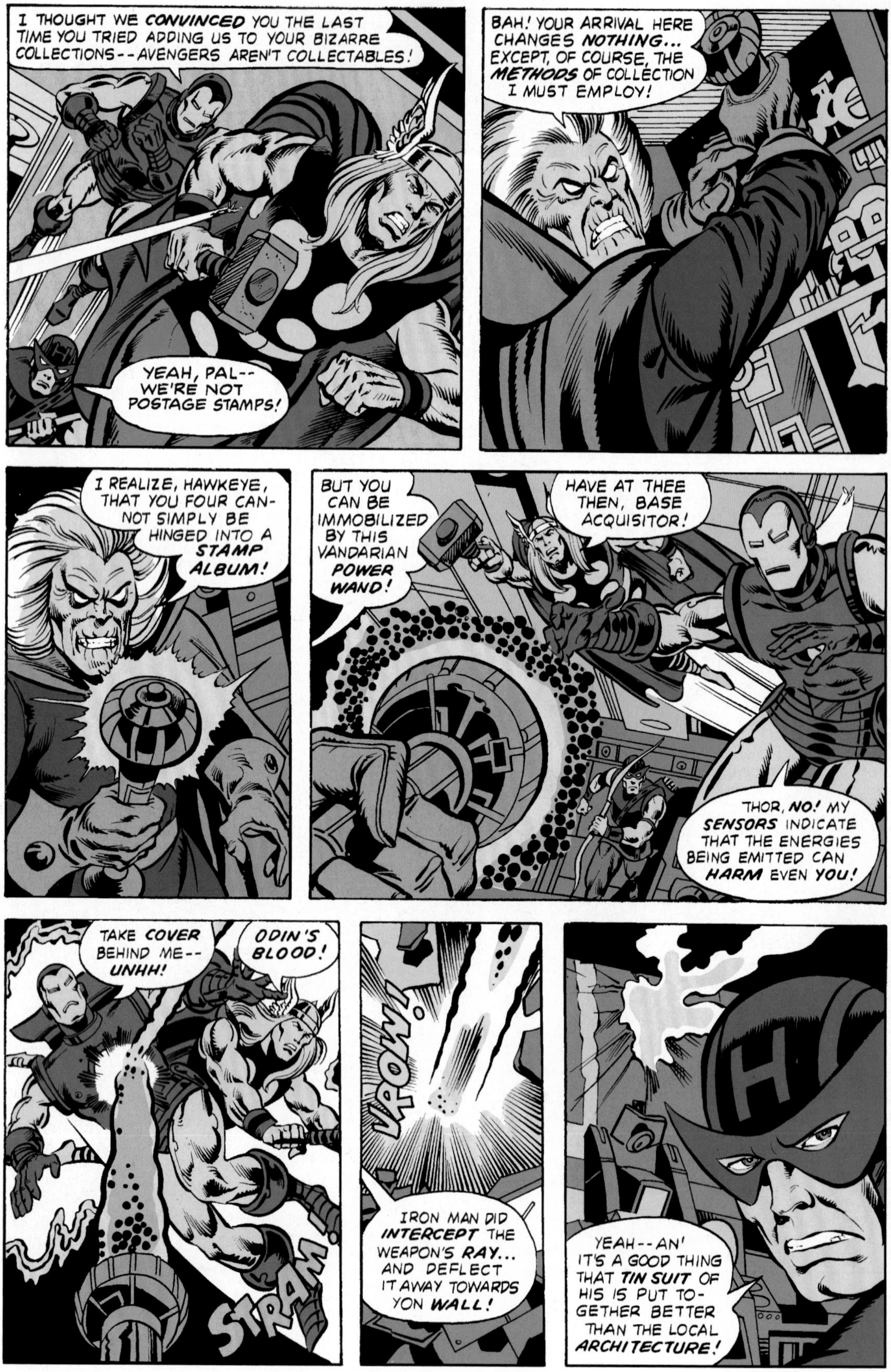
I THOUGHT WE CONVINCED YOU THE LAST TIME YOU TRIED ADDING US TO YOUR BIZARRE COLLECTIONS--AVENGERS AREN'T COLLECTABLES!
YEAH, PAL-- WE'RE NOT POSTAGE STAMPS!
BAH! YOUR ARRIVAL HERE CHANGES NOTHING... EXCEPT, OF COURSE, THE METHODS OF COLLECTION I MUST EMPLOY!
I REALIZE, HAWKEYE, THAT YOU FOUR CAN-NOT SIMPLY BE HINGED INTO A STAMP ALBUM!
BUT YOU CAN BE IMMOBILIZED BY THIS VANDARIAN POWER WAND!
HAVE AT THEE THEN, BASE ACQUISITOR!
THOR, NO! MY SENSORS INDICATE THAT THE ENERGIES BEING EMITTED CAN HARM EVEN YOU!
TAKE COVER BEHIND ME-- UNHH!
ODIN'S BLOOD!
STRAM
VROW!
IRON MAN DID INTERCEPT THE WEAPON'S RAY... AND DEFLECT IT AWAY TOWARDS YON WALL!
YEAH--AN' IT'S A GOOD THING THAT TIN SUIT OF HIS IS PUT TO-GETHER BETTER THAN THE LOCAL ARCHITECTURE!

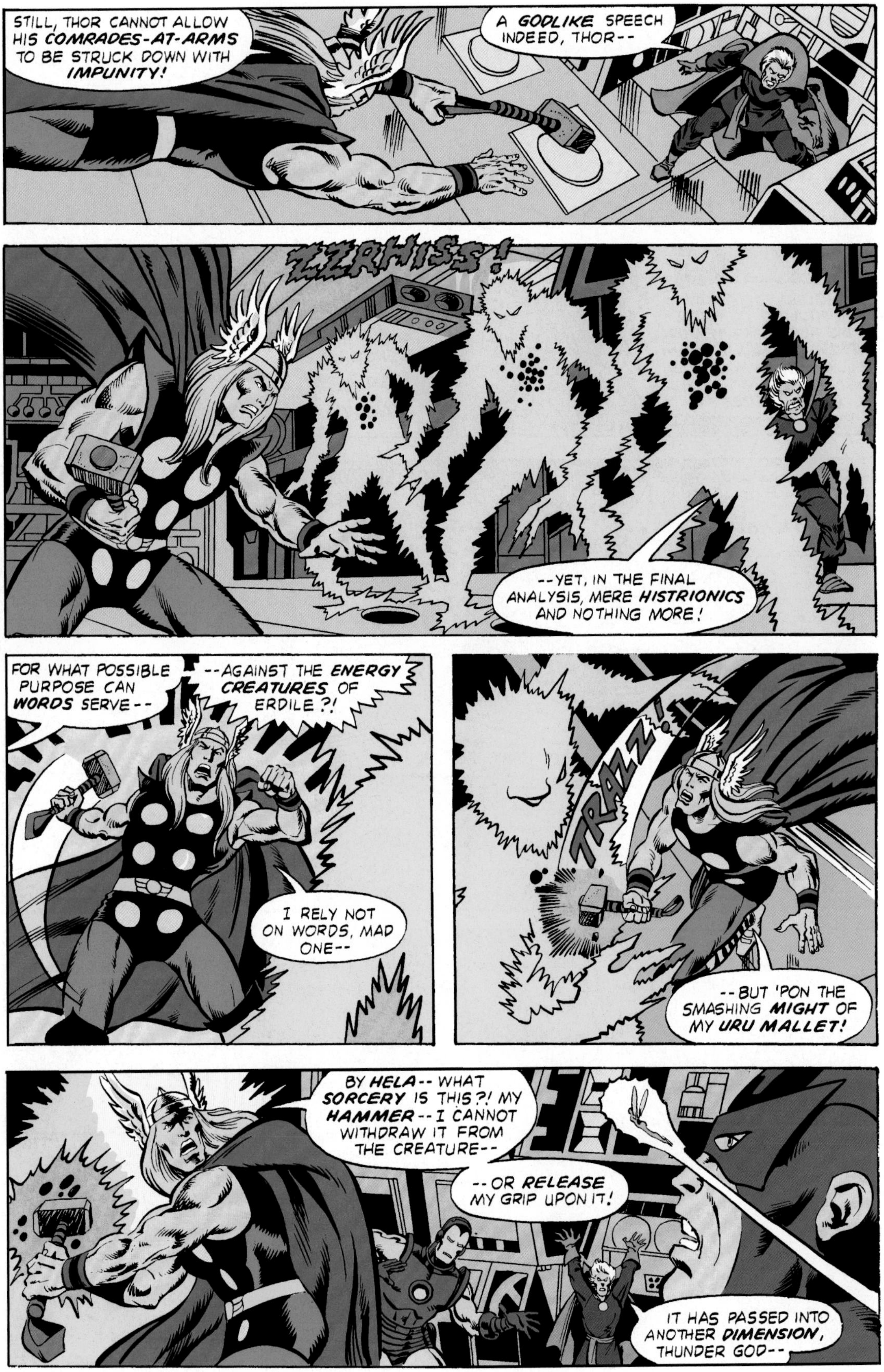
STILL, THOR CANNOT ALLOW HIS **COMRADES-AT-ARMS** TO BE STRUCK DOWN WITH **IMPUNITY!**
A **GODLIKE** SPEECH INDEED, THOR--
ZZRHISSS!
--YET, IN THE FINAL ANALYSIS, MERE **HISTRIONICS** AND NOTHING MORE!
FOR WHAT POSSIBLE PURPOSE CAN **WORDS** SERVE--
--AGAINST THE **ENERGY CREATURES** OF ERDILE?!
I RELY NOT ON WORDS, MAD ONE--
TRAZZ!
--BUT 'PON THE SMASHING **MIGHT** OF MY **URU MALLET!**
BY **HELA**-- WHAT **SORCERY** IS THIS?! MY **HAMMER**-- I CANNOT WITHDRAW IT FROM THE CREATURE--
--OR **RELEASE** MY GRIP UPON IT!
IT HAS PASSED INTO ANOTHER **DIMENSION**, THUNDER GOD--

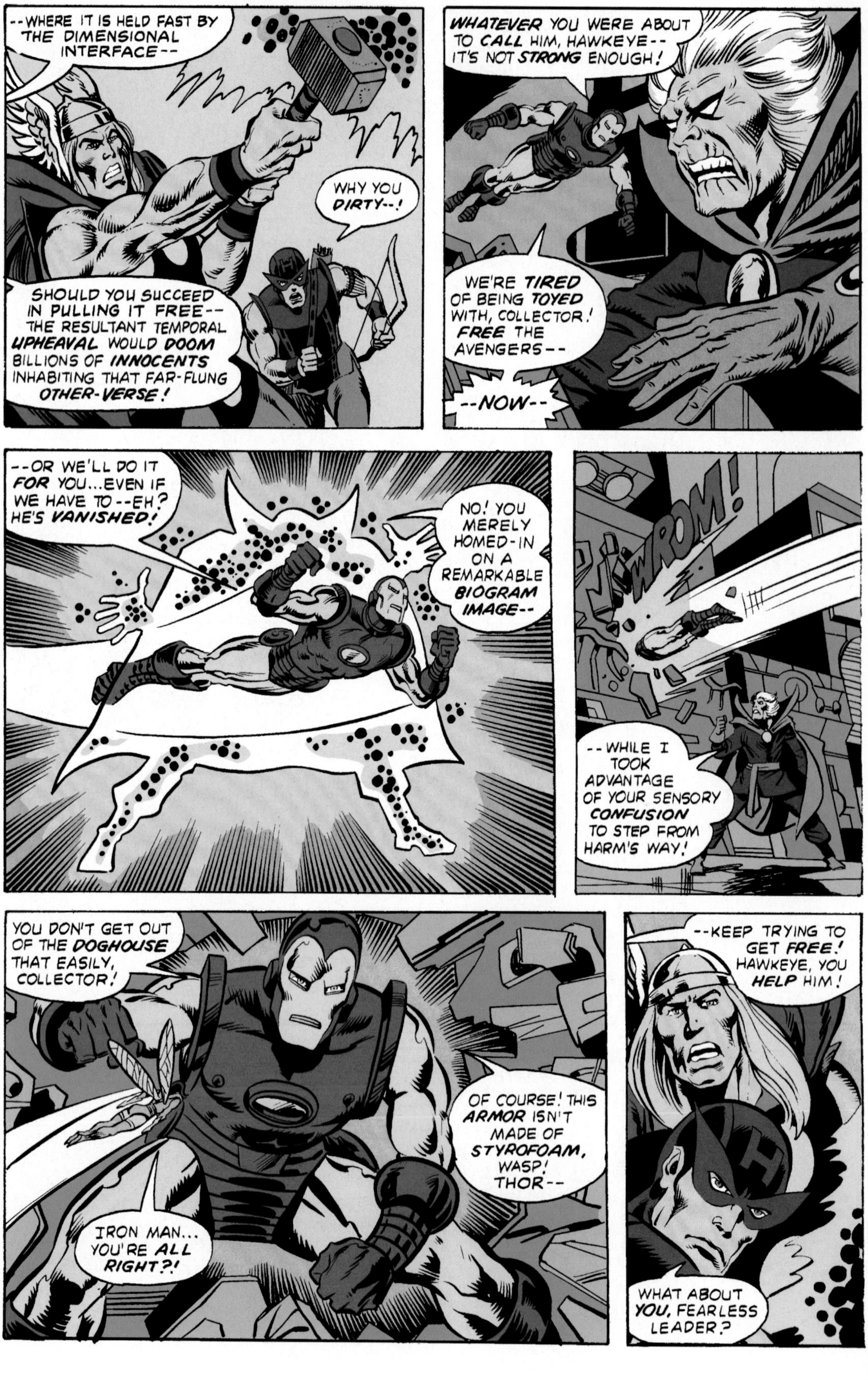
--WHERE IT IS HELD FAST BY THE DIMENSIONAL INTERFACE--
SHOULD YOU SUCCEED IN PULLING IT FREE-- THE RESULTANT TEMPORAL UPHEAVAL WOULD DOOM BILLIONS OF INNOCENTS INHABITING THAT FAR-FLUNG OTHER-VERSE!
WHY YOU DIRTY--!
WHATEVER YOU WERE ABOUT TO CALL HIM, HAWKEYE-- IT'S NOT STRONG ENOUGH!
WE'RE TIRED OF BEING TOYED WITH, COLLECTOR! FREE THE AVENGERS--
--NOW--
--OR WE'LL DO IT FOR YOU...EVEN IF WE HAVE TO--EH? HE'S VANISHED!
NO! YOU MERELY HOMED-IN ON A REMARKABLE BIOGRAM IMAGE--
WROM!
--WHILE I TOOK ADVANTAGE OF YOUR SENSORY CONFUSION TO STEP FROM HARM'S WAY!
YOU DON'T GET OUT OF THE DOGHOUSE THAT EASILY, COLLECTOR!
IRON MAN... YOU'RE ALL RIGHT?!
OF COURSE! THIS ARMOR ISN'T MADE OF STYROFOAM, WASP! THOR--
--KEEP TRYING TO GET FREE! HAWKEYE, YOU HELP HIM!
WHAT ABOUT YOU, FEARLESS LEADER?

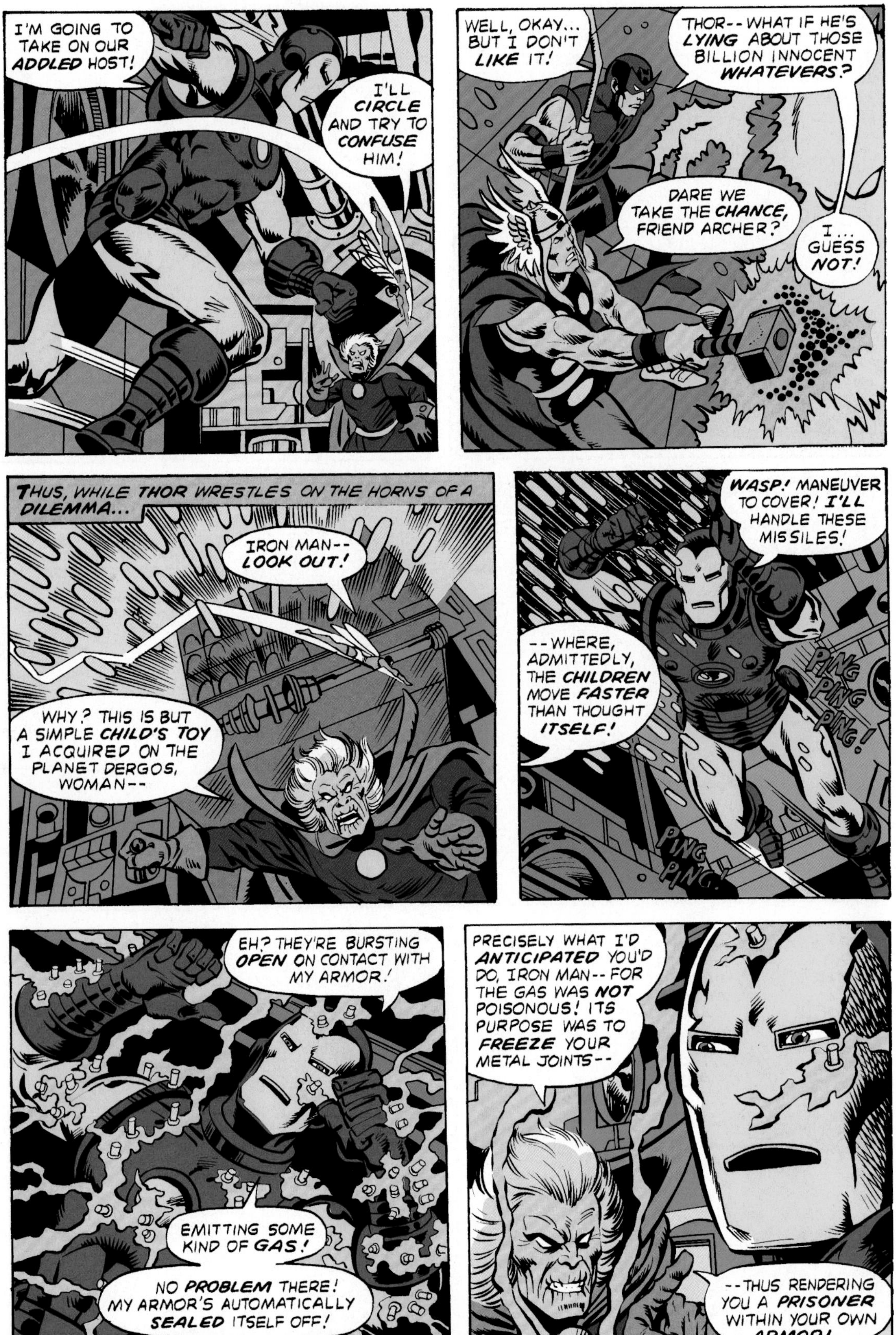
I'M GOING TO TAKE ON OUR ADDLED HOST!
I'LL CIRCLE AND TRY TO CONFUSE HIM!
WELL, OKAY... BUT I DON'T LIKE IT!
THOR-- WHAT IF HE'S LYING ABOUT THOSE BILLION INNOCENT WHATEVERS?
DARE WE TAKE THE CHANCE, FRIEND ARCHER?
I... GUESS NOT!
THUS, WHILE THOR WRESTLES ON THE HORNS OF A DILEMMA...
IRON MAN-- LOOK OUT!
WHY? THIS IS BUT A SIMPLE CHILD'S TOY I ACQUIRED ON THE PLANET DERGOS, WOMAN--
WASP! MANEUVER TO COVER! I'LL HANDLE THESE MISSILES!
--WHERE, ADMITTEDLY, THE CHILDREN MOVE FASTER THAN THOUGHT ITSELF!
PING PING PING!
PING PING!
EH? THEY'RE BURSTING OPEN ON CONTACT WITH MY ARMOR!
EMITTING SOME KIND OF GAS!
NO PROBLEM THERE! MY ARMOR'S AUTOMATICALLY SEALED ITSELF OFF!
PRECISELY WHAT I'D ANTICIPATED YOU'D DO, IRON MAN-- FOR THE GAS WAS NOT POISONOUS! ITS PURPOSE WAS TO FREEZE YOUR METAL JOINTS--
--THUS RENDERING YOU A PRISONER WITHIN YOUR OWN ARMOR!

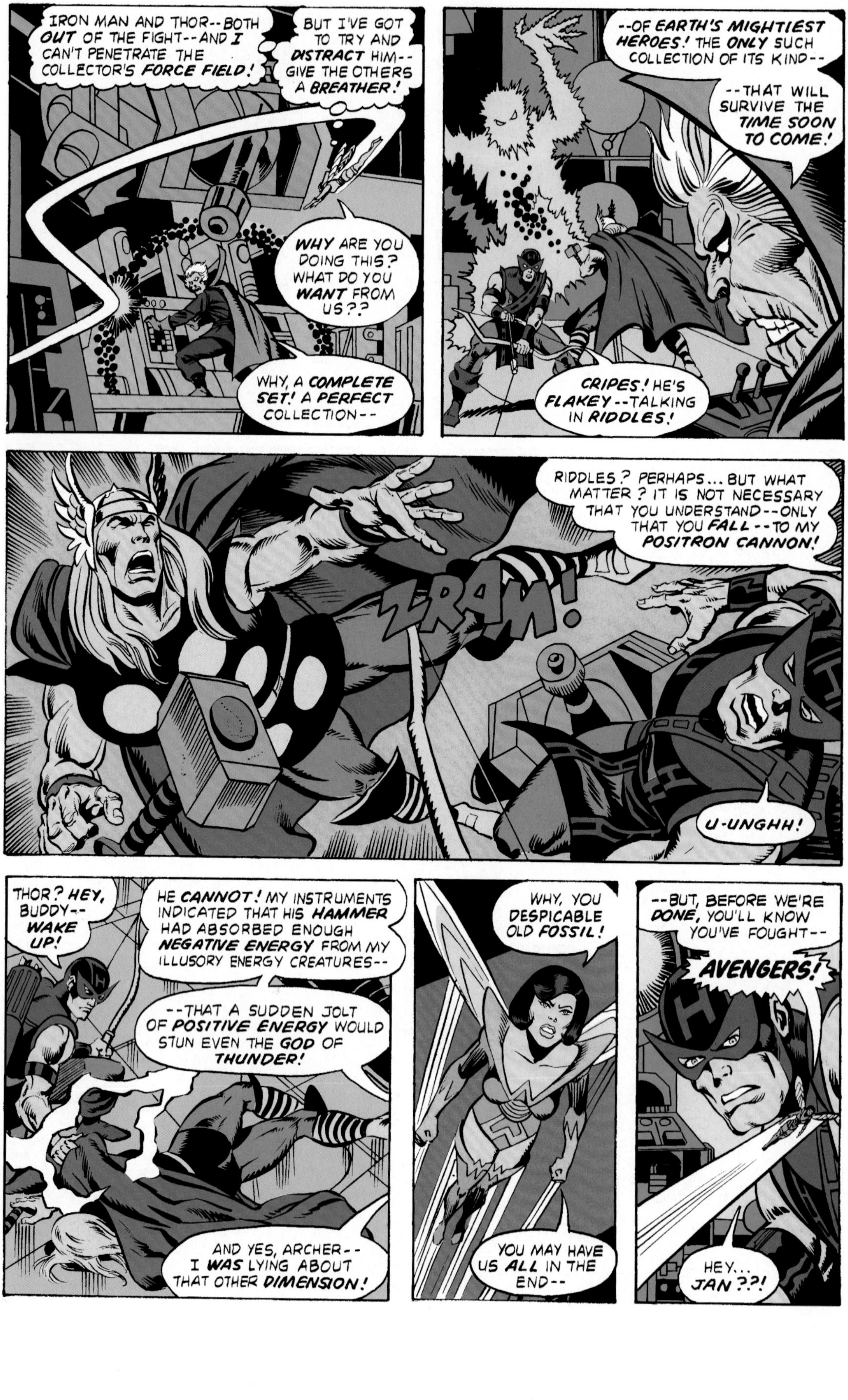
IRON MAN AND THOR--BOTH **OUT** OF THE FIGHT--AND **I** CAN'T PENETRATE THE COLLECTOR'S **FORCE FIELD**!
BUT I'VE GOT TO TRY AND **DISTRACT** HIM--GIVE THE OTHERS A **BREATHER**!
WHY ARE YOU DOING THIS? WHAT DO YOU **WANT** FROM US??
WHY, A **COMPLETE SET**! A **PERFECT** COLLECTION--
--OF **EARTH'S MIGHTIEST HEROES**! THE **ONLY** SUCH COLLECTION OF ITS KIND--
--THAT WILL SURVIVE THE **TIME SOON TO COME**!
CRIPES! HE'S **FLAKEY**--TALKING IN **RIDDLES**!
RIDDLES? PERHAPS... BUT WHAT MATTER? IT IS NOT NECESSARY THAT YOU UNDERSTAND--ONLY THAT YOU **FALL**--TO MY **POSITRON CANNON**!
ZRAM!
U-UNGHH!
THOR? **HEY**, BUDDY--**WAKE UP**!
HE **CANNOT**! MY INSTRUMENTS INDICATED THAT HIS **HAMMER** HAD ABSORBED ENOUGH **NEGATIVE ENERGY** FROM MY ILLUSORY ENERGY CREATURES--
--THAT A SUDDEN JOLT OF **POSITIVE ENERGY** WOULD STUN EVEN THE **GOD OF THUNDER**!
AND YES, ARCHER--I **WAS** LYING ABOUT THAT OTHER **DIMENSION**!
WHY, YOU DESPICABLE OLD **FOSSIL**!
YOU MAY HAVE US **ALL** IN THE END--
--BUT, BEFORE WE'RE **DONE**, YOU'LL KNOW YOU'VE FOUGHT--
AVENGERS!
HEY... **JAN**??!

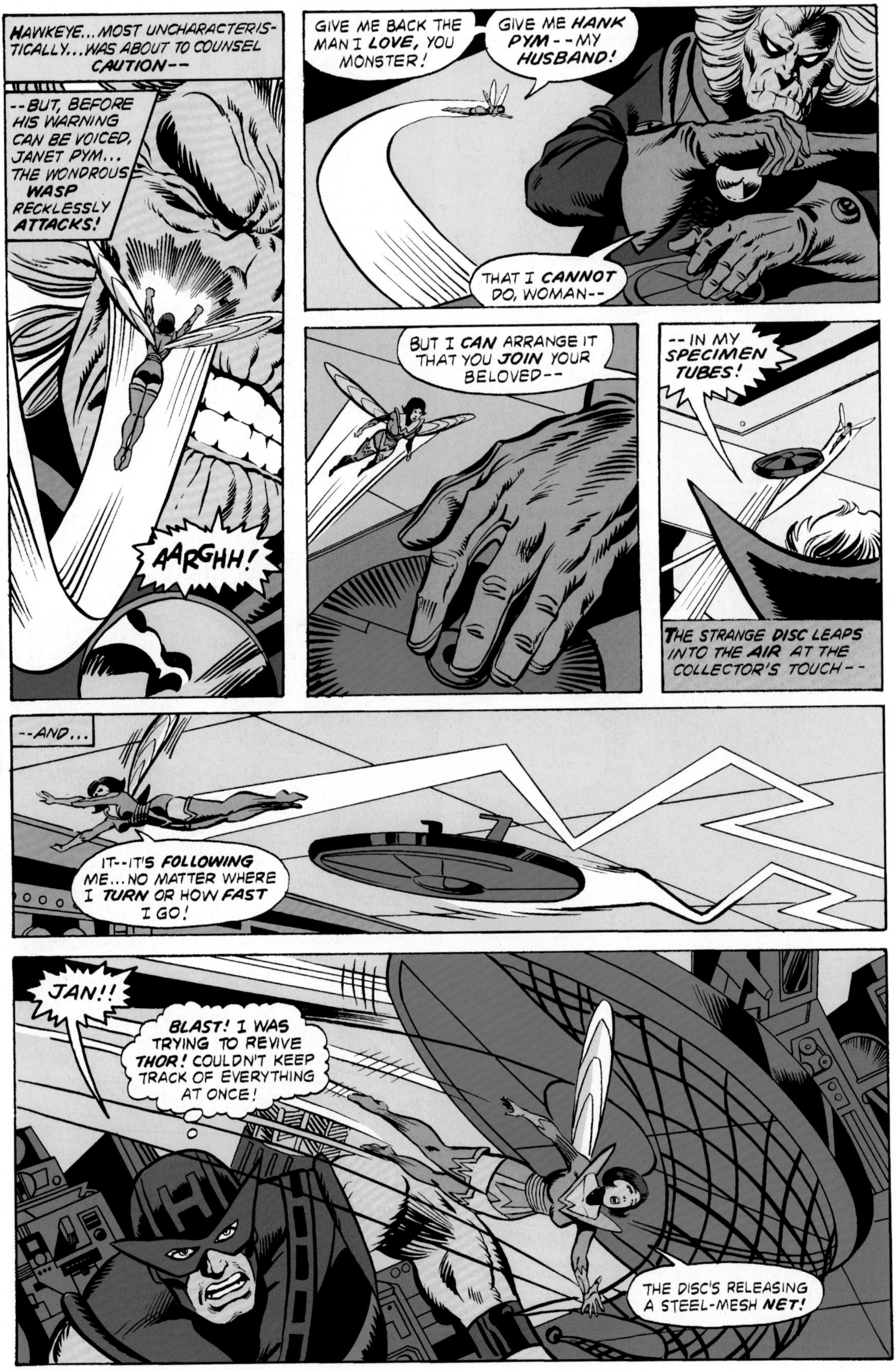
HAWKEYE... MOST UNCHARACTERISTICALLY... WAS ABOUT TO COUNSEL CAUTION--
--BUT, BEFORE HIS WARNING CAN BE VOICED, JANET PYM... THE WONDROUS WASP RECKLESSLY ATTACKS!
AARGHH!
GIVE ME BACK THE MAN I LOVE, YOU MONSTER!
GIVE ME HANK PYM--MY HUSBAND!
THAT I CANNOT DO, WOMAN--
BUT I CAN ARRANGE IT THAT YOU JOIN YOUR BELOVED--
--IN MY SPECIMEN TUBES!
THE STRANGE DISC LEAPS INTO THE AIR AT THE COLLECTOR'S TOUCH--
--AND...
IT--IT'S FOLLOWING ME... NO MATTER WHERE I TURN OR HOW FAST I GO!
JAN!!
BLAST! I WAS TRYING TO REVIVE THOR! COULDN'T KEEP TRACK OF EVERYTHING AT ONCE!
THE DISC'S RELEASING A STEEL-MESH NET!

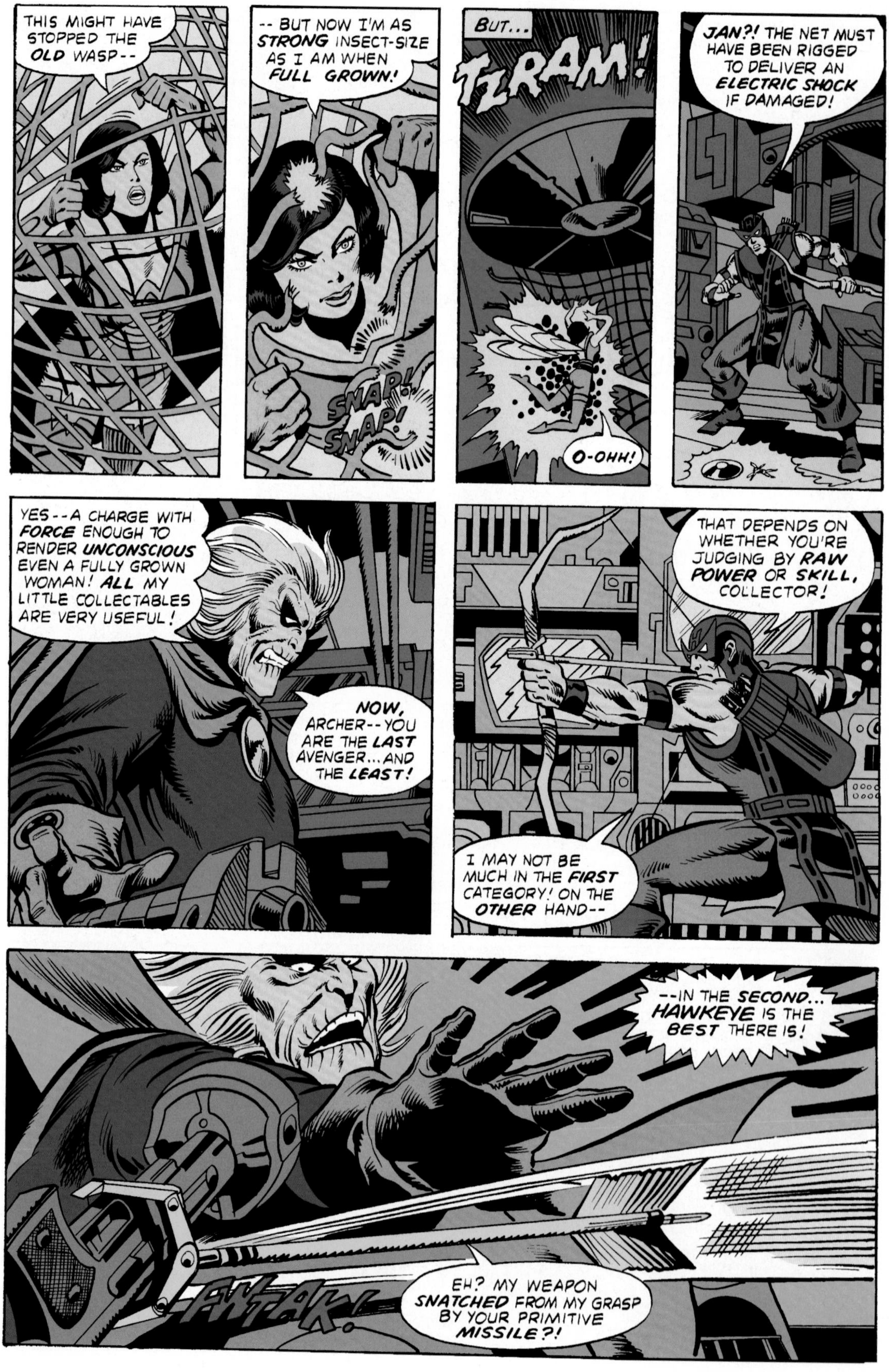
THIS MIGHT HAVE STOPPED THE OLD WASP--
-- BUT NOW I'M AS STRONG INSECT-SIZE AS I AM WHEN FULL GROWN!
SNAP! SNAP!
BUT...
TZRAM!
O-OHH!
JAN?! THE NET MUST HAVE BEEN RIGGED TO DELIVER AN ELECTRIC SHOCK IF DAMAGED!
YES--A CHARGE WITH FORCE ENOUGH TO RENDER UNCONSCIOUS EVEN A FULLY GROWN WOMAN! ALL MY LITTLE COLLECTABLES ARE VERY USEFUL!
NOW, ARCHER--YOU ARE THE LAST AVENGER...AND THE LEAST!
THAT DEPENDS ON WHETHER YOU'RE JUDGING BY RAW POWER OR SKILL, COLLECTOR!
I MAY NOT BE MUCH IN THE FIRST CATEGORY! ON THE OTHER HAND--
--IN THE SECOND... HAWKEYE IS THE BEST THERE IS!
FWTAK!
EH? MY WEAPON SNATCHED FROM MY GRASP BY YOUR PRIMITIVE MISSILE?!

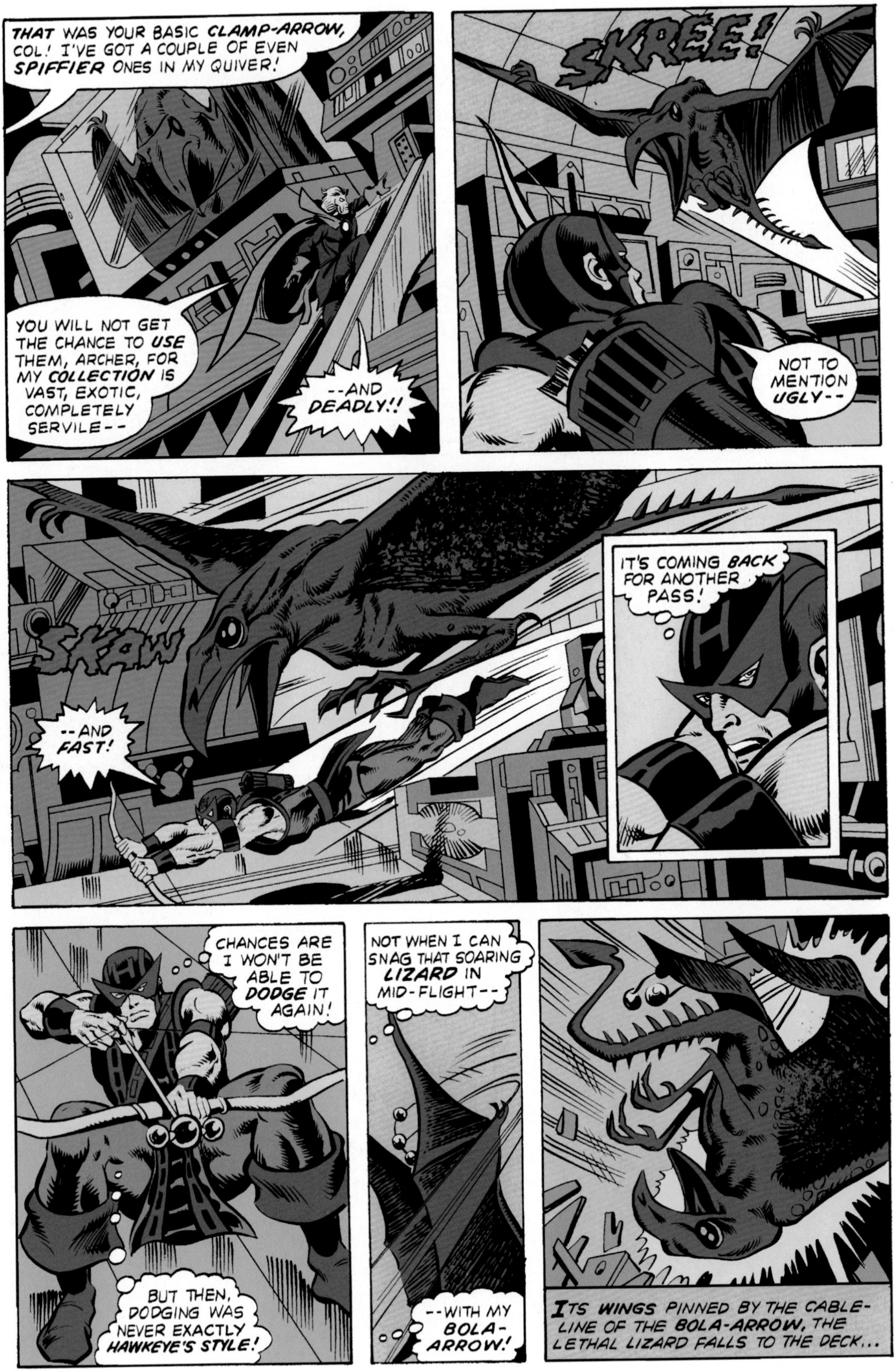

THAT WAS YOUR BASIC CLAMP-ARROW, COL! I'VE GOT A COUPLE OF EVEN SPIFFIER ONES IN MY QUIVER!
YOU WILL NOT GET THE CHANCE TO USE THEM, ARCHER, FOR MY COLLECTION IS VAST, EXOTIC, COMPLETELY SERVILE--
--AND DEADLY!!
SKREE!
NOT TO MENTION UGLY--
SKAW
--AND FAST!
IT'S COMING BACK FOR ANOTHER PASS!
CHANCES ARE I WON'T BE ABLE TO DODGE IT AGAIN!
BUT THEN, DODGING WAS NEVER EXACTLY HAWKEYE'S STYLE!
NOT WHEN I CAN SNAG THAT SOARING LIZARD IN MID-FLIGHT--
--WITH MY BOLA-ARROW!
ITS WINGS PINNED BY THE CABLE-LINE OF THE BOLA-ARROW, THE LETHAL LIZARD FALLS TO THE DECK...

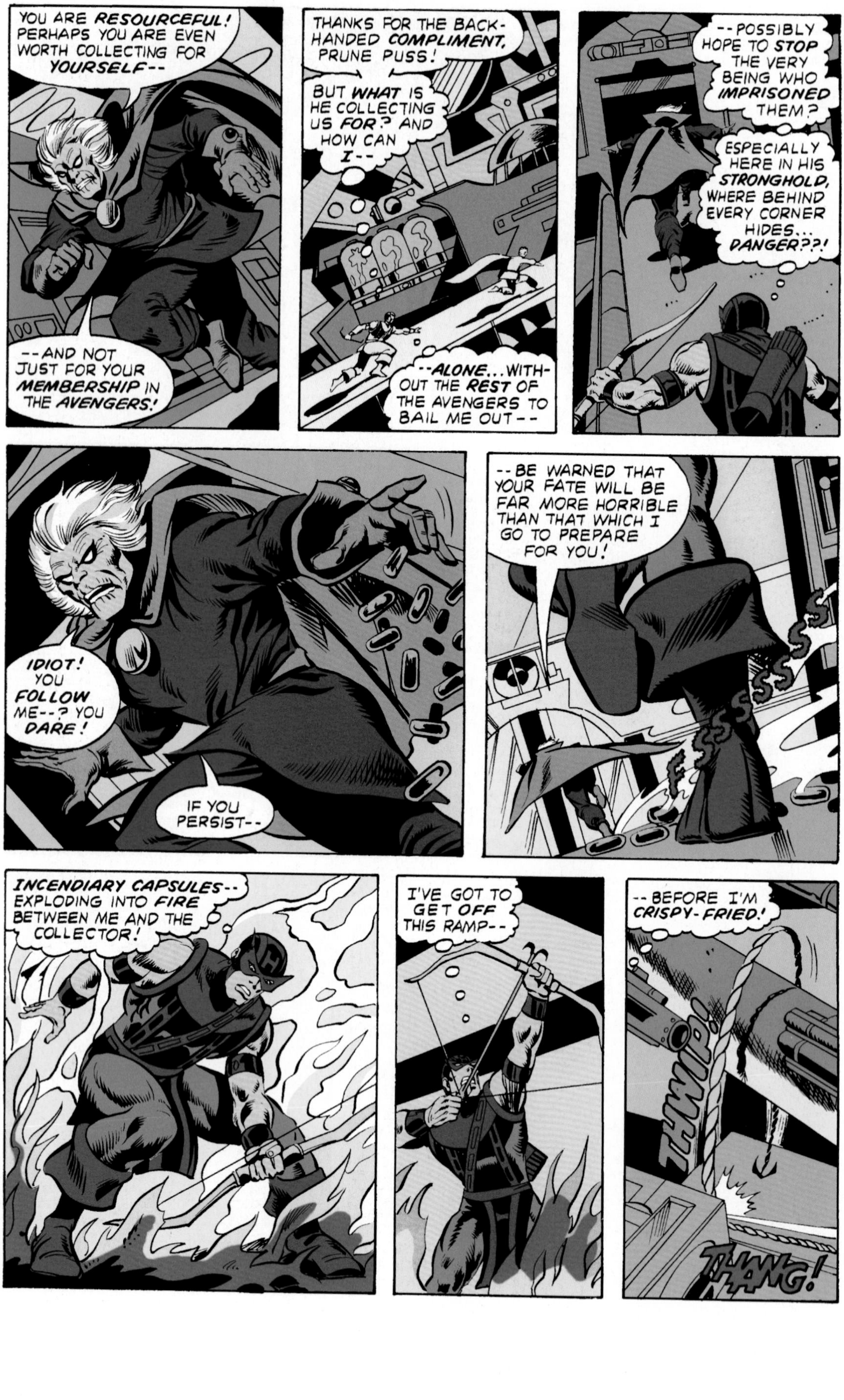

YOU ARE RESOURCEFUL! PERHAPS YOU ARE EVEN WORTH COLLECTING FOR YOURSELF--
--AND NOT JUST FOR YOUR MEMBERSHIP IN THE AVENGERS!
THANKS FOR THE BACK-HANDED COMPLIMENT, PRUNE PUSS!
BUT WHAT IS HE COLLECTING US FOR? AND HOW CAN I--
--ALONE...WITH-OUT THE REST OF THE AVENGERS TO BAIL ME OUT--
--POSSIBLY HOPE TO STOP THE VERY BEING WHO IMPRISONED THEM?
ESPECIALLY HERE IN HIS STRONGHOLD, WHERE BEHIND EVERY CORNER HIDES... DANGER??!
IDIOT! YOU FOLLOW ME--? YOU DARE!
IF YOU PERSIST--
--BE WARNED THAT YOUR FATE WILL BE FAR MORE HORRIBLE THAN THAT WHICH I GO TO PREPARE FOR YOU!
INCENDIARY CAPSULES--EXPLODING INTO FIRE BETWEEN ME AND THE COLLECTOR!
I'VE GOT TO GET OFF THIS RAMP--
--BEFORE I'M CRISPY-FRIED!
THWIP!
THANG!

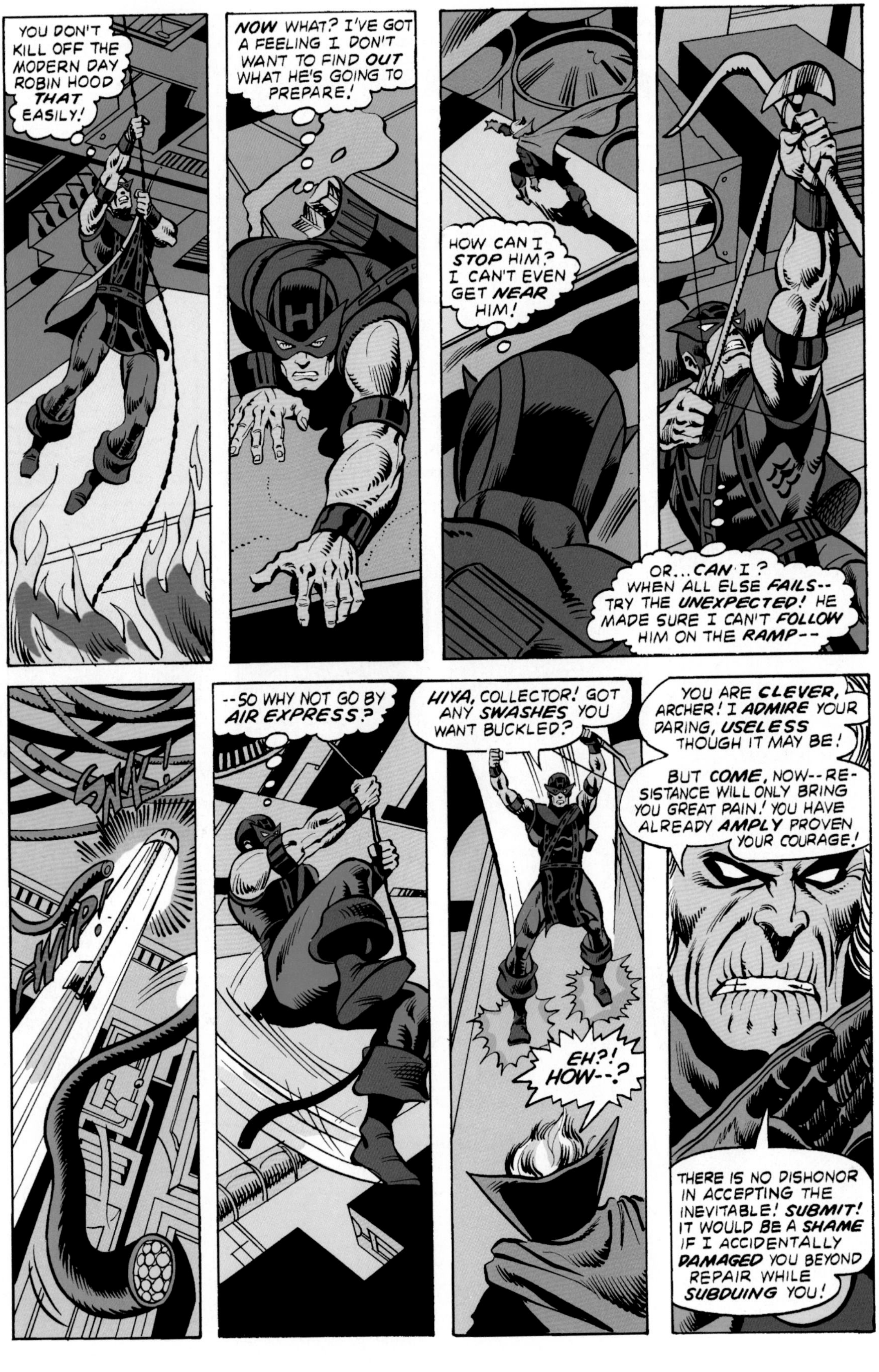
YOU DON'T KILL OFF THE MODERN DAY ROBIN HOOD THAT EASILY!
NOW WHAT? I'VE GOT A FEELING I DON'T WANT TO FIND OUT WHAT HE'S GOING TO PREPARE!
HOW CAN I STOP HIM? I CAN'T EVEN GET NEAR HIM!
OR... CAN I? WHEN ALL ELSE FAILS-- TRY THE UNEXPECTED! HE MADE SURE I CAN'T FOLLOW HIM ON THE RAMP--
SNK!
FWIP!
--SO WHY NOT GO BY AIR EXPRESS?
HIYA, COLLECTOR! GOT ANY SWASHES YOU WANT BUCKLED?
EH?! HOW--?
YOU ARE CLEVER, ARCHER! I ADMIRE YOUR DARING, USELESS THOUGH IT MAY BE!
BUT COME, NOW--RE-SISTANCE WILL ONLY BRING YOU GREAT PAIN! YOU HAVE ALREADY AMPLY PROVEN YOUR COURAGE!
THERE IS NO DISHONOR IN ACCEPTING THE INEVITABLE! SUBMIT! IT WOULD BE A SHAME IF I ACCIDENTALLY DAMAGED YOU BEYOND REPAIR WHILE SUBDUING YOU!

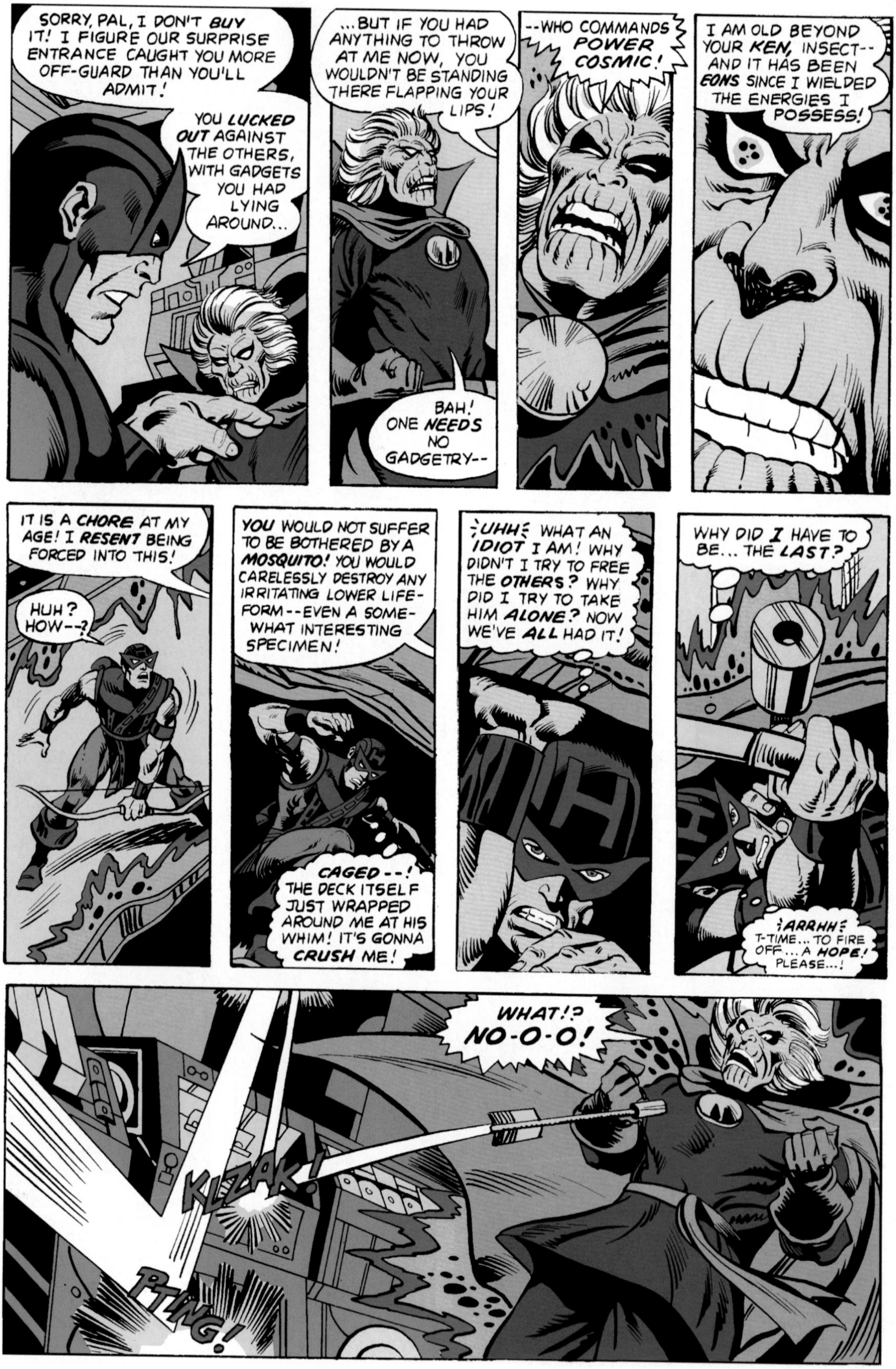
SORRY, PAL, I DON'T BUY IT! I FIGURE OUR SURPRISE ENTRANCE CAUGHT YOU MORE OFF-GUARD THAN YOU'LL ADMIT!
YOU LUCKED OUT AGAINST THE OTHERS, WITH GADGETS YOU HAD LYING AROUND...
...BUT IF YOU HAD ANYTHING TO THROW AT ME NOW, YOU WOULDN'T BE STANDING THERE FLAPPING YOUR LIPS!
BAH! ONE NEEDS NO GADGETRY--
--WHO COMMANDS POWER COSMIC!
I AM OLD BEYOND YOUR KEN, INSECT--AND IT HAS BEEN EONS SINCE I WIELDED THE ENERGIES I POSSESS!
IT IS A CHORE AT MY AGE! I RESENT BEING FORCED INTO THIS!
HUH? HOW--?
YOU WOULD NOT SUFFER TO BE BOTHERED BY A MOSQUITO! YOU WOULD CARELESSLY DESTROY ANY IRRITATING LOWER LIFE-FORM--EVEN A SOMEWHAT INTERESTING SPECIMEN!
CAGED--! THE DECK ITSELF JUST WRAPPED AROUND ME AT HIS WHIM! IT'S GONNA CRUSH ME!
UHH! WHAT AN IDIOT I AM! WHY DIDN'T I TRY TO FREE THE OTHERS? WHY DID I TRY TO TAKE HIM ALONE? NOW WE'VE ALL HAD IT!
WHY DID I HAVE TO BE... THE LAST?
ARRHH! T-TIME... TO FIRE OFF... A HOPE! PLEASE...!
WHAT!? NO-O-O!
KLZAK!
PTING!

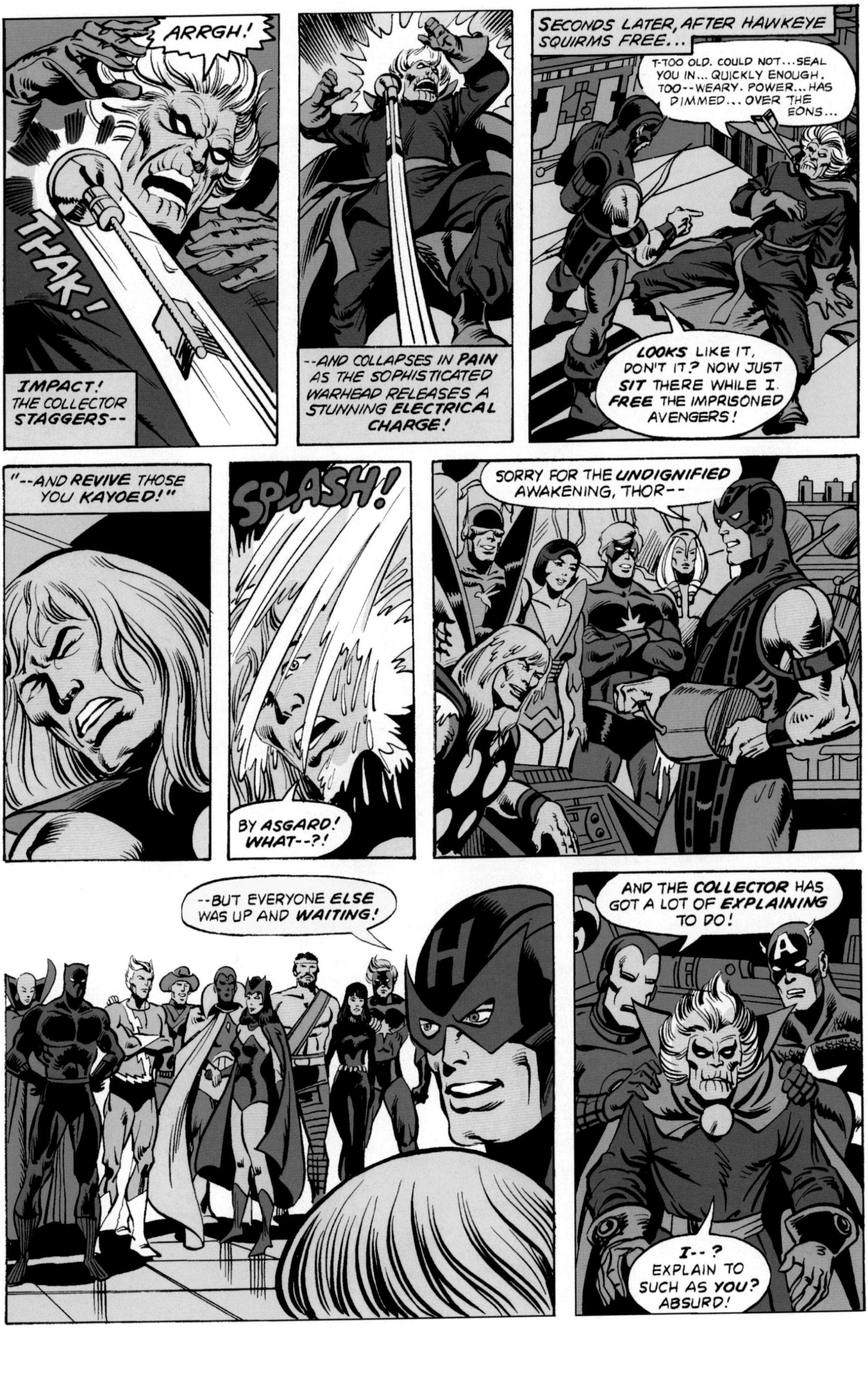
ARRGH!
THAK!
IMPACT! THE COLLECTOR STAGGERS--
--AND COLLAPSES IN PAIN AS THE SOPHISTICATED WARHEAD RELEASES A STUNNING ELECTRICAL CHARGE!
SECONDS LATER, AFTER HAWKEYE SQUIRMS FREE...
T-TOO OLD. COULD NOT...SEAL YOU IN... QUICKLY ENOUGH. TOO--WEARY. POWER...HAS DIMMED... OVER THE EONS...
LOOKS LIKE IT, DON'T IT? NOW JUST SIT THERE WHILE I. FREE THE IMPRISONED AVENGERS!
"--AND REVIVE THOSE YOU KAYOED!"
SPLASH!
BY ASGARD! WHAT--?!
SORRY FOR THE UNDIGNIFIED AWAKENING, THOR--
--BUT EVERYONE ELSE WAS UP AND WAITING!
AND THE COLLECTOR HAS GOT A LOT OF EXPLAINING TO DO!
I--? EXPLAIN TO SUCH AS YOU? ABSURD!

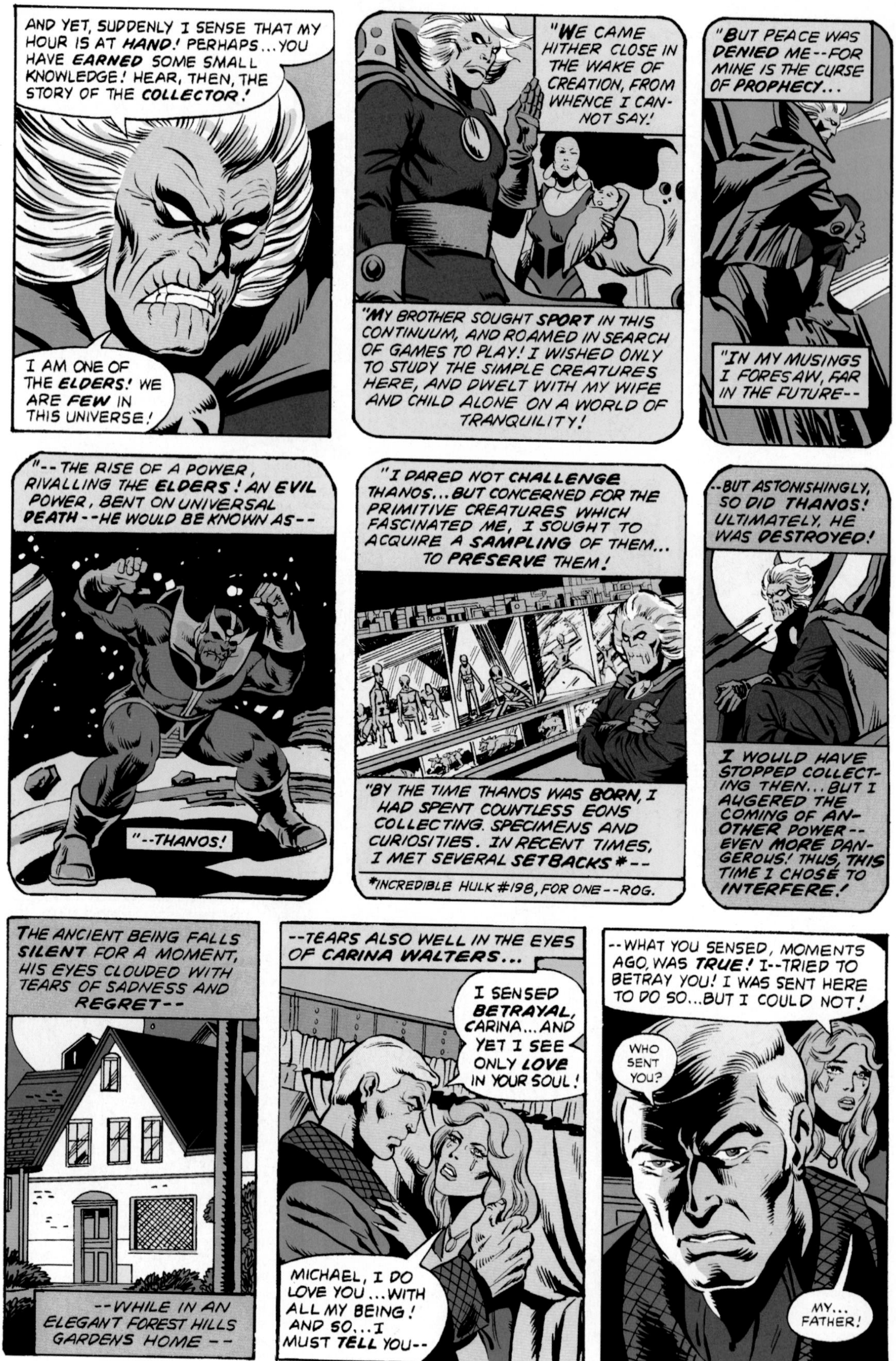
AND YET, SUDDENLY I SENSE THAT MY HOUR IS AT HAND! PERHAPS...YOU HAVE EARNED SOME SMALL KNOWLEDGE! HEAR, THEN, THE STORY OF THE COLLECTOR!
I AM ONE OF THE ELDERS! WE ARE FEW IN THIS UNIVERSE!
"WE CAME HITHER CLOSE IN THE WAKE OF CREATION, FROM WHENCE I CAN-NOT SAY!
"MY BROTHER SOUGHT SPORT IN THIS CONTINUUM, AND ROAMED IN SEARCH OF GAMES TO PLAY! I WISHED ONLY TO STUDY THE SIMPLE CREATURES HERE, AND DWELT WITH MY WIFE AND CHILD ALONE ON A WORLD OF TRANQUILITY!
"BUT PEACE WAS DENIED ME--FOR MINE IS THE CURSE OF PROPHECY...
"IN MY MUSINGS I FORESAW, FAR IN THE FUTURE--
"--THE RISE OF A POWER, RIVALLING THE ELDERS! AN EVIL POWER, BENT ON UNIVERSAL DEATH--HE WOULD BE KNOWN AS--
"--THANOS!
"I DARED NOT CHALLENGE THANOS...BUT CONCERNED FOR THE PRIMITIVE CREATURES WHICH FASCINATED ME, I SOUGHT TO ACQUIRE A SAMPLING OF THEM... TO PRESERVE THEM!
"BY THE TIME THANOS WAS BORN, I HAD SPENT COUNTLESS EONS COLLECTING. SPECIMENS AND CURIOSITIES. IN RECENT TIMES, I MET SEVERAL SETBACKS*--
*INCREDIBLE HULK #198, FOR ONE--ROG.
--BUT ASTONISHINGLY, SO DID THANOS! ULTIMATELY, HE WAS DESTROYED!
I WOULD HAVE STOPPED COLLECT-ING THEN...BUT I AUGERED THE COMING OF AN-OTHER POWER--EVEN MORE DAN-GEROUS! THUS, THIS TIME I CHOSE TO INTERFERE!
THE ANCIENT BEING FALLS SILENT FOR A MOMENT, HIS EYES CLOUDED WITH TEARS OF SADNESS AND REGRET--
--WHILE IN AN ELEGANT FOREST HILLS GARDENS HOME --
--TEARS ALSO WELL IN THE EYES OF CARINA WALTERS...
I SENSED BETRAYAL, CARINA...AND YET I SEE ONLY LOVE IN YOUR SOUL!
MICHAEL, I DO LOVE YOU...WITH ALL MY BEING! AND SO...I MUST TELL YOU--
--WHAT YOU SENSED, MOMENTS AGO, WAS TRUE! I--TRIED TO BETRAY YOU! I WAS SENT HERE TO DO SO...BUT I COULD NOT!
WHO SENT YOU?
MY... FATHER!

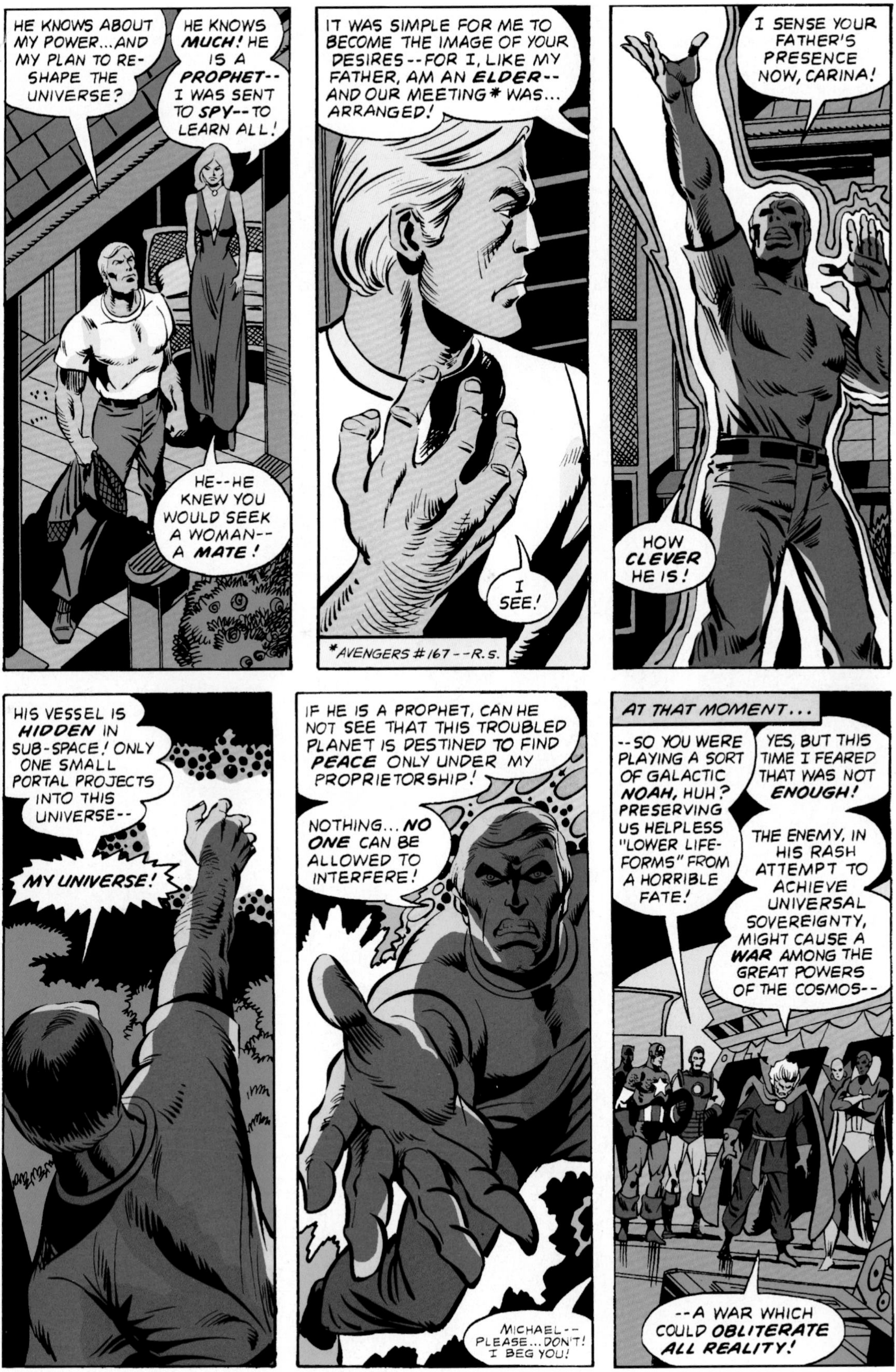
HE KNOWS ABOUT MY POWER...AND MY PLAN TO RE-SHAPE THE UNIVERSE?
HE KNOWS **MUCH!** HE IS A **PROPHET**-- I WAS SENT TO **SPY**--TO LEARN ALL!
HE--HE KNEW YOU WOULD SEEK A WOMAN-- A **MATE!**
IT WAS SIMPLE FOR ME TO BECOME THE IMAGE OF YOUR DESIRES--FOR I, LIKE MY FATHER, AM AN **ELDER**-- AND OUR MEETING* WAS... ARRANGED!
I SEE!
*AVENGERS #167--R.S.
I SENSE YOUR FATHER'S PRESENCE NOW, CARINA!
HOW **CLEVER** HE IS!
HIS VESSEL IS **HIDDEN** IN SUB-SPACE! ONLY ONE SMALL PORTAL PROJECTS INTO THIS UNIVERSE--
MY UNIVERSE!
IF HE IS A PROPHET, CAN HE NOT SEE THAT THIS TROUBLED PLANET IS DESTINED TO FIND **PEACE** ONLY UNDER MY PROPRIETORSHIP!
NOTHING... **NO ONE** CAN BE ALLOWED TO INTERFERE!
MICHAEL-- PLEASE...DON'T! I BEG YOU!
AT THAT MOMENT...
--SO YOU WERE PLAYING A SORT OF GALACTIC **NOAH**, HUH? PRESERVING US HELPLESS "LOWER LIFE-FORMS" FROM A HORRIBLE FATE!
YES, BUT THIS TIME I FEARED THAT WAS NOT **ENOUGH!**
THE ENEMY, IN HIS RASH ATTEMPT TO ACHIEVE UNIVERSAL SOVEREIGNTY, MIGHT CAUSE A **WAR** AMONG THE GREAT POWERS OF THE COSMOS--
--A WAR WHICH COULD **OBLITERATE ALL REALITY!**

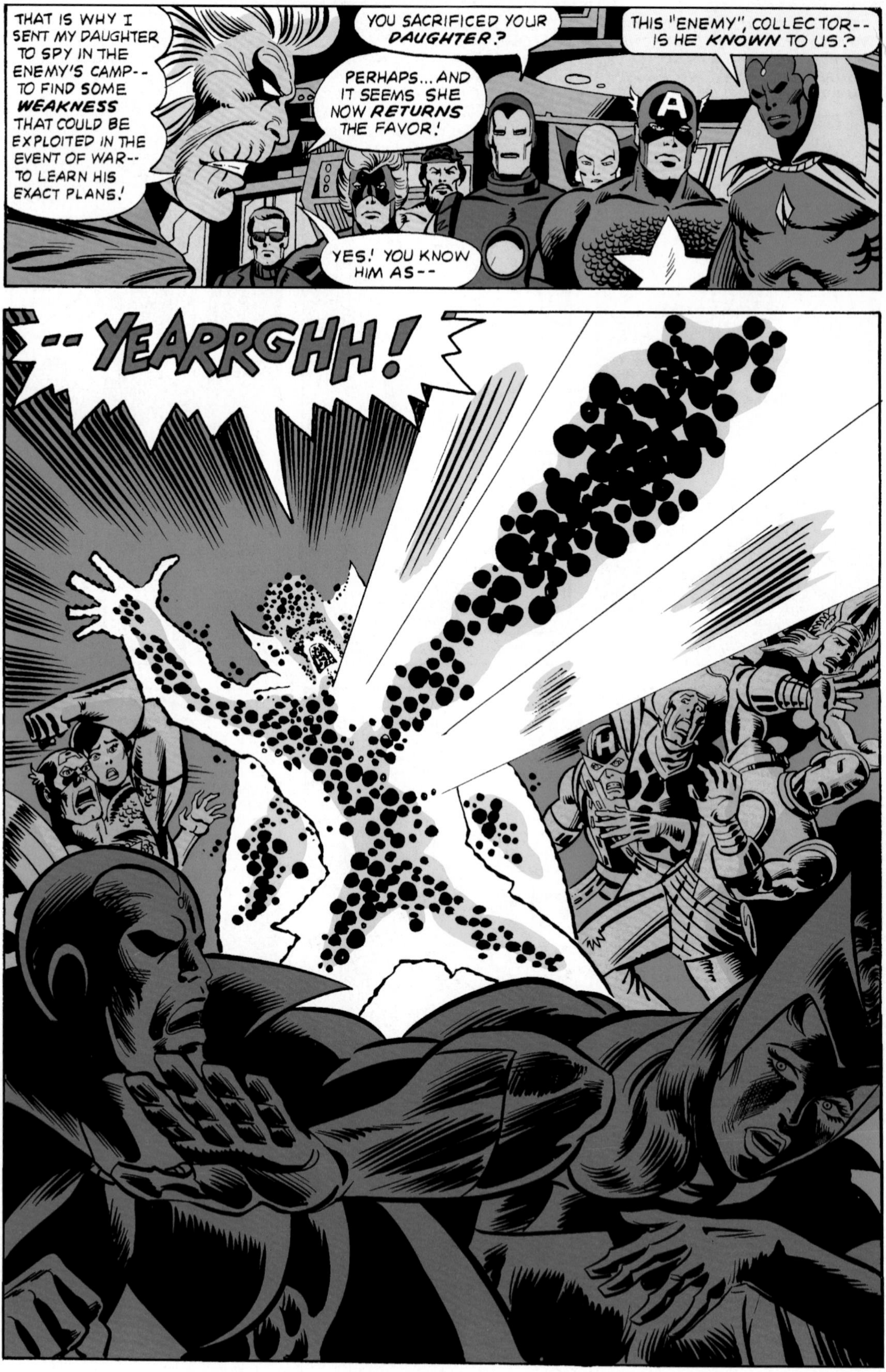
THAT IS WHY I SENT MY DAUGHTER TO SPY IN THE ENEMY'S CAMP-- TO FIND SOME **WEAKNESS** THAT COULD BE EXPLOITED IN THE EVENT OF WAR-- TO LEARN HIS EXACT PLANS!
YOU SACRIFICED YOUR **DAUGHTER**?
PERHAPS... AND IT SEEMS SHE NOW **RETURNS** THE FAVOR!
THIS "ENEMY", COLLECTOR-- IS HE **KNOWN** TO US?
YES! YOU KNOW HIM AS--
--YEARRGHH!

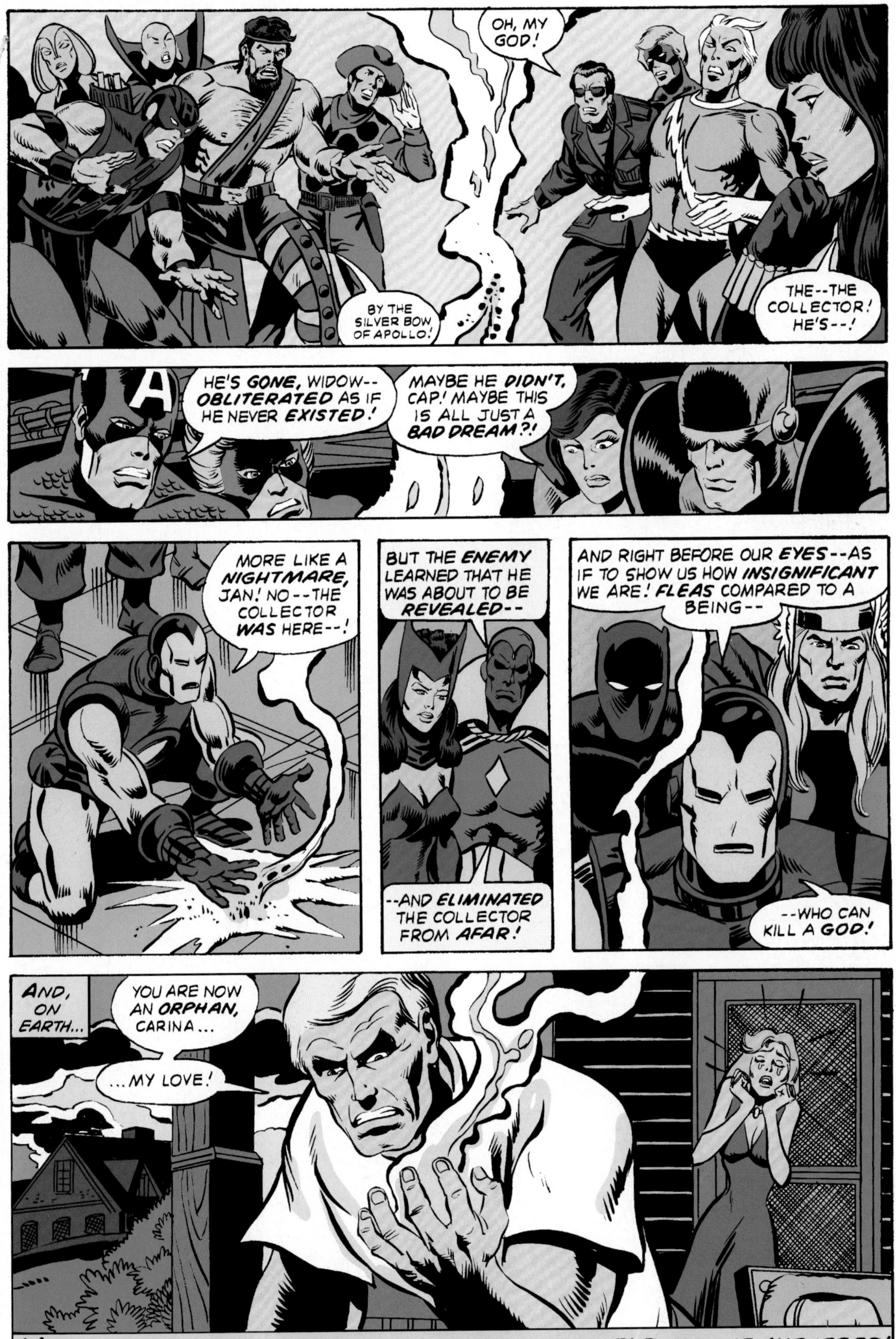
OH, MY GOD!
BY THE SILVER BOW OF APOLLO!
THE--THE COLLECTOR! HE'S--!
HE'S GONE, WIDOW-- OBLITERATED AS IF HE NEVER EXISTED!
MAYBE HE DIDN'T, CAP! MAYBE THIS IS ALL JUST A BAD DREAM?!
MORE LIKE A NIGHTMARE, JAN! NO--THE COLLECTOR WAS HERE--!
BUT THE ENEMY LEARNED THAT HE WAS ABOUT TO BE REVEALED--
--AND ELIMINATED THE COLLECTOR FROM AFAR!
AND RIGHT BEFORE OUR EYES--AS IF TO SHOW US HOW INSIGNIFICANT WE ARE! FLEAS COMPARED TO A BEING--
--WHO CAN KILL A GOD!
AND, ON EARTH...
YOU ARE NOW AN ORPHAN, CARINA...
...MY LOVE!
NEXT: THE ORIGIN OF THE ENEMY AND THE BEGINNING OF THE END FOR THE AVENGERS!

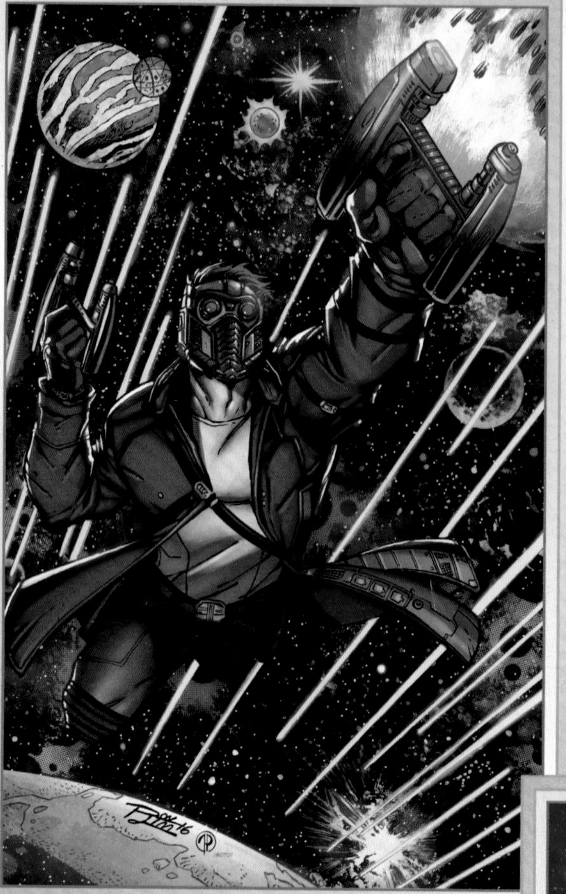

#8 VARIANT BY RON LIM,
TOM PALMER & CHRIS SOTOMAYOR

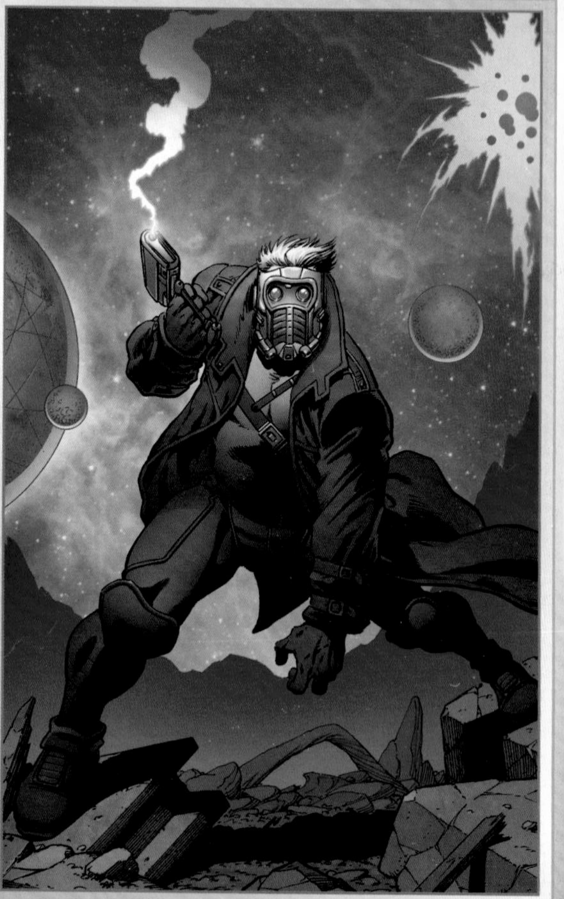

#8 VARIANT BY JIM STARLIN & FRANK D'ARMATA